REAGAN'S FEDERALISM:

His Efforts to
Decentralize Government

Richard S. Williamson

UNIVERSITY
PRESS OF
AMERICA

Center for the
Study of
Federalism

Lanham • New York • London

Library of Congress Cataloging–in–Publication Data

Williamson, Richard S.
Reagan's Federalism : His efforts to decentralize
government / Richard S. Williamson.
p.   cm.
Bibliography: p.
1. Federal government—United States.
2. Intergovernmental fiscal relations—United States.
3. United States—Politics and government—1981–1989.
I. Title
JK325.W47   1989   321.02'0973—dc20   89–35578 CIP

ISBN 0–8191–7534–X (alk. paper)

Co-published by arrangement with the
Center for the Study of Federalism

 The paper used in this publication meets the minimum requirements of
American National Standard for Information Sciences—Permanence
of Paper for Printed Library Materials, ANSI Z39.48–1984.

DEDICATION

TO JANE AND TO LISA, CRAIG AND RICKY

ACKNOWLEDGMENTS

First and foremost I owe a debt to President Reagan, Vice President Bush, and to my colleagues on the White House Senior Staff, Chief of Staff Jim Baker, Counsel Ed Meese, and Deputy Chief of Staff Michael Deaver, for giving me an opportunity to serve in the White House during the first Reagan Administration and for supporting my efforts to further the President's federalism dream.

I also am indebted to an extraordinarily able team who served under me in the White House Intergovernmental Affairs office, all of whom worked long hours and effectively in the effort to decentralize government, and a number of whom helped me with this volume: Deputy Assistant to the President Alan F. Holmer; my special assistant, Penny Eastman; Special Assistants to the President Jim Medas, Steve Rhodes, Rick Neal, Judy Peachee, Bob Gleason; staff assistants Eve Baskowitz, Jocelyn White, Linda Miller Gambatesa and Susan Hawkes; and Gail Golay, who served with great skill and patience as my executive secretary.

I am also indebted to a number of able people who read all or major portions of this manuscript and provided me with helpful suggestions: Steve Farber, Professor Daniel Elazar and Professor John Hall.

I wish to express special appreciation to Sandy Schueftan Kwiecien, who typed this manuscript and patiently retyped it a number of times through its various drafts -- a woman of great skill.

Finally, I wish to express appreciation to Jane Williamson, whose insights, judgment and patience have proven invaluable to me in this project as in so many other endeavors.

TABLE OF CONTENTS

PREFACE

Ronald Reagan fully appreciated the value of decentralized government. He knew that federalism is a cause of enduring importance.

- Federalism fosters social harmony because it reduces government to a manageable scale and makes citizen participation more readily accessible.

- Federalism promotes civic responsibility by fostering citizen participation.

- Federalism helps secure individual rights by providing multiple avenues of redress.

- Federalism provides diversity and allows for local considerations in problem solving.

- Federalism fosters accountability because responsibilities are sorted out. With a national government focusing on national problems, and state and local governments handling their own local problems, the system does not become overloaded and congested.

President Reagan did not achieve all he sought to do on his federalism initiative, but more than skeptics in Washington thought possible. This is the story of those efforts.

Richard S. Williamson
January 1989

INTRODUCTION

Ronald Reagan came to Washington to bring about change! The most ideological United States president in generations and a genuine outsider to the Washington Establishment, Reagan took office with a deep belief in the Founding Fathers' original federalism design of dual sovereignty1/ and an equally firm commitment to translate that belief into action that would decentralize power.

At the outset, critics challenged his constitutional theory and smugly suggested that this Californian, notwithstanding his overwhelming election victory,2/ would learn that the iron triangle of the Federal Establishment,3/ the Washington status quo, was resilient to the reformer dreams of a mere president. Others had tried to reverse the trend of centralized power in Washington. And they had failed. They saw no reason why this congenial former governor with no experience in Washington could succeed where others had not.

The prevailing wisdom for decades in Washington was that the classical arguments for federalism were nonsense. The Founding Fathers' design of dual sovereignty may have had value as the thirteen colonies began to congeal after the Revolutionary War but those horse and buggy days were long gone. The elite in Washington felt that state and local governments had neither the capacity, competence nor compassion to handle most problems. After two hundred years, they believed, the United States had become a single highly interconnected nation that required na-

---

1/   See Raoul Berger, _Federalism: The Founders' Design_ (University of Oklahoma Press, Norman, Oklahoma) 1987. See also, W.B. Allen and Gordon Lloyd, ed., _The Essential Antifederalist_ (University Press of America, Inc., Lanham, MD, 1985), and Walter Berns, _Taking the Constitution Seriously_ (Simon and Schuster, New York, 1987), pp. 78-85.

2/   Election results were: Reagan 50.7%, Carter 41%, Anderson 6.6%. Reagan received 489 votes in the Electoral College and Carter 49.

3/   The so-called iron triangle in Washington is the special interests, congressional committees and Executive department bureaucracies. These three groups work together in their shared self-interest of greater concentration of power in the federal government.

tional solutions for everything from foreign policy to fire protection.

But that common wisdom was not monolithic. Ronald Reagan's own experience in California had greatly strengthened his belief in the urgent need to decentralize power. By the time he took office as President, a number of other political leaders were signaling their belief that something had to be done to make government work again. As liberal Democratic Governor Bruce Babbitt of Arizona said, "If the federal government would worry about national defense and let the states worry about the highways, we'd be more secure and have better roads."4/

Frustrated by the inability to get America moving, in 1979, President Carter had pointed a finger toward the national malaise among the people.5/ Reagan simply did not accept that. He embraced the view of the Advisory Commission on Intergovernmental Relations that the intergovernmental system was overloaded. Reagan wanted to get government closer to the people. And that meant getting responsibility, power and resources back to state and local governments.

In many areas of his federalism agenda, Ronald Reagan did fail. There were many disappointments. Occasionally, even conservative Republicans in Congress who were philosophical soul mates of Reagan were more concerned with protecting their congressional turf or satisfying a Washington special interest group than supporting decentralization. Quite often, state and local officials, however frustrated with Washington controls, favored the devil they knew over trying to fend for themselves. There were many setbacks. Most dramatic was our failure to achieve the federalism initiative outlined by President Reagan in his 1982 State of the Union Address. Nonetheless, there also were many victories. There were many accomplishments. Some were a result of Reagan Administration efforts; some the consequence of a budget squeeze that had gone out of control. In the end, much of President Ronald Reagan's dream to decentralize government was achieved.

Ronald Reagan confounded his critics. Through block grants, regulatory reform, tax reform and fiscal federalism, the Reagan

---

4/   Governor Bruce Babbit, The Washington Post, February 22, 1982.

5/   Jimmy Carter, Address to the nation, July 15, 1979. See Jimmy Carter, Keeping Faith: Memoirs of a President (Bantam Books, New York, 1982), pp. 114-121.

Administration has cut back the dominance of the federal government and helped decentralize power. He helped restore vigor, authority and innovation to state government. As New Jersey Governor Tom Kean has said to his fellow governors, "Our time is now."

I first worked for Ronald Reagan in his 1976 run for the Presidency. When he challenged President Ford for that year's Republican Presidential nomination, I was serving as Administrative Assistant and Legislative Counsel to Congressman Phil Crane of Illinois, one of only a handful of members of the Senate and House of Representatives to join the Reagan team. I traveled from Washington to help Reagan's campaign in a number of states including my native Illinois. It was at the Executive Club in Chicago during that campaign that Reagan first outlined a sweeping $90 billion plan to return programs to the states.6/ At the convention, I helped coordinate the conservative delegates' efforts to shape the platform.

When Reagan made his second run for the Presidency in 1980, I was in private law practice. Soon I again was caught up in the Reagan campaign, serving as Deputy to the National Campaign Chairman, Senator Paul Laxalt. And, again, I worked in drafting the platform at the convention.

From my personal dealings with Reagan in the '76 and '80 campaigns, especially my platform work, there was absolutely no question in my mind that as President he would be committed to decentralizing power. His experience as governor of California and his philosophy made this a priority for him. Therefore, I was particularly delighted that after the 1980 election he asked me to join his White House Senior Staff as Assistant to the President for Intergovernmental Affairs.7/

It was from that post that I was able to be a participant and observer of President Reagan's persistent efforts to restore the

---

6/ Ronald Reagan, Address to the Chicago Executive Club, Chicago, Illinois, September 26, 1975.

7/ Actually, I first served as Special Assistant to the President and Deputy Chief of Staff to Jim Baker. However, three weeks after his inauguration, the President promoted me to the White House Senior Staff as Assistant to the President for Intergovernmental Affairs, where I served until June, 1983, when I became U.S. Ambassador to the United Nations Offices in Vienna, Austria.

proper balance to the intergovernmental system. I now realize that while I was Reagan's senior aide for his federalism agenda in the first years of his presidency, there were many opportunities I failed to fully utilize. The Administration made mistakes. But, due to the President's commitment and his political skills, we did a lot. A historic shift has taken place. As Democratic Governor Bill Clinton of Arkansas said in 1987, "Whether you agree with President Reagan or not, he has made Governors important again."

In this volume, I attempt to draw upon my perspective as a participant and observer of this process to explain what we did in a manner that provides both analysis and perspective.

President Reagan's federalism efforts to decentralize power have had profound effect upon the delivery of care and services. While not realizing all of his goals, he has shaken the status quo and challenged presumptions. State and local governments are experiencing a renaissance of innovation and leadership.

John Herbers, long-time New York Times reporter and one of the leading observers of state and local governments recently wrote:

"State and local governments, with a new sense of independence from the federal government, have been taking on new responsibilities in the 1980's -- a change that promises to be both more profound and more permanent than most people have recognized."8/

Whether in the end the Reagan era will result in a more permanent decentralized government or be transitory is yet unknown. But it is my hope that the observations in this book can at least put together in a single volume the scope of how we tried to decentralize government during the early years of the Reagan Administration. Perhaps thereby it can enlighten the on-going debate of precisely what is the proper role of the various levels of government in our federal system.

8/   John Herbers, "The New Federalism: Unplanned, Innovative and Here to Stay," Governing, Vol. 1, No. 1, p. 28.

CHAPTER 1

FEDERALISM: A NEW BEGINNING

President Ronald Reagan believed in what he had said during the campaign. "Everything that can be run more efficiently by state and local governments we shall turn over to local governments, along with the funding sources to pay for it."1/ It wasn't just rhetoric. He really believed.

This mystified most of the Washington Establishment. In this era of modern sophisticated politics with millions of dollars to spend in presidential campaigns for pollsters, political consultants and media advisors, the common wisdom had developed that issue papers, television ads and candidate speeches were all parts of a whole driven by the polls, not genuine commitment. Then along came Ronald Reagan.

Reagan realized the climate in America viewed politicians as lacking principle. He felt comfortable poking fun at politicians too ready to shift their views to satisfy the voters because he so obviously was an exception to that rule. He once told this story about a flip-flop politician:

> There was a fellow running for Congress; and he went out soliciting votes and sat down by an old-timer on the courthouse bench in a little town and solicited his vote. He told him what he was there for and when he finished his pitch the old man said: "What do you intend to do about the geese?" The candidate looked, and the courthouse lawn was covered with geese. He said: "Well, now that's a lovely sight, isn't it? I think they should be protected." And the old man said: "You just lost my vote. They mess up the lawn; they chase the kids; they peck at their legs. They ought to be destroyed." So the candidate moved over to another bench, sat down beside another old-timer, made the same pitch and when he finished, he got the same question: "What are you going to do about the geese?" "Well," he said, "look at them out there messing up the lawn. I think they ought to be destroyed." The old man said: "You just lost my vote. I raise geese. They're an important part of this community." The candidate moved to the third

---

1/   Ronald Reagan, Acceptance Speech, Republican National Convention, Detroit, Michigan, July 17, 1980.

bench, made the same pitch and, believe it or not, got the same question about the geese. This time, he put his arm around the fellow's shoulders and said, "Brother, on that question, I'm with you."2/

As Reagan said on another occasion, "The reason there is a cynical lack of confidence in government is because too many politicians are elected to office but never try to carry out their campaign promises."3/ Well, Ronald Reagan was intent on doing what he told the voters he'd try to do while on the campaign trail.

Reagan's world view grew out of his own experiences. His philosophy was well rooted in America's heritage. And he has an old fashioned view that he should say what he means, and mean what he says, even if he is a politician.

At the same time, Ronald Reagan as a former leader of the Screen Actors Guild also knew about negotiating, the give and take of different interests. As the President often told those of us on his staff, he wasn't one of those conservative hard liners who believed in jumping off cliffs. He would always take something rather than nothing.

This posture of Reagan as a firm ideologue, yet one willing to horse trade and compromise to get something done kept Congress off balance. It even kept the White House staff off balance. When Reagan drew a line in the sand, we often weren't sure ourselves how firm it was. Indeed, some of the most colorful intramural skirmishes amongst the staff resulted from tension between the so-called "pragmatists" on the staff and the so-called true "Reaganauts."

On the one hand were the so-called "pragmatists" like Chief of Staff Jim Baker, Legislative Liaison Ken Duberstein and OMB Director Dave Stockman who all felt they were realists. Experienced in Washington, they felt their skills at the traditional log-rolling of the legislative process gave them a sense of when compromise was required. On the other hand were the so-called "Reaganauts" such as Presidential Counselor Ed Meese, Domestic

---

2/   Ronald Reagan, appears in A Time for Choosing: The Speeches of Ronald Reagan 1961-1982 (Regnery Gateway, Chicago, 1983), p. 135.

3/   Ronald Reagan, speech, October 15, 1974, in Joseph R. Holmes, The Quotable Reagan (JRH & Associates, Inc., San Diego, CA, 1974), p. 134.

Advisor Marty Anderson and myself. We tended to have deep philosophical roots that brought us into politics in the first place
and long time personal relationships with Ronald Reagan.

One group would lead the charge for compromise to get the "deal"
while the other would defend the principles to protect the
President's traditional positions. In point of fact, that dicho-
tomy is overly simplistic. But the general tension did exist.
And Ronald Reagan seemed comfortable with it. He wanted both
ideological issue development and practical political advice. He
used us, our varying perspectives and talents. And, in the end,
he would make the decision of when to hold firm, when to negotiate and when to fold.

While there were substantial accomplishments in the efforts to
decentralize, one of my major mistakes in advancing the
President's federalism agenda was during the negotiations with
state and local officials on his major 1982 State of the Union
Address initiative. I should have drawn Reagan more directly
into the process. This could have resolved some of the internal
tensions and helped resolve some of the disputed issues between
the administration and the state and local officials. It was a
significant opportunity missed.

Since Ronald Reagan is both ideologue and compromiser, any understanding of his efforts to decentralize government must begin
with some sense of his federalism philosophy. His belief in
federalism was deep rooted in theory, in our nation's experience,
and -- importantly -- on his own experiences while Governor of
California.4/ All three elements fashioned in Reagan a consis-

---

4/   Lou Cannon, political writer for the Washington Post
      and long-time Reagan watcher and biographer, relates a
      conversation with Reagan about his days as a spokesman
      for General Electric in the 1950's that reveals his
      experience even then in the benefits of decentraliza-
      tion. The President of GE was Ralph J. Cordiner, who
      had pioneered decentralization of his vast company.
      Reagan says approvingly of Cordiner, "He was the man
      who really was the leader of decentralization of in-
      dustry and business. They had 139 plants in 38
      states, and he was the one that had the courage as the
      Chief Executive Officer and Chairman of the Board to
      say to the managers of those plants, 'I want you to
      run them as if they were your plants'. They never had
      to get a ruling from the Board of Directors. There'd
      be a general code of ethics laid down, and this is how
      the theater came about. Cordiner had the idea that
(Cont'd)

tent commitment to decentralize government and get it closer to the people.

Part of Reagan's view was simply anti-government. Both in his private life and while governor of California he had witnessed so many "horror stories" that resulted from big government interference that his instincts indeed were anti-government. He delighted in telling visitors to the Oval Office and staff story upon story of how government had messed up here, there and everywhere. As Reagan once said, "Government does not solve problems; it subsidizes them."5/ There is no question that he feels that when in doubt a problem should be left to the private sector.

This presumption was not only due to Reagan's distrust of big government, but also because he is an optimist who has a sincere faith in the American people, their ingenuity, their charity.

Reagan has a story he often tells about two brothers: one is an optimist and the other a pessimist. Their parents became concerned because one boy always saw the bright side of every situation whereas the other always saw doom and gloom. To try to teach them a lesson, the parents prepared two rooms. One, in which they sent their pessimistic son, was full of brand new shiny toys. The other, in which they sent their optimistic son, was full of manure. A half an hour later they opened the door to the room where they had sent the pessimist. He was crying. They asked him why. The pessimistic boy said he was crying because he had all these nice new toys and if he played with them they'd become scuffed and broken. Then the parents opened the door to the room where they had sent their optimistic son. He was smiling and laughing and digging in the manure. When they asked him how he could be so happy, the optimist said, "Well with all this manure, there has to be a pony somewhere!".

---

not only would they do this television show, but that the spokesman they got to do the theater, which turned out to be me, would a certain number of weeks be put on tour in visiting the plants. The employees, scattered as they were, would realize that the headquarters knew they were there because here's that fellow they saw on Sunday night coming to visit them." Lou Cannon, Reagan (G.P. Putnam's Son, New York, 1982), p. 93.

5/ Ronald Reagan, speech, December 11, 1972, in ed. Joseph R. Holmes, The Quotable Ronald Reagan (JRH and Associates, Inc., San Diego, California, 1974), p. 91.

Ronald Reagan believes there is a pony. He trusts the character of the American people. When the going got tough for President Carter in 1979, he blamed the situation on a "malaise" in America. In contrast, in 1980, Ronald Reagan campaigned for a new beginning.

Critics continually attack Ronald Reagan for being just anti-government. They equate this view with being anti-people. They say it shows Reagan's total lack of compassion.

Ronald Reagan is a compassionate man. He simply doesn't equate big government and central government regulation with compassion. To him, a welfare check was not compassionate if a recipient was able bodied and could work.6/ It was not compas-sionate to teach dependency. Except for the truly needy who cannot help themselves, Reagan believes compassion is creating jobs through an expanding economy and teaching skills through workfare programs so people can re-enter the work force and be-come self-reliant.

To Ronald Reagan, it is not compassionate to have nameless, face-less bureaucrats in distant Washington designing government pro-grams and setting national standards. To Reagan, compassion was recognizing individual Americans' ability, talent, capacity and interest in having a direct say in helping to design their gov-ernment programs and setting standards that reflected their local concerns, needs and aspirations. And this could only happen by devolving government closer to the people.

Reagan's federalism goals were an integral part of his internally coherent conservative political ideology. His desire to decen-tralize government generally was reinforced by other aspects of his conservative agenda such as reducing government interference in the marketplace, lowering federal taxes and cutting domestic expenditures. But critics who charged that President Reagan's federalism proposals were just a smokescreen for cutting the budget failed to grasp the profound philosophic importance to Ronald Reagan personally of devolution.

As the White House point man on the federalism agenda, my task of publicly putting his programs in proper perspective was compli-cated immeasurably by some of my colleagues, especially OMB Director David Stockman, who in fact did see the federalism agenda just as a way to cut the budget. This blind commitment by some to cut the budget -- which, of course, was their job --

---

6/ Lou Cannon, Reagan (G.P. Putnam's Sons, New York, 1982), pp. 177-183.

using every tool available, contorting every other initiative to this end, resulted in a breach of faith between the Administration and many key political constituencies including state and local officials. The irony, as I argued at the time, is that if we had been less greedy in trying to cut certain programs so that the Administration's budget proposal would appear lower, often the final budget expenditures from the congressional process could have been lower in fact.7/ Opportunities to "cut deals" with constituencies and Capitol Hill at a given spending level reflecting real cuts were lost as often we sought unrealistic deeper cuts. We failed to get the deeper cuts, and Congress too often sent back spending bills far higher than the level we could have achieved at the outset. Our reach would exceed our grasp. Endemic was a well-intended, but too often short-sighted zeal by some of my colleagues who were responsible solely for the budget, that resulted both in unnecessary breaches of confidence (a political commodity too precious to squander) and higher spending.

But Ronald Reagan and most of us really believed in the importance of decentralizing government. We felt there were inherent virtues of federalism that brought great benefits.

It is as dangerous to conduct a representative democracy under a monolithic central authority as it is to drive a car without brakes down the highway. Restraint mechanisms are highly recommended. The Constitution of the United States provided for institutional restraint by creating a federal system. Powers were dispersed within and among units of government. Sovereign states entered into a compact in which they agreed to entrust general powers to a national government, while retaining local powers for themselves. In turn, states were decentralized to vest appropriate responsibilities in counties, cities and towns.8/ While the debate on federalism often focuses on organizational principles, to Ronald Reagan dispersal of power in government has inherent virtues beyond its service as a functional system.

7/   See the discussion in Chapter Six.

8/   Writing in his autobiography at the age of 77, Thomas Jefferson said:

"Were not this great country already divided into states, that division must be made, that each might do for itself what concerns itself directly, and what it can so much better do than a distant authority ... Were we directed from Washington when to sow, and when to reap, we should soon want bread."

In a sense, federalism is a natural extension of our desire for freedom of association. The ability of people to unite for a common purpose without losing their individuality bonds the character of our society.9/ All of us assign specific functions to entities which can best achieve our defined objective -- the family, the church, businesses, service and fraternal organizations. This division of responsibilities is just as fundamental in government. As we would not assign child rearing and philanthropy to the same entity, nor should one unit of government be responsible for both sewer extensions and national defense, and everything in between. By sorting out responsibilities in both private and public endeavors, we achieve efficiency and accountability. This fosters social harmony and helps secure individual rights.

Because decentralization reduces government to a manageable size and brings it closer to the people, it makes citizen participation easier. People are less frustrated because they have access to the policy making process. Some citizens participate formally by serving in state legislatures, on city councils, zoning boards, advisory committees, etc. Others, just as importantly, make more informal contributions. Most states and localities provide for ballot initiatives and referenda to decide at least some policy issues. Advisory votes also are common at the state and local level. All states have some form of open meeting laws, and most require local budget hearings.10/ As a result of citizen participation, civic responsibility becomes a personal responsibility. People are committed to making their government work because they have a direct involvement in shaping it.

9/ Daniel J. Elazar of Temple University maintains that: American federalism can be traced to the Mayflower Compact of 1620. Because the Pilgrims were about to settle in an area outside the jurisdiction of their patent-issuing company, they drew up an aboard-ship agreement to preserve order through rule of law sanctioned by themselves. It was patterned after their church covenant, which vested religious authority in the congregation. Thus, the Mayflower Compact was an agreement by parties seeking to unite for a common purpose while preserving their respective integrities.

10/ Advisory Commission on Intergovernmental Relations, "Citizen Participation in the American Federal System," In Brief, August, 1979. See also, David Riley, "Government By Initiative," Government Executive, October, 1988, p. 32.

When Congress -- or the national government in general -- tries to replace local political entities, responsibility and accountability are lost. The Washington special-interest groups involved in education replace elected school boards. The transportation lobbies set road priorities rather than city councils. The urban planning consultant influences residential construction more than the local zoning board. With a national government involved in all areas of daily life, people don't know whom to blame when government services go sour. Not only is civic responsibility lost, but people don't even know whom to turn out of office or whom to re-elect. Instead of a representative democracy, the system becomes collectivism in an estranged power structure, with a potential for degenerating into chaos.

Our republic was founded because a distant and monopolistic government in England ignored the desires and rights of the people. Federalism in the new nation was to provide many avenues of redress with each unit of government acting as a check and balance on the others. Our Founding Fathers believed that if government were closer to the people, a permanent ruling class would become much less likely. According to Ronald Reagan, many of the Washington elite felt they were the permanent ruling class. He doesn't agree that they hold a monopoly on wisdom. In fact, his experience as governor of California left no doubt in his mind that the Washington establishment was the problem and not the solution.

But perhaps, diversity is the greatest strength of a decentralized government. States and localities can adjust for the different customs, demographics and climate of their areas. A problem solved in one manner at a given time and place may be solved differently in another period and setting. This promotes efficiency. Programs are implemented only when they are really needed, and they are designed to meet the specific requirements of a particular locale. On the other hand, centralized governments, which to be monolithic, are wasteful. Their bureaucratic overhead diverts funds from real services, and imposes inflexible "solutions" despite a vast disparity of needs. Decentralization permits states and localities to use more innovative approaches, learn from one another, and, in the words of Justice Brandeis, serve as "laboratories of democracy."11/

11/ In a dissenting opinion in New State Ice Co. v. Liebmann, (1932) Supreme Court Justice Louis Brandeis wrote: "It is one of the happy incidents of the federal System that a single courageous state may, if its citizens choose, serve as a laboratory; and try novel social and economic experiments without risk to the rest of the country."

Federalism principles eroded somewhat during the republic's first 150 years, only to be fundamentally altered by the New Deal and the power shift initiated by the New Frontier/Great Society was startling. It accelerated throughout the 1970's as succeeding Congresses become so insensitive to intergovernmental balance that even the most trivial local decisions began to reflect federal priorities. The federal government was burgeoning out of control, and it was time to apply the brakes -- to bring back the institutional restraints embedded in the Constitution. That's what Reagan sought to do.

* * * * *

In a December 1980 report, the bipartisan Advisory Commission on Intergovernmental Relations said:

> "The federal government's influence has become more pervasive, more intrusive, more unmanageable, more inefficient, more costly, and above all, more unaccountable."12/

Other than that, one assumes, things were running smoothly. Three interlocking mechanisms had been used to diminish the role of the states: grant proliferation, revenue usurpation and excessive regulation.

During the 1960's and 1970's, the number of categorical (restrictive, single purpose) grant-in-aid programs to state and local governments mushroomed from under 50 to over 492. The federal tax dollars required to finance these programs drained the total revenue pool so that states and localities found it increasingly difficult to raise revenues and initiate programs on their own. Cut-throat competition for federal dollars ensued, and Washington was able to "leverage" its spending by requiring states to put up matching funds as a condition for receiving the grant.

12/ Advisory Commission on Intergovernmental Relations (ACIR), "A Crisis of Confidence and Competence," The Federal Role in the Federal System: The Dynamics of Growth, A-77, 1980.

The ACIR is a bipartisan organization created by Congress in 1959 to monitor the operation of the American federal system and to recommend improvements.

The national government was mandating spending by states and localities and setting program priorities. Grant money came attached with rules, regulations, and reporting requirements. Compounding the problem, the federal judiciary -- mostly because of the involvement of federal dollars, and mostly with ill-conceived good intentions -- was issuing a series of rulings dictating how states and localities could spend their revenues, and what procedures to follow.

Meanwhile, the federal government was losing its grip on its responsibilities. It became involved in so vast an array of concerns that members of Congress could not concentrate on, nor master more than a fraction of legislative business. They did not have time to adequately study or completely understand uniquely national concerns, such as peace in the Middle East or a comprehensive energy policy. Too much work was delegated to staff. Too many laws were poorly conceived. Too many legislative responsibilities were delegated to bureaucratic rulemakers, with too little congressional oversight.

Every federal department and agency in the Reagan Administration was directed to reduce federal intrusiveness. The President made it clear to members of his Cabinet and department heads that all programs were to be monitored carefully to avoid unintended and undesired effects on state and local government.13/

More formally, the President had a three part plan. The first was the consolidation of categorical programs into block grants.14/ This gave flexibility to state and local governments to target funds within more broadly defined programmatic areas. Second, he established a Task Force on Regulatory Relief and asked Vice President Bush to chair it.15/ While the Task Force was charged with reducing excessive regulations on all segments of society, a major goal was to ease the burdens on state and local governments. Third, he pushed for a major Federalism Initiative to phase out the federal government's role in some areas, as programs and revenue resources were turned over to states and localities.

13/ President Ronald Reagan, Memorandum for Members of the Cabinet and Agency Heads, March 29, 1981.

14/ See generally, Williamson, Richard S., "Block Grants: A Federalist's Tool," State Government, Vol. 54, No. 4, 1981.

15/ Executive Order No. 12291, February 17, 1981.

There is a three-sided Washington power structure made up of special interest groups, the permanent federal bureaucracy, and Capitol Hill committee staff and members known as the Iron Triangle. The Iron Triangle was not pleased by President Reagan's proposed reforms. In protecting the status quo, or expanding federal spending and control, they gain more power, more prestige, and more money. Thus, for every possible area of government endeavor, there is a special interest constituency to keep it in Washington. All too often, the Iron Triangle becomes the Bermuda Triangle for good government.

* * * * *

Secretary of Education Ted Bell had been through the wars. During the Nixon Administration, he was Special Assistant to Health, Education and Welfare Secretary Elliott Richardson. They tried to enact block grants and failed. During the Ford Administration, he was U.S. Commissioner of Education (under HEW). Again, they proposed block grants; again they failed. So when we were formulating President Reagan's first block grants -- two of which involved programs in the Department of Education -- Ted Bell was skeptical. He said to me, "Rich, you know I'm for it, and I'll help all I can, but I've tried this before."

While the Congress did not give the President everything he wanted, the Economic Recovery Program of 1981 did consolidate 57 categorical programs into nine block grants. It was a big victory for federalism. Thereafter, when speaking to groups of state and local officials, Ted Bell often related the story of his initial skepticism, and his delight that events proved him wrong.

However, the difficulties that he had encountered in previous administrations had not gone away. The entrenched federal establishment was not about to roll over and see its power and prosperity diminished. The difficulty was compounded by the fact that many local officials had become so addicted to federal funds, and so liked by-passing their state governments, that they too, became a strong constituent lobby for proliferating federal spending and involvement. The Iron Triangle was becoming a square.

Still, the mood of the country had changed. There was a growing recognition that government had become overloaded and congested and, in part, Ronald Reagan's election was a mandate to clean up the mess. Also, the iron triangle had been jolted. For the first time in over 25 years, in 1980 the Republicans gained control of the United States Senate. The new Republican Senate Committee chairman and the staff did not have an enormous vested interest in the status quo. They were receptive to the leadership of the new President as he sought to decentralize government. So, after a half century of proliferating power in Washington, there was a man in the Oval Office with a deep belief in the virtues of federalism and decentralization. And there was opportunity. Dust-caked copies of the <u>Federalist Papers</u> were suddenly being pulled from shelves for reexamination. Federalism was now part of the debate and it forced America's leaders to take stock of what had become of the American federal system.

CHAPTER 2

RONALD REAGAN IN CALIFORNIA

The title was <u>A Time for Choosing</u>. It was a television address by Ronald Reagan on behalf of Republican presidential candidate Barry Goldwater the week before the 1964 elections. For half an hour, Mr. Reagan dazzled a nationwide audience with an eloquent conservative agenda for America, and it catapulted him into national political prominence. The choice, he said, was that:

> "either we believe in our traditional system of individual liberty, or we abandon the American Revolution and confess that an intellectual elite in a far distant capital can plan our lives for us better than we can plan them ourselves."1/

Two years later, Ronald Reagan was elected governor of the nation's largest state. On inauguration day, January 5, 1967, he arrived in Sacramento to inherit a ballooning state bureaucracy, and taxes --particularly property taxes-- that were skyrocketing.2/

The California budget was hemorrhaging. Reagan's predecessor, Governor Edmund Brown, had switched part of the state's accounting systems to the accrual method to meet the state constitution's mandate for a balanced budget while expenditures were kept on the cash basis. As Reagan said, "They were using fifteen months' worth of income to cover twelve months' worth of expenditures."3/   The state's budget deficit was actually $194 million. In his inaugural message in Sacramento, Reagan said:

1/   Full text reprinted in Reagan, Ronald, <u>Where's the Rest of Me?</u>, (Kartz Publishers Edition, New York, 1981), pp. 302, 312.

2/   Spending for social welfare alone had risen 247% during the decade prior to his election.

3/   Ronald Reagan, "Why the Conservative Movement Is Growing," Address to the Southern GOP Leadership Conference, Atlanta, Georgia, December 7, 1973, appearing in <u>A Time for Choosing, The Speeches of Ronald Reagan 1961-1982</u> (Regnery Gateway, Chicago, 1983), p. 144.

"Our fiscal situation has a sorry similarity to the situation of a jetliner out over the North Atlantic, Paris-bound. The pilot announced he had news -- some good, some bad -- and he would give the bad news first. They had lost radio contact; their compass and altimeter were not working; they didn't know their altitude, direction or where they were headed. Then he gave the good news -- they had a 100-mile-an-hour tail-wind and they were ahead of schedule."4/

For the eight previous years, the California bureaucracy had grown by an average of five thousand new employees a year. Welfare costs were going up almost four times as fast as revenues. As Reagan has said, "In 1967, our Administration took over a government that had been a 'Little Sir Echo' to the great society experiments in Washington."5/

At the national level, President Lyndon Johnson was at the apex of his political power, advancing his social legislation. Liberalism and centralization were in full power. Power and revenue were flowing ever more relentlessly toward Washington. After some 35 years of shifting balance, the federal system had been bent out of shape. Now it appeared that a thriving liberal coalition was determined to break it.

Governor Reagan set out to institute sweeping reforms at the state level. He pledged that he would get the state's financial house in order, provide tax relief, rein in spending, and devolve many decision-making responsibilities from Sacramento to local units of government.6/ As for Washington, he said that he would

---

4/   Ronald Reagan, "The Creative Society," Inaugural Message as Governor of California, Sacramento, California, January 5, 1967, appearing in A Time for Choosing, The Speeches of Ronald Reagan 1961-1982 (Regnery Gateway, Chicago, 1983), p. 67.

5/   Ronald Reagan, "Why the Conservative Movement Is Growing," Address to the Southern GOP Leadership Conference, Atlanta, Georgia, December 7, 1973, appearing in A Time for Choosing, The Speeches of Ronald Reagan 1961-1982 (Regnery Gateway, Chicago, 1983), p. 144.

6/   Addressing a luncheon of the California Association of County Supervisors on November 13, 1968, Governor Reagan said:

(Cont'd)

work "to make the state an effective bulwark between the people and the ever-encroaching federal government."7/ Reagan set, even then, the goals to "secure less restrictive controls on federal grants, and work for a tax retention plan that will keep some of our federal taxes here for our use with no strings attached."8/ That this was during the height of the Great Society, and given the political climate at the time, there were surely those who said, "It'll never fly, Orville."

* * * * *

To the amazement of many, when Governor Reagan left Sacramento in 1974, California had a $554 million budget surplus.9/ He had become the greatest tax cutter in the state's history by providing the people with over $5.7 billion in tax relief.10/ And he held the number of state employees virtually constant while both

---

"When I spoke to you in 1966 [the year of his election], I outlined my concept of and my belief in home rule -- my conviction that the closer the government is to the people it serves, the more effective, the more efficient, and the more economical it can be. I am here today to renew that commitment. And, I am here to thank you for your cooperation and your assistance in making it more of a fact during the past two years ... thanks in large measure to the cooperation and efforts of your association, we were able to give our people some measure of property tax relief ..."

7/   Governor Ronald Reagan, Address to the California Republican Assembly, April 1, 1967, Long Beach, California.

8/   Ronald Reagan, "The Creative Society," Inaugural Message as Governor of California, Sacramento, California, January 5, 1967, appearing in A Time for Choosing, The Speeches of Ronald Reagan 1961-1982 (Regnery Gateway, Chicago, 1983), p. 67.

9/   The Reagan Record 1967-1974, op. cit., p. 7.

10/   Summary of Actions and Programs of Governor Ronald Reagan's Administration, 1967-1974, (Sacramento, California, December 1974), p. 1.

the population and level of services expanded.11/ As acknowledged by the Los Angeles Times:

> "The entire thrust of the Reagan Administration has
> been to reduce or at least contain the role of govern-
> ment in the lives of Californians, as measured primar-
> ily by the taxes it collects. The basic goal has been
> to pare back or at least hold the line on government
> spending."12/

All the while he was decentralizing government, as evidenced by
an increase in the percentage of state budget devoted to local
assistance -- from 52% to 65.5%.13/   He provided diversity.14/
For example, he recognized that local agencies should have primary responsibility for enforcing minimum state and federal air
quality standards; he sought legislation giving state financial
assistance to local governments to finance effective
programs.15/   To foster accountability, Governor Reagan signed
legislation requiring the state to assume full cost of any new
programs imposing expanded costs on local governments, and to
reimburse localities for revenues lost from new sales or property
tax exemptions.16/   Also, he opposed a ballot proposition which
gave a state commission veto power over local governments on
coastal development.17/   To promote civic participation and re-

---

11/ The Reagan Record 1967-1974, op. cit., p. 13.

12/ Ibid, p. 1.

13/ Ibid, p. 51.

14/ In an address to the Economic Club of New York on
January 17, 1968, Governor Reagan said:

> "As society grows more complex, administration should
> become decentralized. While the problems facing agri-
> culture in the Midwest share common elements with the
> problems of California's agriculture, there are great
> dissimilarities which make rules from Washington dif-
> ficult and at times impossible to apply equitably.
> The same holds true for our urban problems, our prob-
> lems which face the people of the United States."

15/ The Reagan Record 1967-1974, op. cit., p. 40.

16/ Ibid, p. 50.

17/ Ibid.

sponsibility, he initiated a policy through the Department of Public Works to involve local government and citizens in decisions as to where, and whether, to build freeways.18/ He also called for coastal legislation which would help local governments identify areas of environmental concern.19/

To assure that the theme of decentralization reached all areas of government, the state Council on Intergovernmental Relations was upgraded under an Executive Reorganization Plan.20/ This gave local governments greater responsibility in helping to shape state policy.

Agriculture, for example, was the state's largest and most important industry, and Governor Reagan helped provide protection from indiscriminate development to almost 14 million farm acres. This was done through grants to local governments to assure that land remained in agricultural production, and by tax relief to farm owners. The Reagan Administration supported a proposal for improving the state's pest prevention system, and developed it in cooperation with county agricultural commissioners.21/

Counties also were instrumental in a plan to curtail drug abuse. A federal-state-private Governor's Inter-agency Council on Drug Abuse was established, and legislation was enacted to develop coordinated, county-wide community drug abuse control plans.22/

As a result of these and innumerable other actions, government in California at all levels became more efficient. Forty-five of the state's 58 counties were able to reduce their property taxes.23/ It was the first comprehensive property tax relief

---

18/ Ibid.

19/ Ibid.

20/ Governor Ronald Reagan, Address to the California Association of County Supervisors luncheon, November 13, 1968.

21/ The Reagan Record 1967-1974, op. cit., p. 22.

22/ Ibid, p. 28.

23/ Summary of Actions and Programs of Governor Ronald Reagan's Administration, 1967-1974, op. cit., p. 1.

program in state history, and it saved home owners and businesses $2.4 billion.24/ In Sacramento -- faced with a Democratically-controlled legislature with a proclivity for reckless spending -- Governor Reagan vetoed 994 bills, saving some $15.5 billion during his eight years in office.25/

But in no area did Reagan make more dramatic reform than in California's welfare system. These reforms demonstrated the capacity of the state to deal with a politically and fiscally complex problem where the federal government had failed. Repeatedly while in the White House, Reagan would refer to his accomplishments in welfare reform in California to reinforce his arguments to Congress regarding the capacity of state governments to tackle big problems and the beneficial flexibility in state solutions rather than nationwide norms.

In his first Inaugural Address he had said, "In the whole area of welfare, everything will be done to reduce administrative overhead, cut red tape, and return control as much as possible to the county level. And the goal will be investment in, and salvage of, human beings."26/ Having gotten the state house in order during his first years in Sacramento, in 1971 he focused on the urgent need for welfare reform.

California's welfare system had run amuck -- in large part due to federal regulations. The number of people on welfare was soaring. In 1961, the welfare case load was 620,000. In 1971, when Reagan proposed his reforms, the caseload was 2.3 million and increasing by 40,000 a month.27/ California Budget Director

---

24/ He sponsored and signed legislation to increase home-owner exemptions; provide property tax refunds to senior citizens; and reduce business inventory tax by 50 percent.

25/ During his eight years in office, Governor Reagan had only one veto overridden, and that was on a non-spending piece of legislation.

26/ Ronald Reagan, "The Creative Society," Inaugural Message as Governor of California, Sacramento, California, January 5, 1967, appearing in A Time for Choosing, The Speeches of Ronald Reagan 1961-1982 (Regnery Gateway, Chicago, 1983), p. 65.

27/ Peter Hanaford, The Reagans: A Political Portrait (Coward-McCann, Inc., New York, 1983), p. 16.

Verne Orr28/ warned that if the case load continued to grow California would be bankrupt.

In August, 1970, during his gubernatorial re-election campaign, Reagan appointed a fifteen-member task force of state officials and private citizens to review federal, state and county problem areas in welfare. And during that campaign against Assembly Speaker Jesse Unrah, Reagan made welfare reform a central issue stating, "Welfare is the greatest domestic problem facing the nation today and the reason for the high cost of government."29/

On March 3, 1971, Reagan's welfare reforms were sent to the legislature. The package contained seventy specific proposals. It outlined both how to tighten the welfare system and acknowledged that welfare recipients who were truly needy were underpaid. The four goals of the Reagan welfare proposals were:

∘ Increase assistance to the truly needy who have nowhere else to turn to meet their basic needs.

∘ Require those who are able to work to seek a job or job training.

∘ Place Medi-Cal benefits on the same footing as health benefits received by persons not on the program.

∘ Strengthen family responsibility as the basic element in our society.

When he unveiled his welfare reform package, Reagan said:

"The crisis in Welfare and Medi-Cal presents a challenge to all Californians. We simply cannot sit idly by and do nothing to prevent an uncontrolled upward spiraling of the welfare caseload. ...[T]he system does not adequately provide for the truly needy. Virtually everywhere in California, the truly needy are barely subsisting, many below the poverty line, while thousands of the less needy with other sources of income and various exemptions and disregards are getting a disproportionate share of the available money."30/

28/ During President Reagan's first term Verne Orr served as Secretary of the Air Force.

29/ Lou Cannon, Reagan (G.P. Putnam's Sons, New York, 1982), p. 173.
(Cont'd)

The California Democratic leadership denied the governor his request to present his welfare reform proposals to a joint session of the legislature. Therefore, Reagan began his campaign for welfare reform by addressing the Town Hall, a major Los Angeles civic forum.31/ He then went up and down California speaking to political and community groups and talking to the press. While campaigning for public support for his proposals, he implemented those he could through executive order.At the time, President Nixon's Family Assistance Plan was pending in Congress. And a substantial portion of the California legislature favored such a federal takeover of the welfare fiscal mess.32/ But Reagan, even though he stood almost alone, spoke out against the Nixon plan and continued to press for a state solution to the problem.

On June 28th, Assembly Speaker Bob Moretti approached Reagan to begin face to face negotiations for a compromise bill. Reagan felt Moretti had approached him to negotiate because of the public pressure he had generated for his reform proposals by going over the heads of the legislature and going directly to the people. This was a technique he would later employ often when in the White House for budget cuts, tax cuts and other major initiatives.

Reagan, with the assistance of aides Ed Meese and Robert Carleson,33/ bounded out the California Welfare Reform Act with Moretti. There was compromise, but Reagan was confident he

---

30/ Lou Cannon, p. 177.

31/ Old Reagan hands such as Ed Meese and Peter Hanaford believe that Reagan got more coverage from his Town hall speech than he would have by addressing the Legislature. First, some newspapers and television stations resented the Democratic leadership denying Reagan's request to address a joint session. Second, by denying Reagan's request, the speech became like a book banned in Boston. Everyone wanted to know what was in it.

32/ Cannon, p. 178.

33/ Robert Carleson later served as U.S. Commissioner of Welfare in the Nixon and Ford Administrations and Special Assistant to the President under Marty Anderson in the Reagan White House. He proved an invaluable ally on federalism initiatives, especially the block grant initiatives.

achieved 70 percent of what he wanted. For Reagan, this reform package was among the high points of his governorship. The new welfare program was easier to administer than its predecessor. The truly needy who continued to receive AFDC benefits received an increase of their welfare grants that ultimately averaged 43 percent.34/ As longtime Reagan observer and biographer, Lou Cannon has written, "By almost any yardstick -- liberal, conservative or managerial -- the law has been a success."35/

During his two terms as governor, Ronald Reagan also had become a national spokesman for a new generation of governors, state legislators, mayors and county officials. They had come to realize that the mushrooming federal programs reflected Washington's lack of trust for state and local officials as their partners in our federal system. Reagan was speaking out against the bloated bureaucracy in Washington. He was speaking out against a federal government unresponsive to the needs and concerns of the citizens. But just as surely, he was speaking out about his belief and trust in the American people and our basic institutions. Foremost among these institutions are state and local governments which can be more responsive to the needs and desires of the citizens.

During his eight years as governor, Reagan had been a regular attendee of National Governors' Association meetings. During those years the nation's governors were predominantly Democratic and liberal.36/ Nonetheless, Reagan developed personal affection and respect for the talents of his colleagues. One among them with whom he worked on a variety of NGA resolutions, Governor Paul Laxalt of Nevada, would become the national chairman of each of Reagan's three Presidential campaigns and his best friend and collaborator in Congress during Reagan's White House years.

34/ Peter Hanaford, p. 18.

35/ Lou Cannon, p. 182.

36/ During Reagan's last two years as governor, there were thirty-seven Democrats among his peers. And among the Republicans the leaders were the quite able but more liberal William Milliken of Michigan, Robert Ray of Iowa and Daniel Evans of Washington.

Reagan also saw NGA meetings as a platform to explain his basic philosophy about the role of the federal government. For example, at his last NGA meeting in July, 1974, Governor Reagan held a special news conference to attack legislation pending in Congress to create federally supervised land-use planning. Reagan already had sent letters to the President and to members of Congress urging defeat of the Jackson-Udall land-use bill. At his press conference at the NGA meeting in Seattle, he said:

> "Land-use planning is so intricately bound up with the question of basic property rights that the only proper place to deal with it is at the state level. And, a land-use plan which works well in one state may not in another. Surely, it should be for the individual state to decide, and not rest in the hands of a bureaucrat or social engineer in Washington."37/

While governor, Reagan also served a term as a member of the Advisory Commission on Intergovernmental Relations. The staff member who accompanied him to these meetings and occasionally represented him was Ed Meese, later, of course, Counselor to the President and then Attorney General.

Ronald Reagan's experience for eight years as governor of California and his exposure to the talent and innovation in other states through his work with the National Governors' Association and ACIR gave him an appreciation and perspective radically different than that of the Washington establishment. Unlike politicians, journalists and other opinion leaders in Washington, Ronald Reagan knew the capacity of the states for responsible leadership, innovation and performance had grown and matured. For him, federalism wasn't just an abstract philosophy he embraced. To Ronald Reagan, the need and value of decentralized government was an imperative he knew and had experienced.

* * * * *

37/ Peter Hanaford, The Reagans: A Political Portrait (Coward-McCann, Inc., New York, 1983), p. 48.

Responsible government at the state level is the prerequisite to any revitalized federalism. And Reagan's experience of increased talent and capacity in the California state government was not unique.

> Those who looked at the states in the 1930's or even in the early 1960's and decided that they lacked the capability to perform their roles in the federal system because they operated under outdated constitutions, fragmented executive structures, hamstrung governors, poorly equipped and unrepresentative legislatures and numerous other handicaps should take another look at the states today.38/

Growth in the capacity of state governments during the 1950's, 1960's and 1970's was remarkable. Financially, the states became more resourceful; institutionally, they reorganized; and politically, they became vigorous and viable. It frustrated Reagan as President, however, that the elitist Washington establishment clung to the antiquated stereotypes of bumbling courthouse pols and continued to treat state governments as administrative provinces. Gradually, though, it became clear that the states had changed. One of the first to notice was _Washington Post_ columnist David Broder. He wrote that:

> "The contrast between the stumbling of the national government and the improving performance of state and local government is a largely unreported story. Individual states have moved out ahead of the federal government, justifying again their claim to be 'laboratories of democracy.'"39/

California under Reagan had not been alone in showing state leadership. By the 1970's, a wide range of social, health and education programs had evolved in the states. Many were devoted particularly to urban needs. Mass transportation, environmental issues, penal reform, consumer protection measures, and tax reform were all state innovations. The states were initiating many programs that would later be copied by the federal govern-

---

38/ Advisory Commission on Intergovernmental Relations, _In Brief: State and Local Roles in the Federal System_, ACIR, Washington, D.C. (November 1981), p. 3.

39/ Cited by Doyen, Ross O., "The Transformation of the States; Yes, Virginia, There is a Case for the 'New Federalism,'" _The Washington Post_, October 25, 1981.

ment.40/ For example, California initiated a program of compen-
satory education for disadvantaged children before the federal
Elementary and Secondary Education Act of 1965.41/ Pennsylvania
began the program of re-training the unemployed after which the
federal Manpower Development and Training Act was patterned.42/
And in 1966, Kentucky passed a civil rights bill broader in scope
than the federal Civil Rights Act of 1964.43/ The states were
demonstrating that they could provide leadership to the nation,
going well beyond the policies of the federal government.

Additionally, states were showing a great deal of diversity in
the administration of federal grants when given the flexibility
they needed from Washington. Delaware, for example, used
Community Service Block Grant (CSBG) and Low Income Energy
Assistance funds to provide shelter for the homeless. Arizona
earmarked discretionary CSBG funds for emergency services, with a
special emphasis on emergency food services. Texas used discretionary funds to employ unskilled and unemployed workers in a
project to move homes scheduled for demolition from a flood
plain, rehabilitate them, and make them available to the homeless
poor. And in Georgia, CSBG money was used to help community
action agencies cover the cost involved in distributing surplus
food.44/

As far back as 1967, Terry Sanford, former governor of North
Carolina, noted in his book, Storm Over the States that:

40/ National Governors' Conference, Innovation in State
     Government: Messages from the Governors, National
     Governors Conference, Washington, D.C., June, 1974;
     and Council of State Governments, "Innovations from
     the Laboratories of Democracy," State Government News,
     August 1976, pp. 2-3.

41/ Sanford, Terry, Storm Over the States, (McGraw Hill,
     New York, 1967), p. 67.

42/ Sundquist, James L., Making Federalism Work, The
     Brookings Institute, Washington, D.C., 1969, p. 261.

43/ Ibid.

44/ Bechtel, William, "States Well Prepared to Run
     Expanded Humanitarian Relief Programs," Governor's
     Bulletin, NGA, Washington, D.C., April 1, 1983.

"The States have served the people well. There is a
long list of solid and reassuring achievements in
every state to bear out this conclusion. They have
the capacity to serve even better..."45/

The transformation was attributed, in large part, to a new breed
of state officials.

First, there were the governors. By the 1970's they were better
educated and more thoroughly trained for their respon-
sibilities.46/ Many had served in the Congress, so they
understood the intricacies of federal programs, bureaucratic
procedures, and funding mechanisms.47/ Broder wrote that it was
his "subjective view that there is more and more qualified leadership to tap at the state level" and "it is certain that some of
the arguments of an earlier day supporting transfer of functions
to the federal government -- arguments that praise the represent-
ativeness and professional character of federal administrators --
may eventually be undercut by trends underway in the states."48/

Constitutionally, the office of the governor was substantially
strengthened. By 1986 only three states limited their governorships to two year terms (Vermont, Rhode Island and New
Hampshire). Only three states limited their governorships to one

---

45/ Sanford, Storm Over the States, op. cit., p. 58.

46/ For a general discussion, see, Sabato, Larry, Goodbye
to Goodtime Charlie, (Lexington Books, Lexington,
Massachusetts, 1978).

47/ A 1975 article in State Government noted:

An increase in the importance to the states of federal programs of various sorts and a corresponding
increase in the value of the Governor's understanding
of the intricacies of federal programs, bureaucratic
procedures, and funding mechanisms should increase the
extent to which congressmen are perceived ... as among
the best-qualified candidates for governor.

See Hain, Paul L. and Smith, Terry B., "Congress: New
Training Ground for Governors," State Government, Vol.
48, Spring 1975, pp. 114-115.

48/ Broder, David S., "The 'New Federalism' Fades Away,
and With It An Opportunity," The Washington Post,
April 14, 1982, p. A-23.

term or banned immediate succession (Virginia, Kentucky and New Mexico). The average annual salary increased from $16,180 in 1955 to $46,883 in 1980. Forty-nine states provided their governors with the ability to veto all legislation and 43 provided a line #tem veto -- a power which Ronald Reagan had as governor and which he repeatedly has said should be given to the president. In 47 states the governor had sole authority to propose a budget.49/

Gubernatorial staffs grew from an average of 11 persons in 1956 to 34 in 1979, and in 41 states an average of nearly 4 people in each governor's office were involved in federal-state relations.50/ The quality of state administrators rose as well. By the '70's the heads of state agencies were substantially younger, better educated and more professionally qualified than their predecessors.

By 1978, the proportion of agency heads with less than a college degree had dropped from 34 to 11 percent. Those with graduate degrees had risen from 40 percent to 58 percent. A tradition of career service was growing. Half of the agency heads began work in state government before they were 30 and had reached the top of their agency before they were 50, most often within the same agency. In addition, the proportion of agency heads who held their positions by popular election declined from 13 percent in 1964 to 9 percent in 1978, thereby enhancing gubernatorial appointive authority.51/

Also, the number of state employees rose tremendously. In 1960 there were 1.4 million; by 1970 there were 2.3 million; and by 1980 there were 3 million. State payrolls increased from $545 million in 1960, to $1.6 billion in 1970, to $4.3 billion in 1980.52/

49/ Advisory Commission on Intergovernmental Relations, In Brief, op. cit., p. 6.

50/ Advisory Commission on Intergovernmental Relations, "State and Local Roles," op. cit., p. 110.

51/ Hebert, F. Ted and Wright, Deil, "State Administrators: How Representative? How Professional?" State Government Quarterly, Volume 55, 1982.

52/ Statistical Abstract of the United States, 1982-83, U.S. Department of Commerce, Bureau of the Census, Washington, D.C., p. 304.

The transformation of state executive branches was paralleled in their legislative branches. As noted by Alan Rosenthal, director of Rutgers University Eagleton Institute of Politics, "The people who serve as state legislators are not what they used to be. The new breed is young, well educated, bright, hard-working, aggressive, and sometimes zealous."53/

State legislatures of old were justifiably the target of much criticism. They met infrequently. Their committees were a jumble of overlapping jurisdictions. Compensation, staffing and budgets were poor, so research and bill drafting was a primitive process. There was little legislative oversight of programs. The malapportionment of legislative chambers caused a disparity between actual population distribution and legislative seats. As a result, the legislatures were not adequately or accurately reflecting the wishes of the people.54/

The 1960's and early 1970's, however, saw sweeping reforms. As a result of the Supreme Court's Baker v. Carr 55/ and Reynolds v. Sims 56/ decisions, state legislatures were apportioned on "one man, one vote" principles; and the Voting Rights Act of 1965

53/ Rosenthal, Alan, Legislative Life, (Harper & Row, New York, 1981), pp. 57, 60.

54/ David Broder of the Washington Post stated:

"It was not very long ago that the typical state legislature was a collection of part-time amateurish politicians, meeting for 60 days every other year, with little staff or information resources of their own, ratifying the governor's budget and passing whatever bills were uppermost on the lobbyists' minds."

See Broder, David S., "New States of Power," The Washington Post, August 1, 1982, p. B-7.

55/ 639 U.S. 186 (1962).

56/ 377 U.S. 533 (1964).

broadened the franchise.57/ The effect was that state legislatures today represent no demographically different constituency
than does the Congress. Women and blacks are represented in a
higher proportion in state legislatures than in the Congress.
Also, there is no longer an anti-urban bias.58/ After the 1970
census, every state reapportioned its legislature, and for the
first time the urban-suburban majority became predominant in the
legislatures as it was in the country as a whole.59/

57/ One author noted in 1966 that:

"Reform of American governmental institutions is normally preceded by decades of discussion, with advances
made in fits and starts when made at all. So it was
with the state legislatures -- until 1962. The back-
ground papers for the 1955 American Assembly on "The
Forty-Eight States" cited the misrepresentativeness of
state legislatures as urgently requiring remedy, and
gave the faulty legislative apportionments then prevailing as a principal block to public confidence in
state government itself. Baker v. Carr, in 1962,
began a series of court decisions that upset long-
entrenched patterns of representation and led down the
road to apportionment in all state legislatures on the
principle of 'one man, one vote.' This radical development solved what was thought to be the number one
problem, a problem annually becoming more acute as the
nation's population grew and became more mobile."

See, Jones, Hechert, "Dimensions of State Politics,"
State Legislatures in American Politics, The American
Assembly, Columbia University, New York, 1966.

58/ The Executive Director of the National Conference of
State Legislatures stated in 1981 that:

"Local people tell me they prefer having their interests considered by the legislature rather than having
somebody in the bureaucracy making the decisions,
whereby they have no chance for impact."

Mackey, Earl S., "Reagan's Policies Bring Cities,
States Together in a Marriage of Convenience,"
National Journal, December 19, 1981, p. 2226.

59/ Sabato, Goodbye to Goodtime Charlie, op. cit., p. 81.

State legislatures also revised their structures and operations with the help of the Citizens' Conference on State Legislatures. The Citizens' Conference on State Legislatures was formed in 1965 as a non-profit, non-partisan, private organization to help state legislatures make the transition from archaic, unrepresentative bodies to more modern, representative institutions. A study conducted by the Conference in 1969 recommended many changes regarding the length and frequency of sessions, staffing, compensation, facilities, procedures, and size of House and Senate.60/

Another significant development was increased oversight of federal funds. Prior to 1975, a survey by the Advisory Commission on Intergovernmental Relations indicated most state legislatures paid very little attention to how their federal funds were being spent.61/ That changed dramatically as grants-in-aid grew to 25% of state budgets. By the late 1970's, most legislatures were involved in the appropriation of federal funds. The involvement was expanded to include program evaluation, review of administrative rules, and sunset reviews. In many states, the legislature acquired the power to temporarily suspend, veto, or require modification in proposed administrative rules.62/ Oversight of funds became an important component of federalism because it was a legislative check and balance on the executive branch of government.63/

60/ In addition to the Citizens Conference, many other groups were involved in making similar recommendations for changes in legislatures, including The American Assembly, the American Political Science Association, The Advisory Commission on Intergovernmental Relations, the Council of State Governments, and the National Conference of State Legislatures.

61/ Advisory Commission on Intergovernmental Relations, The Intergovernmental Grant System as Seen by Local, State and Federal Officials (A-54), Washington, D.C., p. 101.

62/ Wiltsee, Gerbert L., "The State Legislatures," The Book of States 1976-1977, Council of State Governments, Washington, D.C., p. 181.

63/ State Senator Harold Schreier of South Dakota described the oversight process as:

The most important question facing state legislatures if they wish to remain a viable part of the federal
(Cont'd)

The growing responsibility of the legislatures was made possible because of a fundamental change in their internal operations. Rutgers University's Alan Rosenthal noted in 1974 that:

> "Legislatures are more likely to meet annually than biennially. They spend more time in session than before. Professional staff has increased. Research agencies nearly everywhere are larger, many of the important standing committees have assistance and leaders in more than half of the states have full-time staff support. Facilities are better. Salaries are higher. Procedures have become more efficient, and more public. Electronic data processing, in one form or another, is widespread. Legislative office space is more attractive and larger numbers of able individuals are willing to make personal sacrifices in order to serve. Probably more than other American political institutions, state legislatures have recently undergone significant change."64/

In 1969, only 26 state legislatures met annually. By 1980, 43 did so,65/ and nine were in session throughout the year.66/ During the late 1960's and 1970's, there was a 130% increase in the number of legislative employees so that by 1980 total staffing was approximately 25,000.67/ This enabled individual members to be better informed and equipped to deal with the increasing number of constituent problems brought to their attention.

---

system and incidentally, if the country wishes to remain a bastion of check and balance systems of three co-equal branches of government.

See Advisory Commission on Intergovernmental Relations, In Brief: State and Local Roles in the Federal System, ACIR, Washington, D.C., November 1981, p. 8.

64/ Rosenthal, Alan, Legislative Performance in the States, (The Free Press, New York, 1974), pp. 2-3.

65/ ACIR, "State and Local Roles," op. cit., p. 77.

66/ California, Illinois, Massachusetts, Michigan, New Jersey, New York, Ohio, Pennsylvania, and Wisconsin; see Wiltsee, Book of States, op. cit., p. 182.

67/ Wiltsee, Book of States, op. cit., p. 181.

With legislatures taking on more responsibilities and spending more time on their jobs, there was both demand and justification for increased salaries. The recommendation by the Citizens Conference was that no legislative salaries be below $10,000 a year with legislators in larger states receiving $20,000 to $30,000 a year. Fringe benefits also were greatly expanded.68/ The potential advantages to increased legislator salaries were that members would not have to be affluent to take on the job; turnover would be reduced resulting in retention of experienced legislators; and temptation to accept bribes would be decreased.

Finally, the size of legislatures was reduced in many cases. The Illinois House of Representatives, for instance, decreased from 171 to 118 members. This promoted more meaningful debates by giving individual legislators more opportunity to express opinions.

Also, the public interest groups (PIGs) representing state officials and headquartered in Washington helped improve their quality and effectiveness through research assistance, interstate communication and cooperation. These groups gave state officials cohesive voices in federal decision making. One of their prime functions, of course, was to get more federal grant-in-aid money from the Congress. This had the undesirable effect of centralizing the debate in Washington over what government at all levels should do and finance. Rather than the program merits being debated in state capitols, they were debated on Washington's Capitol Hill by lobbyists hired by governors and state legislators. Nevertheless, the unifying of state officials enabled them to become more professional, reform their organizational structures, and regain their respect.69/

These state and local organizations, the PIGs, located in Washington at times proved invaluable allies and, at other times, tremendous obstacles to the Reagan Administration's efforts to decentralize government. Some, such as the very able NGA Executive Director Steve Farber and NACO Executive Director

---

68/ For example: California supplies state cars, gas and telephone credit cards; Illinois supplies a pension for service of at least eight years; and Colorado supplies free ski passes.

See generally, Rosenthal, Legislative Life, op. cit..

69/ For a general discussion see Haider, Donald H., When Government Comes to Washington, (The Free Press, New York, 1974).

Bernie Hillenbrand, understood the concerns of the governors and county officials, the political momentum of Ronald Reagan and the federal fiscal crisis and constructively worked to forge sensible compromise given these competing considerations. Other public interest groups, especially the cities' representatives, tended to take a posture of massive resistance to any decentralization. They failed to grasp the changing climate and, I felt, proved both an unthinking obstacle to the Reagan Administration and failed to successfully represent the best interests of their own constituencies.

The National Governors' Association and the National Conference of State Legislatures became potent and respected voices. NGA alone had a professional staff of over 100, monitoring federal legislation and coordinating gubernatorial congressional testimony. Additionally, individual states opened Washington offices, and by 1980 there were 31 such offices to represent their respective governors.[70]

The public interest groups representing cities and counties also grew in the 1960's and 1970's and became more effective. As with state officials, they helped local officials become more professional and enabled them to share ideas and administrative techniques. This was important because it came at a time when local governments were growing nearly as fast as state governments. Employment by local governments almost doubled between 1960 and 1980 -- from 4.2 million to 7.9 million. Thus, cities and counties had over twice the number of employees as state governments. Their payrolls went from $1.7 billion to $10.4 billion.[71]

In contrast, federal civilian employment remained relatively constant -- from 2.4 million in 1960, to 2.9 million in 1970 and 1980.[72] With states and localities having such large staff support, they were obviously prepared to take over new responsibilities from the federal government. Indeed, in administering

---

[70] Trost, Cathy, "States' Lobbyists Want Bucks to Stop at Home," USA Today, January 7, 1983.

[71] Statistical Abstract of the United States, 1982-83, op. cit., p. 304.

[72] These figures do not include members and employees of Congress, Central Intelligence Agency, temporary Christmas help of the U.S. Postal Service, and National Security Agency. See Statistical Abstract of the United States, op. cit., p. 265.

-36-

federal grants, they were, in essence, providing the services that the federal government was enacting. And, this pervaded all the various units of government -- the state, the county, the city, and the township.

It is perhaps a coincidence, but the evolving role of the states was reflected in presidential politics. Through Franklin Roosevelt, the most prominent route to the White House was by first serving as a governor. The 1950's, '60's and early '70's saw a dramatic shift. Contenders for the office came primarily from the United States Senate -- military hero Dwight Eisenhower and Governor Nelson Rockefeller being the notable exceptions. It was indicative of the dominance of the federal government over the nation's agenda.

By the mid 1970's, however, governors were again on the ascendancy as the states were reclaiming their role in our federal system. Governor Jimmy Carter of Georgia was elected in 1976. The election in 1980 was the first time since 1944 (Roosevelt and Dewey) that both major parties gave their nominations to men who had come to prominence through being a governor. And on Inauguration Day in 1981, a former governor of California -- a strong advocate for the states -- succeeded the former governor of Georgia in the Oval Office.

There is no question in my mind that a key reason Reagan federalism could successfully devolve responsibility was this tremendous growth in the capacity of state and local governments. As Reagan said near the end of his second term as governor, "I believe we have the talent and the capacity to solve whatever problems we face, in the cities of the states."73/ Reagan continued to speak out on the need for such devolution when he left office in Sacramento.

* * * * *

73/ Ronald Reagan, speech, June 25, 1973, ed. Joseph R. Holmes, _The Quotable Ronald Reagan_ (JRH and Associates, Inc., San Diego, California, 1974), p. 27.

The people had come to recognize a sincerity, consistency and momentum in Ronald Reagan's approach to government. With a solid eight-year record of achievement in state government, Governor Reagan left Sacramento to criss-cross the country speaking out on the issues. Again, there would be a national time for choosing.

* * * * *

In the middle of Ronald Reagan's first term as governor, there had been a change in control of the White House. There was movement on the federalism front at the national level as a new Republican administration eventually gave birth to revenue sharing in 1972.74/ Governor Reagan felt that this was a productive first step, yet his underlying philosophy differed substantially from the thrust of President Nixon's "New Federalism." While the ultimate goal of revenue sharing was to bestow federal dollars on state and local governments, Ronald Reagan said on "Meet the Press" that "the federal government should simply restore sources of revenue to the states."75/

In a speech to the Chicago Executive Club on September 26, 1975, he said:

"What I propose is nothing less than a systematic transfer of authority and resources to the state -- a program of creative federalism for America's third century."

By February, 1976, he had begun to put a structural framework on his philosophical goal. In a "White Paper on Federalism," he wrote:

"The federal programs that I believe should be carefully considered for transfer to the states (along with the federal tax resources to finance them) are those which are essentially local in nature. The broad areas that include the most likely prospects for transfer are welfare, education, housing, Food Stamps,

---

74/ Advisory Committee on Intergovernmental Relations (ACIR), "General Revenue Sharing: An ACIR Re-evaluation," A-48, 1974.

75/ Ronald Reagan, Meet the Press, September 12, 1971.

Medicaid, community and regional development, and revenue sharing. These programs represent approximately one-fourth of the current activities of the federal government."76/

Above all, he was saying that Washington was taking too many tax dollars. Not only was the federal government stifling the economy, punishing savings and individual initiative, but resources to provide for human needs were being usurped from state and local governments.

Then in July of 1980, Ronald Reagan received the Republican nomination for President.77/ In his acceptance speech -- the first chance that a presidential nominee has to present his platform to the nation -- he said:

"Everything that can be run more efficiently by state and local governments we shall turn over to local governments, along with the funding sources to pay for it."

In the meantime, there had been a reversal in the fortunes of federalism. Block grants proposed by President Ford had been rejected, more strings were being attached to both categorical programs and the block grants enacted under President Nixon, and General Revenue Sharing (GRS) to the states had been discontinued under President Carter. The reality of Democratic control of both ends of Pennsylvania Avenue and the federal budget deficits caused GRS's demise. Without doubt, the deficits resulted in no small part from the exorbitant rate of growth in categorical programs. During the decade of the 1970's, the number of categorical programs leaped from 130 to 492. Diversity, accountability, efficiency and all the virtues of federalism and decentralization were being trampled.

So in election year 1980, the stage was set for a confrontation. It was to be a show-down between an incumbent Democratic administration which had ended revenue sharing to the states and was proliferating federal power and authority, and a Republican nominee who favored limiting government, and who wanted to go even further than bestowing revenues on the states; he wanted to return actual tax sources.

76/ Ronald Reagan, White Paper on Federalism, February 8, 1976.

77/ July 16, 1980.

Federalism was a consistent theme throughout the campaign. Typical of candidate Reagan's rhetoric following a meeting with Republican mayors in June, 1980:

"Sometimes I think Congress and Washington regulators lose sight of the fact that Americans live at the local level.

This remains true despite four decades of centralization of power and resources at the federal level of government. It is at the local level that their problems occur. And, it is in their individual communities -- and not in Washington -- that the solutions to these problems will be found.

The solutions will be found by mayors like these, and other officials. It is they who best know the unique needs of their separate communities. They are the elected representatives who are most accessible to the people. They are therefore the most knowledgeable and, more important, the most accountable to their constituents. They are in the best position to set and respond to the priorities of their cities -- provided they are given the authority and discretion to respond, and greater local access to revenues."78/

On election day in November, the people voted a mandate for change.79/ This time, they chose what Ronald Reagan had advocated on behalf of Barry Goldwater's losing effort sixteen years earlier.

78/ Ronald Reagan, remarks made in Seattle, Washington, June 8, 1980.

79/ Ronald Reagan won 44 states and 489 electoral votes to Jimmy Carter's 49.

CHAPTER 3

REAGAN'S SIX YEAR QUEST FOR THE PRESIDENCY

Less than one year after stepping down as governor of California, Ronald Reagan challenged President Gerald Ford for the Republican nomination for President. Generally, the Washington establishment failed to take Reagan's candidacy seriously. New York Times columnist James Reston wrote on November 20, 1975, the morning Reagan formally announced his candidacy, "The astonishing thing is that this amusing but frivolous Reagan fantasy is taken so seriously by the news media and particularly by the President. It makes a lot of news, but it doesn't make much sense."1/ To the Washington crowd, it may not have made much sense. But to a lot of Republican primary voters Reagan's candidacy and his message had compelling logic. By the time of the convention in Kansas City, Reagan actually had won more primary votes than the incumbent President. And while Reagan narrowly lost the delegate votes for nomination -- 1070 for Reagan and 1187 for Ford -- that 1976 campaign laid the groundwork for his successful effort four years later.

Of particular importance to Reagan's later federalism efforts while President, was a major address entitled "Let the People Rule" which he delivered to the Chicago Executive Club on September 21, 1975. The speech wreaked havoc in that campaign but formed the philosophical foundation for his efforts as President to redefine federalism and decentralize government.

In preparation for that speech a conscious decision was made that it would not be another routine campaign pitch. In anticipation of his approaching official announcement of candidacy, the Chicago Executive Club was seen as a forum for Reagan to set forth his vision for America. The top campaign leadership of John Sears, Mike Deaver, Peter Hanaford and Lyn Nofziger wanted to frame the populist Ronald Reagan, who opposed the government elite in Washington, in contrast to Gerald Ford, a long time

---

1/ Jules Witcover, Marathon: The Pursuit of the Presidency 1972-1976 (The Viking Press, New York, 1977), p. 90.

-41-

member of the Washington buddy system.2/ Jeff Bell, Director of Research, was assigned the task of drafting the address.

In his standard speech, Reagan would discuss his welfare reforms in California and express his belief that states and local governments could better perform this and most other tasks than a distant bureaucracy in Washington. The Chicago Executive Club speech would be an opportunity to expand on this theme of the need for decentralized government.

Reagan took the draft speech and substantially reworked it. He made notations; changing phrases and adding examples. This was typical of Reagan. Presidential scholars later would note that Reagan wrote more of his speech text than any other President in the twentieth century with the possible exception of Woodrow Wilson.

Those of us on his senior staff were powerfully reminded of Reagan's proclivity to work and re-work his speeches within weeks of arriving at the White House. After the election, during the transition before the inauguration, Jim Baker set up a group to block out a plan for Reagan's first 100 days. The group was led by David Gergen and included Richard Wirthlin, Rich Beal and me.3/ We suggested that soon after inauguration day it would be important for the new President to go to the nation and lay down a marker of exactly how bad an economic mess he had inherited. Inflation and interest rates continued in double digits, the

---

2/   John Sears served as Reagan's Campaign Manager in the 1976 campaign and in the early stages of the 1980 campaign. Mike Deaver would go on to serve as Assistant to the President and Deputy Chief of Staff during Reagan's first five years in the White House. Peter Hanaford served as Director of Research in the 1976 and 1980 campaigns. Lyn Nofziger would serve as Assistant to the President for Political Affairs in 1981.

3/   David Gergen would serve as Assistant to the President for Communications in Reagan's first term. Richard Wirthlin, Reagan's long-time pollster, did not enter the Administration but continued to do polling for the White House throughout the Reagan Presidency under the sponsorship of the Republican National Committee. And Richard Beal, a talented professor from Brigham Young University, joined the White House as Special Assistant for the President for Policy Planning under Ed Meese.

budget was running wild, etc. We felt this was important because soon thereafter we planned for the President to go before a joint session of Congress to present his Economic Recovery Program that would contain profound proposals for reform.4/ We thought it valuable to have that marker established so that as the consequent economic recovery was realized Reagan would get full credit for his achievements.

Gergen had served in both the Nixon and Ford White Houses. He employed the same procedures for preparing the address as he had known in those previous Administrations. Under his supervision a draft speech was prepared and circulated to the White House senior staff and relevant cabinet members for comments and suggestions. Substantial input was received and a re-draft completed. Then the day before the February 5th date when the new President was to present his speech, "The State of the Nation's Economy", on national television it was given to the President for his review.

After a luncheon meeting on the day of the speech, Reagan retired to the residence to review his address. At about 6:00 pm, only two hours before the new President was scheduled to address the nation for the first time since taking office, Reagan came down and asked if someone could please retype his speech because he had made a few changes. The staff, especially those newer to the Reagan team, were horrified. He had completely re-written two-thirds of the speech. He had added facts and examples and re-structured substantial portions of the address. The question was briefly raised among the staff whether the scheduled speech should be cancelled and rescheduled. But that suggestion was quickly dismissed for fear it would show we didn't have our act together. All hands were mobilized to check and double check every fact, and fast. After all, this was no longer private citizen Ronald Reagan on the "mashed potato circuit." He was now the leader of the free world. He was President. Everything had to be totally accurate; fully documented.

It turned out that Reagan's facts as well as his changes of thrust and phrasing were right on the money. He gave his address flawlessly and established the marker of exactly how desperate the economic situation was that he had inherited from Jimmy Carter. Thereby he set the stage for his sweeping economic proposals that would soon follow.

4/ President Reagan did address a joint session of Congress on February 18, 1981 and set forth his program for economic recovery in an address entitled, "America's New Beginning."

But from then on, President Reagan was never given a draft speech just forty-eight hours before scheduled delivery. He usually met with the speech writers when an address was first put on the calendar so that he could lay out exactly what he wanted in the speech. Then he'd get the draft many days before the date of delivery to allow him time to re-work it, usually substantially. Reagan was experienced as a writer for the ear from his days in radio and giving speeches around the country for General Electric. It was a great talent. And to fully utilize it and to allow him an opportunity to feel comfortable with the final text of major speeches, we simply built in plenty of time for the best speech writer in the White House, Reagan himself, to do his magic. After all, it's not just his natural delivery that earned Ronald Reagan the honorary title "The Great Communicator."

Similarly back in 1975, Reagan took the draft speech for the Chicago Economic Club and re-crafted it. The end result was a populist assault on centralized government in Washington and a call for devolution. He first defined the problem as the huge ever-growing federal government. "This collectivist, centralizing approach, whatever name or party label it wears, has created our economic problems," he said:

> "By taxing and consuming an ever-greater share of the national wealth, it has imposed an intolerable burden of taxation on American citizens. By spending above and beyond even this level of taxation, it has created the horrendous inflation of the past decade. And by saddling our economy with an even-greater burden of controls and regulations, it has generated countless economic problems, from the rising of consumer prices to the destruction of jobs, to choking off vital supplies of food and energy.

> As if this were not enough, the crushing weight of central government has distorted our federal system and altered the relationship between the levels of government, threatening the freedom of individuals and families."

Later in his address, Reagan outlined his proposals to correct the problem.

> "The problem must be attacked at its source. ...we can and must reverse the flow of power to Washington; not simply slow it or paper over the problem with attractive phrases or cosmetic tinkering...

>What I propose is nothing less than a systematic
>transfer of authority and resources to the states -- a
>program of creative federalism for America's third
>century."5/

Reagan then identified welfare, education, housing, food stamps,
Medicaid, community and regional development and revenue sharing
as a few of the potential programs for devolution to the
states. He said, "Transfer of authority in whole or part in all
these areas would reduce the outlay of the federal government by
more than $90 billion, using the spending levels of fiscal
1976."6/ Reagan also said the transfer of the programs from the
federal to state governments would be accompanied by "a transfer
of federal tax sources along with them."

Then Reagan added his central belief that the people should
rule. He said, "The decision as to whether programs are or are
not worthwhile -- and whether to continue or cancel them -- will
be placed where it rightfully belongs: with the people of our
states." This was the philosophic core of our later proposals
when Reagan was in the White House both with the block grants of
1981 and the $44 billion swap and transfer program outlined in
the 1982 State of the Union Address.

>"The present system is geared for maximum expenditure
>and minimum responsibility. There is no better way to
>promote the lavish outlay of tax money than to trans-
>fer program and funding authority away from state and
>local governments to the federal level. This insures
>that recipients of aid will have every reason to spend
>and none to conserve. They can get political credit
>for spending freely, but don't have to take the heat
>for imposing taxes.

5/   Ronald Reagan, "Let the People Rule," Address to the
     Chicago Executive Club, Chicago, Illinois, September
     26, 1975. (Italics added.)

6/   Reagan also identified various federal functions that
     he would not transfer to the states: national
     defense, space, Social Security, Medicare, federal law
     enforcement, veterans affairs, TVA, and several agri-
     culture, energy, environmental-protection and trans-
     portation programs.

The object is to reverse this: to join ... the spending and taxing functions together whenever feasible,
so that those who have the pleasure of giving away tax
dollars will also have the pain of raising them. <u>At
the same time we can sort out which functions of government are best performed at each level. And that
process, I hope, would be going on between each state
and its local government at the same time.</u> 7/

So back in 1975 Reagan outlined the need to decentralize government; to sort out functions of government between the various
levels in our intergovernmental system. He laid out a scheme for
transferring programs and mentioned the need to accompany that
with a transfer of revenue sources. And he stated the need to
tie spending and taxing functions together at the state and local
level, not in distant Washington, so that the people could rule
and decide their own priorities. It was the people who should
decide which programs prosper and which are eliminated. Back in
his 1964 speech for Barry Goldwater, Reagan had said, "A government agency is the nearest thing to eternal life we'll ever see
on this earth."8/ By sorting out functions, decentralizing government and tying spending and taxing together, Reagan believed
that eternal life for government programs would end for those the
people did not want or need. Through decentralizing government,
the people would rule.

With this speech in 1975, Ronald Reagan indeed had set forth
profound proposals to radically reverse the trend from ever increasing centralization of government in Washington to decentralization. It frontally assaulted the common wisdom of forty
years. In one document it laid a blueprint for returning power,
authority and resources back from the federal government to state
and local governments. While it was a blueprint, we would draw
on it five and a half years later once Reagan reached the White
House; back in 1975 it became a political albatross.

As an addendum to the Chicago Executive Club speech was attached
a list of 24 programs as candidates for transfer with current
federal expenditures of $81.9 billion (and projected growth
bringing the total to $90 billion).

7/   Ronald Reagan, "Let the People Rule", Address to the
      Chicago Executive Club, Chicago, Illinois, September
      26, 1975. (Italics added.)

8/   James S. Brady, ed., <u>Ronald Reagan: A Man True to His
      Word</u> (The National Federation of Republican Women,
      Washington, D.C., 1984), p. 80.

Weeks later on November 20, 1975, Reagan officially announced his candidacy for President saying, in part:

> "[T]he root of [America's] problems lies here -- in Washington, D.C. Our nation's capitol has become the seat of a "buddy" system that functions for its own benefit -- increasingly insensitive to the needs of the American worker who supports it with taxes. ...
>
> If America is to survive and go forward, this must change. It will only change when the American people vote for a leadership that listens to them, relies on them, and <u>seeks to return government to them</u>. We need a government that is confident not of what it can do, but of what the people can do."<u>9</u>/

Clearly, the Chicago speech had not been an aberration. It merely was a more detailed design of how Reagan saw he could "return government" to the people. He intended to challenge the status quo. For, as Reagan said, "Status Quo -- that's Latin for 'the mess we're in'."<u>10</u>/

In political campaigns it is generally understood that the more detailed and explicit a candidate's recommendations the more exposed he is to attack from his opponents. While the Chicago Executive Club speech had laid out a philosophic framework and used illustrative examples, the addendum had been specific in identifying 24 programs. This gave the campaign of Gerald Ford an inviting target to exploit.

Throughout the next couple of months, many of us involved in the Reagan camp trumpeted the Chicago Executive Club speech in recruiting converts to the campaign as a populist imperative for Reagan's candidacy. It received warm receptions from conservative audiences throughout America. But soon after Reagan's formal announcement we were put on the defensive. While the general philosophy was music to many Republican ears, the specifics created prickly problems in some states, notably in New Hampshire, the location of the all-important first primary that had no state income tax.

<u>9</u>/ Ronald Reagan, Address to the National Press Club, Washington, D.C., November 20, 1975. (Italics added.)

<u>10</u>/ James S. Brady, editor, <u>Ronald Reagan: A Man True to His Word</u> (The National Federation of Republican Women, Washington, D.C., 1984), p. 81.

A couple of days after his announcement of candidacy, Reagan appeared on ABC's program "Issues and Answers." Correspondent Bob Clark went to the heart of the political issue, asking "In candor, wouldn't you have to tell the people of New Hampshire that you are going to have to increase your tax burden and that probably means either a sales tax or a state income tax?"

Reagan replied, "But isn't this a proper decision for the people of the state to make?"11/

While a sound policy reply, it was a slippery slope toward a political quagmire. As the primary date approached, New Hampshire State Senate President Alf Jacobson and House Speaker George Roberts, both Ford supporters, held a press conference in Concord. The plan, Roberts said, "would cost the people of New Hampshire tens of millions of dollars just to maintain the existing mandated programs at their present level" and would force New Hampshire "to eliminate many necessary programs, to add to the local property-tax burden, or to institute a state sales tax, a state income tax, or both."12/ The political fat was in the fire. The possibility of a sales or state income tax was political dynamite in New Hampshire. From then on, Reagan was forced to play defense in the snows of New Hampshire.

Those of us in Washington saw Reagan's momentum disappear. Day after day the "$90 Billion Plan" dominated the news. The Ford campaign exploited with great skill the opportunity we had given them. The Chicago Executive Club speech had gone beyond policy framework to troublesome specifics in its addendum. In New Hampshire it wasn't just an issue, it had become the entire campaign.

Jules Witcover, in his excellent book on the 1976 campaign, Marathon, reports a song written in the press bus in New Hampshire, to the tune of "Give Me The Simple Life":

11/ Jules Witcover, Marathon 1972-1976: The Pursuit of the Presidency (The Viking Press, New York, 1977), p. 379. Witcover has an excellent chapter in his book devoted to the "$90-Billion Problem." See also, Rowland Evans and Robert Novak, The Reagan Revolution (E.P. Dutton, New York, 1981), p. 43.

12/ Witcover, Marathon 1972-1976, op. cit., p. 380.

"Cut 90 billion, make it a trillion,
Just call me Ron the Knife;
This Old Vaudevillian can save you a zillion
I'll give you the simple life.

Aid to the old Folks, it's good as gold, folks,
I'll keep you free from strife;
Barry's a cruel hoax, I won't play his jokes,
I'll give you the simple life.

And all those cheats who want a free ride,
I'll guarantee to turn them loose;
And all who break the law will be fried
Just watch me cook their goose.

I may be crazy, but I'm not lazy,
I campaign from dawn to night;
Fresh as a daisy, by keeping it hazy,
I'll give you the simple life."13/

On election eve some of Reagan team gathered at the New Hampshire Highway Motel in Manchester. Others of us joined together at the home of one of our colleagues in Washington, Tom Malatesta. We thought Reagan would narrowly hold on and win. And if he beat incumbent President Ford at the starting gate, we all believed Ford's campaign would quickly fold and Reagan would be the nominee. But the final results showed it was Ford who had narrowly won with 54,824 to 53,507 for Reagan. A consensus throughout the political community was that the "$90 Billion Plan" had snatched defeat out of the jaws of victory for Reagan in New Hampshire. For all of us it was one of the longest, saddest political nights of our lives.

Ford went on to win Florida and Illinois. But Reagan came back to win the North Carolina primary and from then on made it a real horse race. In the end, of course, Ford narrowly captured the nomination. And as we approached another Reagan presidential candidacy in 1980 we were all mindful of avoiding a repeat of the "$90 Billion Plan" trap.

In the first week of January, 1980, Ed Meese lead three days of issue briefings for Reagan in the campaign headquarters near the Los Angeles Airport in preparation for the campaign ahead. A handful of us were there for the entire three days: John Sears, Marty Anderson, Peter Hanaford, Doug Bandow, myself and a few

---

13/ Ibid., pp. 387-8.

others.14/ Most of the policy advisors just joined us for discussions in their area of expertise: Richard Allen and Fred
Ikle, for example, on foreign policy and Jack Kemp, Art Laffer
and Dick Whalen on economic issues.15/ During these discussions
the issue of decentralization was raised. In light of the 1976
experience with the Chicago Executive Club speech the question
came up as to whether the whole federalism issue should be down-
played this time out. Reagan made clear to all of us that he
believed deeply in the need to return power to the people through
decentralization. He would not back away from this commitment
during the campaign. But he also said he would be more cautious
about avoiding specifics. So the course was set. Federalism
would be a Reagan issue in the 1980 campaign.

Our brief luncheon breaks during the three days of briefings were
an informal buffet arrangement when we sat at random. By the
third day I had become very impressed both with how Meese had
organized the substantive presentations as well as the breadth
and scope of Reagan's own knowledge of most of the areas discussed. That third day I happened to be sitting next to Reagan.
He regaled us with stories. But near the end of lunch I had a
chance to raise something with him about which I had become increasingly convinced. I said "Governor, you know an awful lot
more substantively about these important issues than the press
ever gives you credit for. We should get more of your expertise
into your speeches." Reagan turned to me and smiled, almost a
grandfatherly smile, and said, "Rich, I appreciate the compli-
ment. But you know, I've been selling things for a long time. I

14/ Doug Bandow was a research assistant to Marty Anderson
in the campaign. He later went to the White House on
Marty's staff.

15/ Richard Allen who had been on Nixon's NSC staff, was
Reagan's top foreign policy advisor in the 1980 campaign and in 1981 served as Assistant to the President
for National Security Affairs. Fred Ikle had been
Director of the Arms Control and Disarmament Agency
under President Ford and went on to serve as
Undersecretary of the Department of Defense in the
Reagan Administration. Congressman Jack Kemp was the
congressional leader of the Kemp-Roth tax cut legislation. Professor Art Laffer was the theoretician of
the tax cuts and served on President Reagan's Economic
Advisory Board. Richard Whalen is an author and
international economics expert who had served in the
Nixon Administration and was an informal advisor to
the White House throughout the Reagan Administration.

know what I'm doing." And, of course, he did. Casting himself as the citizen-politician he could touch a responsive chord with the voters he'd never achieve if he talked to them as a great expert with a grasp of minute details and subtle substantive nuances. From that day on, when I heard him talk publicly about issues -- and often wished he had a better grasp of all the details and full implications of the subject -- I remembered that earlier brief exchange. Reagan did know how to touch the common man. As the saying goes, "God must like the common man because he made so many of them."16/ Ronald Reagan, notwithstanding his celebrated fame as an actor and later as a politician, always sees himself as a common man and never wanted to endanger his link to those other common men, the American people. He recognized better than anyone that this was his greatest political strength.

As Reagan had directed, decentralization was an issue he often raised in the 1980 campaign. As Reagan said during the primaries, "I don't believe in big, centralized federal government. I believe that the federal government has attempted to do far too many things -- that there are federal programs that should be returned to the states, along with the tax resources to pay for them. I believe that the federal government is too interventionist."17/

He established an unprecedented structure to involve Republican governors in his Presidential effort. Under the direction of Governor Pete du Pont of Delaware, governors provided a steady stream of policy advice and political support to the Reagan-Bush campaign. (Pete du Pont later proved a loyal friend, advisor and advocate for me personally and our federalism agenda when Reagan reached the White House.) Similarly, we established a bipartisan Mayors for Reagan Committee co-chaired by Mayor Pete Wilson of San Diego, California and Mayor Richard Carver of Peoria, Illinois.18/ There also was a Mayors' Urban Advisory Task Force. Indicative of Reagan's views on the intergovernmental

---

16/ The actual quote from Abraham Lincoln is, "The Lord prefers common-looking people. That is the reason He makes so many of them."

17/ Elizabeth Drew, Portrait of an Election: The 1980 Presidential Campaign (Simon and Schuster, New York, 1981), p. 110.

18/ Wilson was elected to the U.S. Senate in 1982. Dick Carver joined the Reagan Administration as an Assistant Secretary of the Air Force in 1983.

system were remarks he made following a meeting with mayors in June, 1980:

"The solutions will be found by mayors. ...It is they who best know the unique needs of their separate communities."19/

The thrust of the federalism framework he had outlined in such detail at the Chicago Executive Club during the 1976 campaign, continued to be echoed throughout 1980. If anything, we found the electorate even more disillusioned with Washington and centralized government in that federal city after four years of Jimmy Carter. One of the lines Reagan often used in the 1980 campaign was that "There's enough fat in the government in Washington that if it was rendered and made into soap, it could wash the world."20/

In July, Ronald Reagan received the Republican nomination for President.21/ In his acceptance speech -- the first chance that a Presidential nominee has to present his platform to the nation -- he stressed the themes of cutting government growth and getting control of the federal budget. He discussed the needs to revitalize our national defense and provide leadership in the free world. And, importantly, he reiterated his strong desire for "a rebirth of the American tradition of leadership at every level of government."22/ In that speech, he also set forth in a few sentences the theme that would become the cornerstone of his federalism policy upon taking office.

"Everything that can be run more effectively by state and local government we shall turn over to state and local government, along with the funding sources to pay for it. We are going to put an end to the money-merry-go-round where our money becomes Washington's

---

19/ Ronald Reagan, remarks made in Seattle, Washington, June 8, 1980.

20/ Elizabeth Drew, Portrait of an Election: the 1980 Presidential Campaign (Simon and Schuster, New York, 1981), p. 269.

21/ First ballot nomination, July 16, 1980, Republican National Convention, Detroit, Michigan.

22/ Ronald Reagan, acceptance speech delivered to the Republican National Convention, Detroit, Michigan, July 17, 1980.

money, to be spent by states and cities only if they spend it exactly the way the federal bureaucrats tell them to."23/

In 1980, unlike 1976, the Reagan campaign was careful not to present a detailed agenda of specific programs for transfer from the federal government to state and local governments. But the theme was crystal clear. Candidate Reagan repeatedly addressed the several basic imbalances in the federal system. The federal government had become overloaded by assuming more responsibilities than it could manage. There had been a breakdown in accountability between the voters and those who decide how to spend our tax dollars. And the reward system had become so distorted that state and local officials were often judged by their effectiveness in intergovernmental lobbying rather than in governing.24/

I later learned from Governor George Busbee, the popular Democratic leader of Georgia, that during the summer of 1980 he had sought out his neighbor and old friend Charles Kirbo, President Carter's closest friend and confidant. Busbee had argued that Carter should get out front on the federalism issue. He told Kirbo, and later members of the Carter White House staff, that even the Democratic governors wanted to cut back on federal interference. And, he told them that he and other Democratic governors were convinced that the voters would respond most favorably to a call from Carter for decentralizing government. Busbee would later tell me that after a couple runs up that hill he gave up. He heard nothing back. It was clear from the Carter campaign that President Carter totally disagreed substantively and/or politically with the judgment of his own party's governors.

The stage was set for a confrontation. It was a show-down between an incumbent Democratic administration which had ended revenue sharing to the states and was proliferating federal power and authority, and a Republican nominee who favored limiting government, and who wanted to go even further than bestowing revenues on the states; he wanted to return actual tax sources.

23/   Ibid.

24/   See Richard S. Williamson, "1980: The Reagan Campaign
      -- Harbinger of a Revitalized Federalism," Publius,
      Vol. 11, No. 3-4, Summer, 1981, p. 147.

On election day, the people voted a mandate for change.25/ That evening we had a "command center" in the Century Plaza Hotel. Dick Wirthlin was receiving data from exit polls around the country and posting the results to the small group of senior campaign staff in the suite. We were in an ebullient mood. Since the second debate a couple of weeks earlier, the numbers had held firm with a comfortable lead for Reagan. We were convinced we would win. But what we were not prepared for was the size of Reagan's crushing victory over Carter: 44 states went to the Reagan-Bush team. Even more amazing and totally unexpected, the Republicans won the Senate.26/

When Reagan arrived in the suite after having had dinner with William French Smith, Holmes Tuttle, Justin Dart and other long-time California friends, he seemed flabbergasted by the Senate victories. He was delighted. He said a number of times, "I simply can't believe it" and "Isn't it wonderful."

While most of us shared his pleasure at the GOP gains in Congress, it was the Reagan-Bush victory we savored. I don't think any of us fully appreciated how crucial the new make up of Congress would be for the early success of Reagan's legislative proposals, including his federalism efforts to decentralize government. As journalist Elizabeth Drew would write:

> "[T]he Republicans had taken control of the Senate -- something that not even the Republicans had dreamed possible -- and had picked up a sufficient number of seats in the House to insure that the prevailing ideology will be conservative. Moreover, the Republicans who will gain positions of power in the Senate -- the committee and subcommittee chairmanship -- are for the most part very conservative Republicans. The transfer of power may be orderly, but the atmosphere in

---

25/ Election results were: Reagan 50.7%, Carter 41%, Anderson 6.6%. Reagan received 489 votes is the Electoral College, and Carter 49.

26/ Nine Democratic incumbent Senators, most of them liberal, were defeated. The Republicans held the Senate, 53 to 46. There was one independent, conservative Harry Byrd, Jr. of Virginia.

Washington is that of a place that has suddenly been taken by a conquering army."27/

And Ronald Reagan, the Washington outsider who wanted to cut back the federal city, led that army.

A few years earlier I had edited a book for some conservative friends in the Senate, A CHANGING AMERICA: CONSERVATIVES VIEW THE '80'S FROM THE U.S. SENATE.28/ At the time the views of these Senators were of no great moment. They seemed antiquated and members of a permanent minority. Now one was to be a cabinet member (Richard Schweiker (PA), Health and Human Services), and others would be Senate committee chairmen (Pete Domenici (NM), Budget; Jake Garn (UT), Banking and Currency; Orrin Hatch (UT), Labor; James McClure (ID), Energy; and Paul Laxalt (NV), who had written a commentary overview for the book, was to assume a role unique in American history).

As Reagan's best friend in Congress and a member of the Senate well-liked on both sides of the aisle, Laxalt would serve as a unique ombudsman and interlocutor between the new President and Congress. He also was a tremendous help to me in advancing the federalism agenda. In the spring of 1981, when the administration efforts to decentralize government seemed to lack focus, I sold Jim Baker, Ed Meese and then the President on the idea of creating a short term Federalism Advisory Committee of members of Congress, the Cabinet, state and local officials and private scholars, which my staff coordinated. And I turned to the President's old friend Paul Laxalt to chair the group and give it political weight, prestige and guarantee the President's attentive ear. Laxalt did a terrific job and thereby provided his old friend Ronald Reagan once again with invaluable assistance.

27/ Elizabeth Drew, Portrait of an Election: The 1980 Presidential Campaign (Simon and Schuster, New York, 1981), pp. 339-40. The Democratic majority in the House of Representatives of 143 in 1977 when Carter took office had shrunk to 49 with the 1980 elections.

28/ Paul Laxalt and Richard S. Williamson, ed., A CHANGING AMERICA: CONSERVATIVES VIEW THE '80'S FROM THE UNITED STATES SENATE (Regnery/Gateway, Inc., South Bend, Indiana, 1980).

CHAPTER 4

DECENTRALIZING THROUGH BLOCK GRANTS

There wasn't long to savor the exhilaration of election night. The next day the presidential transition began. In Los Angeles, Reagan's personal attorney William French Smith convened a meeting of some of the President-elect's closest friends, the so-called kitchen cabinet, to begin a screening process for cabinet appointees.1/ And the next Monday, Ed Meese was back in Washington to head up the elaborate transition team.

We were officed in cramped quarters in a federal building on "L" Street, a short walk from the White House. The offices weren't particularly clean nor was the furniture new. But in the excitement of forming a new government, no one seemed to care.

The problems for the Reagan transition were complicated. Reagan himself was not only an outsider to Washington, he had prided himself on that fact and campaigned against the federal government. Meese also was a Californian with little experience in D.C. And in a highly unusual situation, Congress had not adjourned before election day, but merely recessed. So in addition to staffing the new Administration and drafting transition reports on the complex matrix of federal agencies and departments, the transition team had to cope with Congress. There was sensitivity on Capitol Hill that President Carter had just suffered a crushing defeat and an unusually high number of Senators and Representatives sitting in the lame duck Congress also had been defeated. They were solicitors for input from the President-elect and his transition leader Ed Meese. At the same time, Reagan and Meese were fully mindful of the limiting properties of their position. They held no office at that time. There could only be one President and one administration. And at that time it was Jimmy Carter's, not Ronald Reagan's.

1/ A number of those who met in William French Smith's office later joined the Administration. Smith became Attorney General in the first term. Charles Wick became Director of the U.S. Information Agency. Caspar Weinberger became Secretary of Defense. William Casey became Director of the Central Intelligence Agency. Ed Meese served as Counselor to the President and then succeeded Smith as Attorney General.

To coordinate the situation, Meese first turned to Bill Timmons. He was an old Washington hand from both the Eisenhower and Nixon White House days, who had directed the Republican Convention operation for Reagan in Detroit. Timmons helped staff and direct the teams of experts that went into the various departments and agencies to assess the situation and produce reports on personnel and substance.2/ Pen James, an old friend of Meese's who had run a small executive search firm in California, at Meese's request, had already been scouting for months for talent to staff the administration.3/ And Meese personally not only supervised all these functions, but got involved daily in issue development for the new Administration as well as analysis of whatever mischief the lame duck Congress was up to.

Ed Meese loves meetings. Some of his critics argue he loves them too much. But I've never known anyone else who could listen to such a wide variety of presentations, assimilate the data, sort it out and then lay out the options concisely and fairly. I would later see this ability of Meese to hear conflicting briefs and then sum up with a verbal "mini-memo" often in Cabinet meet-

---

2/   Some of these transition reports were extremely helpful, others not. For example, upon his nomination as
Secretary of State, Alexander Haig dismissed most of
the State Department transition team and pretty much
ignored their recommendations. In contrast, the transition report on the Federal Trade Commission had a
profound effect. In addition to some issue coordination and serving on Jim Baker's White House transition
team, I served as a Senior Advisor to the FTC transition team in part because a substantial portion of my
private law practice had been antitrust. That group
was ably led by economist James Miller. The FTC transition report was thorough and made a number of strong
recommendations. Later when Miller became FTC
Chairman, that report served as a road map for his
successful tenure.

3/   For an excellent discussion of the staffing of the
first term of the Reagan Administration, see Helene
von Damm, At Reagan's Side: Twenty Years in the
Political Mainstream (Doubleday, New York, 1989), pp.
126-152.

ings.4/ He is unfailingly patient, polite and fair. Over time, I grew to respect this talent enormously and to appreciate how valuable this skill was to keep conflicting Cabinet members happy while summing up and focusing the options for Reagan to make his decision.

To help him on the issue matters and in dealing with Congress, Meese set up a 7:00 am meeting of the senior issue people at the transition offices. Some days it was moved even earlier and we'd begin and end these hour long meetings before the sun rose. From sitting in those meetings, talking to friends on Capitol Hill, and visiting with colleagues working in other areas of the transition team, it often was hard to see how it could possibly all come together. Like Alice in Wonderland, we were running twice as fast just to stay in the same place.

Two weeks after the election, President-elect Reagan came to Washington. With guidance from Paul Laxalt, Reagan had set up a masterful schedule. He visited President Carter in the Oval Office. One night Katherine Graham, powerful publisher of the Washington Post, hosted a small dinner party for the Reagans at the F-Street Club with a guest list of leaders of the permanent Washington establishment from areas of business, civic, media and political life. It was intended to introduce them to the Reagans and vice-versa. And it was meant to show the permanent Washington establishment that unlike Jimmy Carter, the Reagans intended to make Washington their real home over the next few years, even if their hearts remained in California. Another night, conservative columnist George Will hosted a dinner party in his home.

Reagan also used these visits to begin his courtship of Congress. He was very mindful of the political necessity to work with Congress, establish a dialogue of mutual respect, develop some rapport. He wanted to avoid a contentious relationship with Congress like that which had developed between President Carter and Capitol Hill. Los Angeles Times Washington Bureau Chief Jack

---

4/ When William Clark was Reagan's Chief of Staff in California, he developed a format whereby gubernatorial decision memorandums would be condensed to a single page. It was a format Reagan appreciated. Upon arriving at the White House, efforts continued to keep decision memorandums short and concise for Reagan. Bill Clark later served in a variety of public offices: Justice on the California Supreme Court, Deputy Secretary of State, National Security Advisor and Secretary of the Interior.

Nelson has a wonderful story about Carter's problems with Congress. "Shortly after the 1976 election," Nelson reports, "Peter Bourne, a Georgian who became a White House aide, told me he was worried that Carter would treat Congress like it's the Georgia Legislature, and Congress will treat him like he's the Georgia governor. Bourne's fears were founded."[5] Reagan was anxious to do better. On Reagan's first full day in Washington, he went to Capitol Hill and had separate meetings with the respective party leadership. I was one of those who accompanied him.

The meeting with House Republican Leader Bob Michel and his senior colleagues was light-hearted and jovial. Then, we went to visit Speaker Tip O'Neill in his large ornate office. The Speaker seemed stiff and ill-at-ease. Perhaps, this was because he and Reagan had never met before. Perhaps, it was because Reagan's political views were dramatically opposed to O'Neill's own and he had just beat the stuffing out of O'Neill's candidate Jimmy Carter. Or perhaps, it was because O'Neill was wary of the new political landscape in the House where the Republicans plus the Southern Democrats might be able to forge a ruling coalition on key issues. Whatever the reason, it took a while and some good Irish jokes for Reagan to loosen up the Speaker. But eventually these two great story tellers were swapping yarns much to their own and our delight.

These two men had a lot in common. About the same age, both were born into modest Irish families. Both had worked hard and prospered. Both had a twinkle in their eye and loved to tell stories. But whereas Reagan had entered politics late in life (running for governor of California at age 54) after a successful career as an actor, Tip O'Neill knew no other life than politics. He had run for the city council while still an undergraduate at Boston College. He was elected to the Massachusetts legislature at age 24. He served there for 16 years, becoming Speaker of the Assembly. Then in 1952, he won the congressional seat vacated by John Kennedy when he went on to the Senate. Tip O'Neill was an old fashioned organization pol who had served his constituents, served his apprenticeship, and worked his way up the ladder. Reagan had started his political career relatively late in life and near the top as governor of California, the largest state in the union. And Reagan knew precious little about precinct, ward or county organizations. He was a media candidate who spoke to the people.

5/ Jack Nelson, "The Reagan Legacy," in ed. Paul Duke, Beyond Reagan: The Politics of Upheaval (Warner Books, New York, 1986), pp. 83-103.

But more fundamentally, Tip O'Neill was an old fashioned unreconstructed New Deal liberal, and proud of it. Whereas Ronald Reagan, who had once supported FDR, had become a solid conservative. I can remember at least a half dozen times while in the White House after a telephone conversation with O'Neill or a meeting when Reagan would turn to us and say, sometimes in amusement and sometimes in utter frustration, "He really believes that stuff. He's just an old fashioned liberal through and through."

While the two remained friends "after six o'clock" they often were in tough political battles. O'Neill saw a lot of his precious beliefs challenged by Reagan. And he witnessed a lot of what he believed in swept away. The political tide was with Reagan. And while it might not have been a tidal wave, it was big enough to change substantially the political landscape through increased defense spending, budget cuts, tax cuts and devolution of domestic programs.

But in that first meeting in the fall of 1980, it was clear that Speaker O'Neill saw himself as the seasoned veteran and Ronald Reagan as the rookie. Near the end of their visit, Reagan said that he hoped to have good relations with Congress and intended to work hard to achieve and maintain those good relations. He went on to note that he had worked well with the Democratic controlled legislature in California and would try to do the same in Washington. O'Neill, the slightly cocky veteran who had seen many occupants of the White House come and go, turned to Reagan and said almost as if to patronize the President-elect, "That was the minor leagues. You're in the big leagues now."6/ Many of us in the room were surprised by O'Neill's tone of voice.

In politics there are no final victories. The Reagan Administration has won some important legislative battles and lost others. But from time to time, especially that first year when Reagan beat back Tip O'Neill and the liberal Democrats to win the Gramm-Latta budget cuts and the Kemp-Roth tax cuts, I'd wonder if the old veteran in the Speaker's office felt the rookie from the minor leagues might just be teaching the "big leagues" a thing or two.

After O'Neill, Reagan went over to the Senate side of Capitol Hill and visited with Senator Howard Baker (TN), the new Majority

---

6/ See the Speaker's recollection of this meeting in Tip O'Neill, Man of the House: The Life and Political Memoirs of Speaker Tip O'Neill (Random House, New York, 1987), p. 332.

Leader, and the new Republican Senate committee chairmen.7/
Baker had kept the suite of offices he had held as Minority
Leader before the election rather than displace the proud
Democratic leader Robert Byrd (WV) from the larger, more ornate
offices Byrd had used as Majority Leader. It was a small thing
perhaps, but a typically thoughtful gesture by Baker. Also,
Baker had a particular attachment to his offices since they had
once been those of Senator Everett Dirksen of Illinois, his
father-in-law, when he had been Senate Republican leader. A
large portrait of Dirksen now hung on one of the walls.

This meeting was extremely high spirited. Many of these new
Senate committee chairmen, Reagan hardly knew. It was a get-
acquainted session. But it was clear from their remarks and
questions that they were looking for direction from the
President-elect whose coat-tails had swept into the Senate the
unprecedented and highly unexpected Republican majority.

Few of these new committee chairmen had ever really expected to
be in a Republican controlled Senate. Like their Republican
predecessors for over two decades, they had expected to serve
their entire Senate career as members of the minority; reacting
and performing damage control rather than setting the agenda and
leading. Similarly, I knew, most of their staff members who soon
would become committee chiefs of staff and majority counsels had
never expected to be in the driver's seat. Consequently, they
weren't used to running their own show. They had not entrenched
their power, indeed most didn't fully comprehend the extent of
their new power as chairmen. They felt especially indebted to
the President-elect who they rightly felt was the cause of their
good fortune. These factors gave Reagan a profound opportunity
in the early years of his Presidency. The independence and resulting resistance that normally existed with powerful entrenched
congressional committee chairmen did not yet exist. While it
overstates the case to say that the Senate was willing to do
Reagan's will, it would be fair to say that the new President had
little resistance to his leadership in that body. With this sort
of receptiveness to his leadership in one body of Congress,

7/   In addition to the elected Republican Senate leader-
     ship and the new Republican committee chairmen, was
     Senator Paul Laxalt. Laxalt, while holding no offi-
     cial leadership post, would continue to sit in all
     congressional leadership meetings with Reagan through
     1986 when he retired from the Senate. This enlarge-
     ment of the leadership by one indicated Paul Laxalt's
     unique value and importance both to his Senate col-
     leagues and to his old friend Ronald Reagan.

Reagan could then leverage, negotiate, court and log-roll the other and, more often than anyone expected, he could get his way. Reagan's legislative success in the early years of his Administration -- including his efforts to decentralize government -- were aided immeasurably by this new political dynamic.

After the meeting with Howard Baker and the new Republican Senate committee chairmen, Reagan visited Senator Robert Byrd (WV) in his office. It was a brief formal meeting. Try as he might, Reagan couldn't relax the stiff Democratic leader. A hard working expert of parliamentary manner, Senator Byrd could not have been more Reagan's opposite.

After that meeting, Reagan hosted a luncheon for all Republican members of Congress and his senior staff in the large, ornate Senate Caucus room, the scene of the earlier Watergate hearings and of the later Iran-Contra hearings. But that day it was a room filled with good cheer. We felt we were part of history. It was a new beginning. And Ronald Reagan was telling the Republicans on Capitol Hill that they were his valued partners in this enterprise to change the direction of America.

Notwithstanding the fellowship and ebullience and anticipation of those early transition weeks, there still was no focus, no vehicle to get things moving once Ronald Reagan moved into 1600 Pennsylvania Avenue. No one seemed fully directed to translating the long-time Reagan rhetoric to legislative proposals. Then appeared a stimulating memorandum written by Congressmen Jack Kemp (NY) and David Stockman (MI) that provided a blueprint and, while this was not a prime intent of the piece, a vehicle to advance Reagan's goal to decentralize government.

The document was entitled "Avoiding a GOP Economic Dunkirk." It attacked as a failure the policies of the Federal Reserve Board during the Carter Administration. It charged that the Carter misery index of double digit inflation and high interest rates might well continue unless the new administration took prompt dramatic action. This, the memo charged, would doom Reaganomics before it had a chance. It also would destroy the Republican party in the 1982 mid-term elections. This analysis, needless to say, was quite arresting.

Working with and observing Stockman operate while he was Director of the Office of Management and Budget, I learned that his modus operandi was to cry "wolf." He did this loudly and often. If a calamitous disaster wasn't at hand, his hot rhetoric always could conjure one up. It had the desired effect, at least at first, of allowing him to arrest the flow of other matters, focus the President on his analysis, and, with reliable certainty, he then would lay out a new bold program to save the Administration (and the nation) which he could direct from OMB.

Sitting and listening to Stockman employ this technique time and time again in Cabinet meetings, Budget Review Board sessions and occasional legislative strategy sessions, I never was certain whether he believed his own rhetoric or not. He always was intense and serious. He always seemed to believe.8/ As time went on and his political status diminished, this strategy was less effective in the internal issue and strategy debates. But the gambit was his favorite which he utilized with predictable regularity.

But during the transition there is no question that Stockman and Kemp solidly hit a responsive chord. Their memorandum called for immediate drastic action or the Reagan Administration would be overwhelmed. "Thatcherization can only be avoided if the initial economic policy package simultaneously spurs the output side of the economy and also elicits a swift revision of inflationary expectations in the financial markets,"9/ they wrote. The memorandum suggested that Reagan declare a national emergency immediately upon taking office.

While the President-elect rejected as too extreme the proposal to declare a national emergency, the "Dunkirk" memo did have the desired effect by Stockman as a job application.10/ In large part due to the drastic warning and bold proposals of the "Dunkirk" memo and in part due to the heavy lobbying of his

---

8/ The best review of the complex and perplexing David Stockman, the public man, is William Greider, The Education of David Stockman and Other Americans (E.P. Dutton, Inc., New York, 1982).

9/ At the time this memorandum was written, Prime Minister Margaret Thatcher's conservative economic policies in Britian seemed to be failing and her political standing was extremely low. Of course, Mrs. Thatcher would rebound and be re-elected twice.

10/ Stockman has written of the "Dunkirk" memo, "It was my resume." David A. Stockman, The Triumph of Politics: Why the Reagan Revolution Failed (Harper & Row Publishers, New York, 1986) p. 73.

friend Jack Kemp, Stockman became OMB Director.11/ As soon as Reagan's intention to nominate him to this post was announced in December, Stockman and a small group of his staff set to work at a feverish pitch.

Of great importance to these pre-inaugural days of planning, one of the ideas that Ronald Reagan had advocated was to join several categorical grants-in-aid into block grants. The categorical aid programs had become one of the principal techniques by which the federal government had siphoned off authority from the states. And Stockman realized that the legitimate claim could be made that proposed block grants would provide substantial savings by eliminating duplicative administrative costs and overly constrictive compliance regulations. Therefore, his budget proposals could include block grants with reduced funding levels. It responded to a federalism goal Reagan had long held and it advanced the important goal of helping rein in a run-away budget. The result was that Stockman became an active advocate of block grants.

Also, Stockman realized that to achieve the sort of sweeping budget cuts and reform that Reagan wanted and we all felt were necessary would be a political impossibility if dealt with individually in succession on Capitol Hill. The political dynamics of special interest groups, congressional committee prerogatives and bureaucratic interest was too strong an iron triangle to permit this. Therefore, David Stockman's masterstroke was to use the first budget resolution for fiscal 1982 also as a reconciliation measure, thereby using the budget process in a way for which it was never intended.

Normally the first congressional budget resolution had been only a broad outline of the President's budget proposal as revised by Congress. It was non-binding. Then the respective appropriations subcommittees proceed to act on separate money bills. This was the step when special vested interests yielded substantial influence to get increased funding. Only then did Congress pass their second budget resolution, which seeks reconciliation of

---

11/ In the early primaries, Congressman Stockman supported the Presidential bid of John Connally of Texas. In the fall of 1980, Stockman, who had once been on the staff of Congressman John Anderson (R-IL) and was a friend who knew Anderson well, played the role of Anderson in mock debate rehearsals with Reagan. Later he played Carter in mock debate rehearsals for the second debate. He did a superb job. This too enhanced his efforts to get the OMB job.

this process and binds the Congress. Stockman's bold and brilliant stroke was to use the cataclysmic nature of the 1980 elections and its momentum to force a reconciliation measure early with the first budget resolution. It was felt that this would keep a lid on the budget and nail it shut before the special interest groups could effectively exert influence over the pet projects in the jurisdictional committees. In other words, the reconciliation tactic was to force an early up or down vote on the entire budget and tie it down. Since block grants were an element in that budget, there was a chance to get them through before the separate special interests affected could fully exert their leverage on the committees with jurisdiction over their concerns.12/

* * * * *

During his first year in office, President Reagan met at the White House with over 1,700 state and local officials. A prominent priority in each of these meetings was to lobby for support for his proposals to enact block grants. His idea was to consolidate single-purpose categorical grants-in-aid to state and local governments with similar programs in broadly defined areas (such as health), and to give flexibility to states and localities to target funds. Block grants thus could alleviate the restrictiveness of categorical grants by allowing funds to be shifted to the most needy programmatic areas as determined by state and local officials. At one meeting with state legislators, the President said that categorical grants reminded him of "that old gag about 'hey, buddy, have you got two tens for a five.'"

At first blush, a categorical grant is a gift from the federal treasury. A program can be implemented by states and localities while being financed -- in whole or in part -- by Washington. In reality, it is a subtle technique used by the federal government to set programmatic priorities while getting some other unit of government to help foot the bill. Categorical grants had become a primary tool for the federal government to usurp power and authority from state and local governments and help transform

---

12/ There is an excellent discussion of the post-election euphoria and Stockman's transition period strategies in Laurence I. Barrett, Gambling With History: Reagan in the White House (Doubleday & Company, Inc., Garden City, New York, 1983), pp. 126-163.

them into mere administrators of federal policy. In all cases, the funds claimed by Washington to finance these projects drain the total revenue pool, making it more difficult for state and local governments to raise revenues and implement programs on their own; and the problem is compounded when financing is only partial for a particular program.

Many grants-in-aid require the grantee to put up matching funds, or, at the least, establish a structure to administer it. Washington determines what functions should be performed by government and at the same time partially shifts the burden. Of course, if Washington should decide to discontinue funding, the state or local government assumes the entire burden because it is stuck with a politically popular program, and a bureaucracy that is extremely difficult to dismantle. In a sense, the federal government has provided "seed money" for the programs it wants planted; but when the seeds germinate, it is left to some other unit of government to pay for cultivation, harvesting, and re-planting year after year.13/

In theory, a state or locality can avoid this trap by refusing the grant in the first place. And, in rare cases this does happen, such as when the state of Wyoming returned a $200,000 Juvenile Justice grant because it would have cost them $500,000 to comply with the accompanying federal mandates and regulations.14/

U.S. Senator Jake Garn (R-UT) often tells audiences that when he was mayor of Salt Lake City, "federal bureaucrats would come to town with a briefcase full of funded solutions to which we had to try to match our problems. It got so ridiculous we finally just stopped applying for grants." Further, Senator Garn recalls, "we turned down millions of dollars in CETA (Comprehensive Employment and Training Act) funds because we were afraid we'd be stuck with unmeetable obligations if the federal government discontinued funding. It's like a narcotic," he says, "the federal government gives you a quick fix, and just about the time you're hooked,

---

13/ For a general discussion see, Kennedy, David J., "The Law of Appropriateness: An Approach to a General Theory of Intergovernmental Relations," Public Administration Review, March/April 1972, pp. 135, 143.

14/ Commission on Federal Paperwork, Federal/State/Local Cooperation: A Report of the Commission on Federal Paperwork (U.S. Government Printing Office, Washington, D.C., July 15, 1977), p. 1.

they withdraw from the program and you have to go cold turkey."15/

But the reality of cutthroat competition for "free" federal dollars by states and localities -- because Washington has usurped their revenue sources -- makes the option of non-participation politically untenable in most cases.

A permanent solution -- the one long advocated by President Reagan and the one which became a major component of his Federalism Initiative -- was to have the federal government recede from programmatic areas and taxes so that other units of government could determine priorities and have revenue sources available to pay for them.16/ As an initial major step, however, President Reagan used the budget reconciliation process to embark on the most ambitious attempt ever to establish block grants. As long-time Reagan advisor Bob Carleson wrote during the transition, federal block grants were a "model for moving... to return authority, responsibility, and tax resources to state governments... (and) it should be made clear that maximum authority and discretion be in the hands of state and local governments."17/ While Congress did not give him everything he wanted, the block grants that were enacted -- nine in 1981, two in 1982, one in 1983 -- were a major victory for decentralizing government.

By the end of Ronald Reagan's first term in the White House, there were twelve federal block grant programs, the most ever. They involved seven functional areas, and accounted for about 15% of the fiscal year 1984 estimated outlays for grants-in-aid. Ten

---

15/ Related in an April 20, 1983 phone conversation by Senator Garn's press secretary, Bill Hendricks.

16/ Robert B. Carleson, who had served as Director of the California Department of Social Welfare under Governor Reagan and later worked in the Reagan White House, wrote in early 1980 that "Eventually, the federal block grants could be supplanted by state funding if the federal government would return some of its taxing authority to the states." Carleson, Robert, "The Alternatives: True Reform or Federalization," Common sense: A Republican Journal of Thought and Opinion, Vol. 3, No. 1, Winter, 1980, pp. 13, 18.

17/ Robert B. Carleson, "Taming the Welfare Monster" in ed. Wayne Valis, The Future Under President Reagan (Arlington House Publishers, Westport, Connecticut, 1981), pp. 110, 112.

of the twelve require no state or local matching funds. The two
exceptions were direct federal-local programs: Urban Mass
Transit Capital and Operating Assistance and the Community
Development Block Grant.18/

During the 1960's and 1970's, block grants -- when they were
proposed at all -- met mostly with failure. At the same time,
categorical grants were mushrooming.19/

Prior to the Reagan Administration, Congress had established only
five block grants, the first two during the Johnson
Administration. The 1966 Partnership for Health Act consolidated
seven categorical programs and, by establishing a system of state
and area-wide health planning agencies, became the major source
of national assistance for health service. The second Johnson
block grant was the 1968 Omnibus Crime Control and Safe Streets
Act. This established a new program rather than consolidating
existing categoricals.20/

President Nixon entered office with an agenda for "New
Federalism" (the term, incidentally, was resurrected by the media
as applying to Ronald Reagan's efforts to improve intergovernmental relations).21/ A two-tiered program was called for:
"General Revenue Sharing" to provide for direct transfers from
the federal treasury to states and localities for discretionary
spending; and "Special Revenue Sharing" which was basically a
proposal for block grants. The former was enacted, the latter
was not. Charging that the "Special Revenue Sharing" provisions

---

18/ A catalog of Federal Grant-In-Aid Programs to State
    and Local Governments: Grants Funded FY 1984
    (Advisory Commission on Intergovernmental Relations,
    December, 1984), p. 3.

19/ See, George E. Peterson and Associates, "The Block
    Grants in Perspective," in The Reagan Block Grants:
    What Have We Learned? (The Urban Institute Press,
    Washington, D.C., 1986), pp. 1-32.

20/ Barfield, Claude, Rethinking Federalism, American
    Enterprise Institute, Washington, D.C., 1981, p. 16.

21/ See President Richard Nixon, State of the Union
    Message, January 22, 1971, Public Papers of the
    President of the United States: Richard Nixon, 1971
    (Washington D.C., GPO, 1972), pp. 54-55.

were designed to dismantle social programs, the Democratic Congress rejected them.22/

However, three block grants proposed during the Nixon Administration did become law.23/ In 1974, seventeen manpower and employment programs which had been administered by six different Cabinet departments and one agency were consolidated into the Comprehensive Employment and Training Act (CETA).24/ In 1974, the Housing and Community Development Act consolidated six programs under the Department of Housing and Urban Development.25/ Finally, in 1974, Congress enacted another block grant -- Title XX of the Social Security Act -- to reform the

---

22/ For a general discussion see General Revenue Sharing: An ACIR Re-Evaluation (Advisory Commission on Intergovernmental Relations, October 1974).

23/ The Nixon block grants differed from President Reagan's in two major ways. First, President Nixon accepted devolution to whatever level of government Congress chose; President Reagan, in general, favors devolution from the federal government to the states, with pass-throughs where appropriate to local governments. Secondly, President Nixon's block grant proposals included new and additional funds referred to as "sweeteners;" President Reagan's block grant proposals were offered during a time of far greater budgetary pressures where less rather than more resources were available.

See Nathan, Richard P., "The Reagan Presidency in Domestic Affairs," (Paper prepared for the Conference on "The Reagan Presidency at Mid-Term," November 19, 20, 1982, Draft September 30, 1982) pp. 9-10.

24/ Ascik, Thomas, Block Grants and Federalism: Decentralizing Decisions, Heritage Foundation Backgrounder, Number 144, Washington, D.C., p. 30. Also see, P.L. 93-203.

25/ For a detailed discussion of CDBG, see Williamson, Richard S., "Community Development Block Grants," The Urban Lawyer, Vol. 14, No. 2, Spring, 1982, pp. 283-284, 290.

disorganized system of federal subsidies to state social welfare services.26/

The block grants proposed by President Ford were all rejected.27/ The White House then switched to Democratic control. President Carter did not propose any new block grants. And the categorical grant again reigned supreme -- not that its prominence had yet been seriously challenged.28/

* * * * *

While these modest attempts at block grants were sputtering, categorical grants were exploding. In 1959 there were some forty to fifty federal grants-in-aid totaling some $6.5 billion and accounting for 1.4 percent of gross national product.29/ By 1970, there were 130 categorical programs and by 1980 there were 492. They pervaded such obviously local concerns as rat control and sewer extensions, and the dollar amount usurped from local treasuries to finance them leaped to $95 billion -- a 1,343 percent increase in just two decades. By 1980, they accounted for

---

26/ Ascik, Thomas, Block Grants and Federalism: Decentralizing Decisions, op. cit., p. 30.

27/ For a general discussion see Block Grants: A Roundtable Discussion (Advisory Commission on Intergovernmental Relations, October 1976), N.B. pp. 19-20.

28/ Even when enacting the Nixon block grants, the Congress did not seem to want to provide flexibility to state and local governments. The grants had both categorical elements and other federal strings attached. Additionally, over the next fifteen years, Congress created numerous other categorical grants which easily could have been made part of the existing block grants. See Ascik, Thomas, Block Grants and Federalism: Decentralizing Decisions, op. cit., p. 30.

29/ Office of Management and Budget (OMB), Federal Grants-in-Aid to State and Local Governments, OMB, Budget and Review Division, Washington, D.C., March, 1981, p. 5.

3.5 percent of GNP.30/ With such exorbitant growth, the 1959 words of Senator Edmund Muskie, former governor of Maine, offer some nostalgic amusement. At a hearing which resulted in the creation of the Advisory Commission on Intergovernmental Relations, he said:

> "There is a feeling on the part of some people that states are always reaching out for federal dollars. There are upward of 40 grant-in-aid programs depending on how they are classified. I don't know how you keep track of them all."31/

By 1980 -- after we had really lost track of national priorities -- that same Advisory Commission on Intergovernmental Relations concluded that:

> "The current network of intergovernmental relations has become dangerously overloaded, to the point that American federalism's most trumpeted traditional traits -- flexibility and workability -- are critically endangered."32/

The block grants proposed by Reagan were designed to curtail this suffocating federal control, and restore the efficiency and accountability of local spending priorities. While some in the Administration championed block grants because of their own budget agenda, most of us, and certainly President Reagan, saw block grants as significant federalism tool. Reagan wanted to come as close as possible to giving state and local officials five ones back for a five and two fives back for a ten.

* * * * *

30/ Office of Management and Budget, Number of Funded Federal Grant Programs in the Catalogue of Federal Domestic Assistance Included in the Budget Concept of Grants to State and Local Governments, OMB Budget Review Division, Washington, D.C., October 28, 1982, p. 5.

31/ Senator Edmund Muskie, Senate Committee on Government Operations, "To Establish an Advisory Commission on Intergovernmental Relations," June 16, 1959.

32/ Ibid.

As noted above, the first block grants proposed by the President were part of his Economic Recovery Program of 1981.33/ And by being part of a larger whole, the block grant proposals achieved their chance to avoid total dismemberment by the special interest groups and survive the legislative gauntlet on Capitol Hill.

President Reagan's economic plan of budget cuts, tax rate reduction, regulatory relief and a stable monetary policy had been outlined in the campaign. Stockman's drafting of the language for the Economic Recovery Program of 1981 began during the transition by reworking the Carter FY 1982 budget. Both Bob Carleson and I worked during the transition with Ed Meese to ensure that the final package would strengthen the intergovernmental system as well as the economy. Meese was committed to decentralization. He often proved an invaluable ally during internal policy and strategy deliberations both during the transition and in the White House. Reagan's total trust in Meese personally and Ed's familiarity with state government from his days in Sacramento as Reagan's Chief of Staff often tipped the scales during these debates. While Meese has a disarmingly soft, congenial personality and wasn't the most organized person, he never hesitated to join an issue and work to advance Ronald Reagan's deeply held philosophic views, including federalism.

In all the components of the final economic plan program, was the underlying theme of federalism. The spending reductions were a reordering of priorities so that the national budget would address truly national needs. The tax cuts addressed the problem created by the federal government usurping revenues which otherwise would have been available to state and local governments. The block grants were a means to give state and local officials spending control, and achieve better services with fewer federal dollars.

Soon after taking office, the President held budget review board meetings to review the work on the economic program, resolve disputed issues and make final decisions. These sessions were held in the cabinet room. Joining the President and Vice President during these meetings were David Stockman and usually a member of his staff; Jim Baker, Ed Meese and several others of us from the White House Senior Staff; and then the respective cabi-

---

33/ Omnibus Budget Resolution passed the House on May 7, and the Senate on May 14, 1981. Omnibus Budget Reconciliation passed the Senate on June 25, and House on June 26, 1981. Conference report adopted by both houses on June 29, 1981. Economic Recovery Tax Act passed both houses on July 29, 1981.

net member whose department would be reviewed. Each cabinet member could bring one budget or program expert from his staff to assist him.

For me, the process was fascinating. Reagan had set up three different power centers to take a cut at the budget. Stockman and OMB were there with a singular intense focus on cutting the budget. Institutionally and personally, an issue was successful or a disappointment to OMB solely to the extent the budget item was cut further. Stockman is a man who needs certainty and during those days he was certain that the only thing that mattered was cutting the budget. The White House Senior Staff were there for broader policy input and the political spin. Chief of Staff Jim Baker is a master politician. More a political facilitator than a theoretician, Baker has a great political feel of what's do-able and what is not. He is a superb negotiator. And he constantly wants results. A restless man who much prefers short verbal briefings to written documents that get into deep analysis and details, Jim Baker loves the complicated political chess game and he is a master at it. He wanted bottom line results. The rest of us from the White House staff played supporting roles to Baker in this endeavor. And the third power center was the respective department or agency under review. Inevitably there were institutional considerations reflecting the permanent bureaucracy of the department, the interest groups it served and congressional relationships, all of which argued for the status quo.

It is a rare cabinet member who isn't co-opted, at least somewhat, by his or her own department. But during the opening weeks of the Administration, this assimilation process was just beginning. The cabinet members were Ronald Reagan's representatives to the departments and not vice-versa. And importantly, most of the cabinet members didn't know their way around yet. Most were not long-time Washington figures.34/ Consequently, between Stockman's intimate familiarity with the budget items from his long years on Capitol Hill as a staff member and then member of Congress, and the greater familiarity of many members of the senior White House staff during these early deliberations, the cabinet member was ill-positioned to defend his budget even if he were so inclined.

34/ The only cabinet members with substantial Washington government experience were Al Haig at State, Bill Brock at USTR, Bill Casey at CIA (none of whose budgets were substantial) and Cap Weinberger at Defense.

As we went through the major budget items one by one, if there was consensus among all three groups from our earlier deliberations on the budget disposition, Reagan with few exceptions would quickly accept that recommendation. However, if there was a dispute he would want a full and frank debate. And he was willing to hear out the full discussion whether the item in dispute was in the billions of dollars or the relatively more modest hundreds of millions.

An example of a disputed item was the Urban Development Action Grant program. Enacted in October 1977, the UDAG program provided various forms of subsidies to encourage private firms to make investments that would create jobs in distressed urban areas. The grants were made to local governments by a central office at the Department of Housing and Urban Development. Tightly defined criteria were designed in Washington to select from among competing applications. Federal funds were not released until the private capital was actually committed.35/ In this debate, HUD Secretary Sam Pierce and most of the White House staff argued for UDAG, while Stockman argued to abolish it.

Early on in the working group level of internal budget deliberations it became clear that the Administration would propose that many programs would be seriously cut or eliminated that were supported by state and local government officials. Certainly, most deserved to be cut. Not only had the categorical grants-in-aid distorted the intergovernmental system and done enormous harm to American federalism, most were inefficient and wasteful. In a situation where the federal budget had busted, there was double digit inflation, and double digit interest rates, control had to be returned to the federal fiscal situation. And generally, the justification for a substantial federal role in these areas was weak. At the same time, I was mindful that the bottom line was not what Ronald Reagan proposed to Congress, but what ultimately Congress disposed of, what Congress finally passed and the President signed into law.

To get the state and local officials support, which might be crucial to ultimate passage, we had to have some programs in their area that the President could save and champion. From many discussions with leading Republican state and local officials and key Reagan supporters on Capitol Hill, the UDAG program and Revenue Sharing emerged as prime candidates. In small meetings

---

35/ See Richard P. Nathan and Jerry A. Webman ed., The Urban Development Action Grant Program (Princeton Urban and Regional Research Center, Princeton, New Jersey, 1980).

with bipartisan groups of mayors and governors, the President repeatedly heard that the UDAG program should be saved. Consequently, before HUD was to be the subject of a Presidential budget review board meeting, Secretary Sam Pierce was encouraged to argue to save the UDAG program when it came up for discussion.

Sam Pierce is a nice man. An attorney with a distinguished career in government as General Counsel to the Nixon Administration's Department of Treasury and in private practice with a Wall Street law firm, he was the only black in the Cabinet. He is not a particularly forceful speaker and gives the appearance at times of not being particularly vigorous. However on this day during the discussion of the UDAG program, Pierce was energetic and effective.

Just before HUD, the budget review board had gone over the Department of Labor's budget. On practically all issues, Secretary Ray Donovan, OMB and the White House staff were in total accord. The entire Department of Labor review went quickly and the President decided on billions of dollars of proposed cuts. Similarly most of the HUD budget was quickly disposed of. But when we came to the UDAG program, a much smaller dollar item, a spirited substantive debate ensued that lasted approximately two hours.

Sam Pierce made a detailed defense of the program. David Stockman made an equally substantive assault on it. The dialogue went back and forth. For those who charge that Ronald Reagan is detached, disengaged or uninterested in details, it is unfortunate that these deliberations were not recorded. The President was alert and interested. He asked questions of Pierce and Stockman and asked for input from his White House staff. Meese, Baker, Marty Anderson, Max Friedersdorf and I all fully participated.36/ The President understood the program and clearly wanted to hear the views of each of us from our respective vantage points. After about 90 minutes of this discussion, David Gergen, who had served in the Nixon and Ford White Houses, turned to me and said that this was the best, most substantive policy debate he'd ever heard around the cabinet table. I was too new at this to make such comparisons, but I did know that this was the sort of full and frank process that would result in informed, reflective Presidential decision-making. Each person who spoke had a legitimate view that added a new nuance to the deliberation. While the decision might be black or white from one perspective or another, in totality, there were conflicting considerations

---

36/ Marty Anderson was then Assistant to the President for Domestic Policy and Max Friedersdorf was Assistant to the President for Legislative Affairs.

and conflicting perspectives. Properly, only the President could decide. It was great to participate in it.

As the debate waned down, the President brought up the comments he had heard from the state and local officials with whom he had recently met. As a former governor who had frequently fought with the federal government, Reagan gave good weight to the views of these officials. In the end, he decided to retain the UDAG program in his 1981 Economic Recovery Program. Many of us felt it had been the direct input from the state and local officials with whom Reagan felt a special kinship that had tipped the scales.

When this process was completed and the President's 1981 Economic Recovery Plan was put together, he had proposed consolidation of nearly ninety programs into seven blocks: Health Services;37/ Preventive Health Services;38/ Social Services;39/ Energy and

---

37/ The Health Services Block Grant was to consolidate 17 federal health service programs administered by the Department of Health and Human Services. The programs to be consolidated, among others, included community and migrant health centers, maternal and child health services, mental health and drug abuse programs, home health, emergency medical hemophilia services, and the sudden infant death syndrome program.

38/ The Preventive Health Services Block Grant was to consolidate eleven federal health promotion and disease and injury prevention programs administered by the Department of Health and Human Services. The programs included high blood pressure control, health incentive grants, risk education, health education, fluoridation, lead-based paint poisoning prevention, family planning services, venereal disease, rat control, genetic diseases, and adolescent health services.

39/ The Social Service Block Grant was to consolidate 12 federal social service programs administered by three federal agencies: the Department of Health and Human Services, the Department of Education, and the Community Services Administration. The programs included Title XX (existing social services block grant), child welfare services, foster care, adoption assistance, child abuse, runaway youth, developmental disabilities, rehabilitation services, and community services.

Emergency Assistance;40/ Local Education Services;41/ State Education Services;42/ and Community Development.43/ These closely resembled the Special Revenue Sharing bills proposed by President Nixon a decade earlier.44/

After congressional consideration, fifty-seven categoricals were consolidated into nine blocks.45/ This somewhat scaled down the President's request, and Congress added several undesirable restrictions. This was tremendously frustrating. After unsuccessfully lobbying one House member on the phone about this issue, I can remember Reagan slamming down the phone and sputtering about how too many Congressmen had been in Washington too long. But like a dog walking on hind legs, it's not whether it's done gracefully, it's just remarkable that it happened at all. Where President Nixon had failed, where President Ford had failed, and

---

40/ The Energy and Emergency Assistance Block Grant was to consolidate two federal programs administered by the Department of Health and Human Services: the low-income energy and the emergency assistance program.

41/ The Local Education Services Block Grant was to consolidate 12 federal education programs administered by the Department of Education. These included financial assistance to meet the special needs of educationally deprived children, handicapped children, children in schools undergoing desegregation, migrant children, and adults lacking basic educational skills. Most funds were to be passed-through to local education agencies, though the states would determine local allocation.

42/ The State Education Services Block Grant was to consolidate over thirty categorical programs that aim to help states improve school performance and the use of resources.

43/ The Community Development Block Grant was to replace the Community Development Block Grant for Small Cities and Rural Areas.

44/ The Reagan proposals contained far fewer restrictions than were in the existing block grant, giving freedom of action to the states. See Ascik, Block Grants and Federalism: Decentralizing Decisions, op. cit., p.29.

45/ P.L. 97-35. The Omnibus Budget Reconciliation Act of 1981.

where other Presidents had been opposed, Reagan succeeded in getting Congress to begin the politically unnatural act of devolving power and authority to state and local governments.

The victory was made possible by the President's strong leadership with Congress and by his ability to form an effective bipartisan coalition with state officials. Indeed, most state officials were now echoing the sentiments that Ronald Reagan had expressed as governor of California, and as a candidate for the Presidency. Washington had too much control. Programs lacked flexibility. Regulations were restrictive. Expenditures were being made for programs that weren't really needed in particular locales. In short, state and local officials believed that they were more capable of making prudent decisions to run their own jurisdictions than federal bureaucrats.46/ Groups like the National Governors' Association (NGA) and the National Conference of State Legislatures (NCSL) were calling for a reordering of priorities and a sorting out of responsibilities among the various units of government.47/

Once the President presented his Economic Recovery Program to Congress on February 18, my job was to explain the block grant proposals to state and local officials and other outside constituencies. Further, my assignment was to lobby state and local

----

46/ As far back as 1974, then National Governors' Conference Chairman Daniel J. Evans said: "It is my judgement that when historians write of the fundamental changes that occurred in the federal system during the last one-third of the 20th century the reaffirmation of the intended role of the states will be the characteristic most commonly noted."

47/ In a joint statement, NGA and NCSL noted: "Having experienced the tax revolt, a powerful grass roots drive to require a balanced federal budget by constitutional amendment, and deep federal aid cuts in the midst of a national recession, we have no illusions about the seriousness of the problems facing government in this decade ... We are ready to negotiate, not as another of the special interest groups that have dominated the Washington agenda for far too long, but as full constitutional partners who represent precisely the same citizens that Washington represents." See National Conference of State Legislatures and National Governors' Association, Joint Statement, Hall of the States, Washington, D.C., November 25, 1980.

officials to gain their support for the Reagan proposals. Such dramatic block grants as those proposed in the Reagan economic package, we felt, needed some expression of support from state and local officials to be credible on Capitol Hill. Furthermore, if we got active support from these officials their lobbying in support of the proposal could be extremely helpful, even crucial, for its success in Congress.

The majority of state and local officials are Democrats. Their help would give us a bipartisan reach. Each of these officials has his own political base and established political organization. Often these local officials who live right there with their constituents have a stronger political base than the Senators and Representatives in distant Washington. Around the country the local press listens to the views of these local officials. Their support for members of Congress is often crucial for members' re-elections. And at the very least, it was important for members of Congress to work cooperatively with their fellow elected office holders and potential rivals.

We tried to leverage the existing discontent of state and local officials with Washington. They had come of age. Their capacity and competence had grown enormously. They were the ones on the front lines delivering services daily to the American people, not federal bureaucrats. And they were the ones who had daily experience with the frustrations, inefficiency and excessive cost of dealing with federal over-regulation and interference. These people are smart, competent, capable officials elected by the very same people who elected the Senators and Congressmen. Yet the federal government treated them as step-children, as idiots lacking compassion and competence. Increasingly, they were mere administrators for Washington programs that, however well-intended, were Rube Goldberg inventions of inefficiency and waste. And often they were the ones blamed for the failure of services by the voters when their hands were tied by red tape and restrictive regulations in Washington.

The President personally met with scores of state and local officials during this period in groups large and small to lobby for his programs. Vice President Bush gave even more of his time to this effort. From 1981 through 1983, I can't remember a single time when George Bush, if in Washington, didn't agree to meet with these people when I put in a request. And he proved a very able salesman. Secretary of the Treasury Don Regan and Stockman also repeatedly helped out. Slowly, we built support from amongst the state and local officials -- bipartisan support.

The single most important group in this effort was the nation's governors. At first I was concerned that some of the senior Republican governors such as Bill Milliken of Michigan and Bob

Ray of Iowa, who both became governors in 1969, might be a problem. They came from the moderate wing of the party and neither
had supported Ronald Reagan in the primaries. But these two men
became among the most effective supporters of Reagan's
programs. First, they shared Reagan's views that the federal
government should get off the backs of state government.
Washington was simply suffocating the ability of their states to
do their job. Second, they knew well that the state governments
were full of competent, able professionals with the capacity and
desire to provide the needed services to their citizens. And
they knew that federal government programs were wasteful and
inefficient. But also these moderate Republican leaders were
loyal Party men. While they might disagree with some of Ronald
Reagan's proposals, they respected his position in the Party and
as President. They were consensus builders, not radicals. With
Reagan in the White House they reliably worked to be helpful, not
divisive. To whatever extent I was able to help the President
advance his efforts to decentralize government, it was in part
due to these two great pros.

Our efforts to gain effective support for the block grant proposals from the nation's governors also benefitted immeasurably from
the fact that the NGA Chairman was Governor George Busbee of
Georgia. A Democrat who had earned broad bipartisan support and
deep respect among his colleagues, Busbee had been for many years
a member of the state legislature before being elected to succeed
Jimmy Carter as governor in 1974. He knew state government well
and his frustration with the federal government was great.
Busbee wanted decentralization. As I've already mentioned, he
had approached Carter during the 1980 campaign to urge him to
make federalism a major campaign issue. But President Carter
never picked up the tune. Therefore, Reagan's song was sweet
music to his ears. He was ready, willing and able to work with
the new Republican President, at least up to a point.

George Busbee is a tall man of courtly manner. A southern gentleman, he is more conservative than the Democratic party nationally, yet a political partisan. He respected institutions, including the Office of the Presidency, but was not intimidated by
Reagan nor willing to be stampeded. He wanted to be an activist
NGA Chairman, a player on the national stage, and had been frustrated by the deaf ear Jimmy Carter had given the governors'
calls for decentralization. In Reagan he saw the opportunity to
advance the governors' agenda and leave his mark. For me he was
an ideal man to work with. He was a straight shooter; candid and
direct. As a Democrat, he helped our political reach both within
the ranks of the governors and on Capitol Hill. He helped get
the job done. And when he disagreed, he always did it without
being disagreeable. Later when he publicly had to break with the
President on some issues, he always had the courtesy to call me

ahead of time to tell me why, how and where he'd go public so that I could brief the President and, when necessary, be prepared to respond. On block grants, Busbee proved a tremendous help.

In late January and February of every year, the state and local government public interest groups have their annual winter meetings in Washington.48/ At these sessions they formally adopt a variety of positions as well as visit their counterparts on Capitol Hill to lobby for their top priorities; usually including efforts to get more federal money. By the time Reagan presented his comprehensive Economic Program to Congress on February 18, some of that winter's meetings already had occurred. But the governors convened just days afterwards. It was an important meeting both because of the particular prominence of the governors and because it was the first chance we would have to gain bipartisan support for the block grant proposals.

I was new at all of this. Busbee took the lead in forging language that could be adopted by consensus in which the governors praised the block grants, acknowledged that thereby there could be real budget savings, and called upon Congress to adopt the Reagan proposals. This was a tremendous boost to our efforts. It was bipartisan. It avoided the potential of letting block grants become a divisive liberal/conservative issue. It forged an alliance between the new President and the state chief executives against the Washington establishment.

At the same time, on behalf of his colleagues, Busbee issued a warning to the President. Traditionally the governors all come to the White House for a business meeting with the President

---

48/ The primary public interest groups, the so-called PIGs, are the National Governors' Association (NGA), the National Conference of State Legislatures (NCSL), the National Association of Counties (NACo), the United States Conference of Mayors (USCM), and the National League of Cities (NLC). The Reagan White House also worked closely with the National Association of Towns and Townships (NATaT) and the more conservative American Legislative Exchange Council (ALEC).

during their winter meeting.49/ At that meeting Busbee reported on the resolution which would be adopted. He talked about his personal enthusiasm and that of his colleagues for block grants. The categorical grants-in-aid were usurping their authority and forcing administrative waste. He even commented that the governors could accept the proposed 20 percent budget cuts in the line items proposed to be joined into block grants. But he warned that such budget cuts were acceptable only if the flexibility and freedom of the block grants as proposed by Reagan survived the legislative gauntlet. If Congress perverted the block grants by retaining substantial portions of the over-regulation and interference that existed in the current categori-cal grants-in-aid then NGA as an organization could not support the block grants. Indeed, Busbee said, if such undue encum-brances were forced on the block grant proposals, some of the governors, including himself, would oppose them.

With the President demonstrating political strength by getting NGA support in stark contrast to his predecessor, other state officials joined the fray against the "iron triangle" and the fifty year trend of power gravitating to Washington. As stated in the August, 1981 issue of Governors' Bulletin (published by NGA):

> "Seven months after taking office, President Reagan has changed the direction of the federal aid system ... [The block grants] represent some progress toward greater flexibility for state and local officials at a time when aid to state and local governments is shrinking."50/

49/ Traditionally the governors also come down one evening during the winter meeting for a state dinner at the White House. For Reagan, this happened to be the first state dinner of his new Administration. There-fore, since I was the senior aide dealing with his guests, my wife and I were invited to that dinner. It was part business and great pleasure. While I attend-ed other state dinners since none could match the excitment of that first evening of dinner, entertain-ment and dancing in the White House.

50/ NGA, Governors' Bulletin, August 7, 1981, p. 2.

Local government leaders, however, were less enthusiastic about the President's block grant proposals.51/ They had become accustomed to bypassing their state governments and going directly to Washington for funds.52/ Because they liked this arrangement, they feared that the President intended to dramatically curtail or eliminate the federal government's relationship with local governments. At an April 12, 1981 meeting with the President in the Cabinet Room, Mayor John Rousakis, an old line partisan who is the popular and effective mayor of Savannah, noting that the President was proposing that Community Development Block Grant funds for small cities would be channeled through the states, loudly protested saying, "We're concerned that we [larger cities] may be next."

Reagan himself was sympathetic to the concerns of local officials. While governor, he had been opposed to efforts by the California legislature to impose unreasonable restrictions on local governments. For example, while opposing greater California state government control over education, he had said in 1973, "I believe in local control of education and the (state) legislature has mandated too many programs on local education. In order to get money, the (state) legislature has said to each school district, 'you have to spend every dollar exactly as we tell you.' This itself is backward."53/ But while Reagan believed "the more government we can keep at the local levels in local hands, the better off we are,"54/ he also believed that the federal government should not go far in interfering with intrastate issues. It was up to the local governments and their state

---

51/ See "Will Cities' Link to Washington Be Cut? Views From White House Differ on Reagan's New Federalism," Francis Viscount and Fred Jordan, National League of Cities, Nation's Cities Weekly, Vol. 4, No. 21, Washington, D.C., May 25, 1981.

52/ See James W. Fossett, "The Politics of Dependence: Federal Aid to Big Cities," in Lawrence D. Brown, James W. Fossett and Kenneth T. Palmer, The Changing Politics of Federal Grants (The Brookings Institution, Washington, D.C., 1984), pp. 108-163.

53/ Ronald Reagan, speech, April 12, 1973, in ed. Joseph R. Holmes, The Quotable Ronald Reagan (JRH & Associates, Inc., San Diego, CA, 1974), p. 57.

54/ Ronald Reagan, speech, April 12, 1973, in ed. Joseph R. Holmes, The Quotable Ronald Reagan, op. cit., p. 87.

capital to sort out these issues, not Washington. Consequently, while the block grants provided some protection for local units of government by mandating some pass through to them, the protections did not go far enough for many local officials.

Throughout the debate, critics of state governments arose like the Flat Earth Society on Columbus Day. They argued that with block grants, cities which had suffered under the often heavy hand of federal bureaucrats would now be afflicted with the worse fate of arbitrary mandates by allegedly incompetent state governments -- despite the ample evidence that state and local governments are every bit as sophisticated as the federal government. They argued that state legislatures have an anti-urban bias -- despite the fact that with the Supreme Court "one man, one vote" rules,55/ state legislatures represent no demographically different constituency than does Congress.

Our job at the White House was to educate. In May and early June 1981, we sent national mailings to city and county officials. HUD Secretary Sam Pierce, HHS Secretary Dick Schweiker, and Education Secretary Ted Bell held consultations with key local officials. The President held six White House meetings with representatives of the National League of Cities, the U.S. Conference of Mayors, and the National Association of Counties.

In reality, the 1981 block grants did not drastically alter the federal-local relationship.56/ In the health and social services area (which covered four of the seven proposed blocks), for example, almost all the programs already were going directly from the federal government to the states. Counties and some cities had long been receiving federal monies through the states to administer health and social service programs.

55/ Baker v. Carr, 639 U.S. 186 (1962), and Reynolds v. Sims, 377 U.S. 533 (1964).

56/ While speaking to the National League of Cities in November, 1982, the President highlighted the federal-local relationship of working together: "We've held many working sessions about the challenges we face and together we've made significant improvements in this Administration's original federalism proposal ... Perhaps of greatest importance ... you collectively have driven home the absolute need for some programs and some funds to pass directly from Washington to your city without taking a detour by your state capitol."

The two block grants proposed for education did mean a shift to federal-state funding in an area that had previously been federal-local in nature. However, the President's proposal included a mandatory requirement that 75 percent of the funds be passed through to local governments, based on an historical formula, during the first three years of the program. This time frame provided local governments with the transition they wanted to develop a state-local relationship.

However, it was the Community Development Block Grant (CDBG) that was at the heart of the state-local debate. CDBG as proposed by the President was really two separate programs under one title. Of the $4.16 billion requested by the Administration to fund the program, $500 million was to be allocated for the Urban Development Action Grant (UDAG) program. The President proposed that HUD continue to administer UDAG in its current form on a competitive basis. Of the remaining $3.65 billion allocated for CDBG, 70 percent would continue to go directly from the federal government to cities, over 50,000 in population. This portion of CDBG would continue to be administered by HUD.

Key Republican mayors were the first to get on board. Dick Carver, mayor of Peoria, was a past President of the U.S. Conference of Mayors -- the first Republican to have held that post in decades. In 1981, the articulate, ambitious Carver was President of the National Conference of Republican Mayors and Municipal Officials and proved an energetic ally. Margaret Hance was mayor of Phoenix, the largest city with a Republican chief executive. She is a smart, no-nonsense, articulate politician.57/ Hance was an effective ally and advocate address-ing big-city concerns. Bill Hudnut, Republican mayor of Indianapolis was a former member of Congress. As President of the National League of Cities in 1981, he had a platform and broad respect. These three mayors served as a core group with whom the White House worked closely in 1981. They, in turn, suggested strategies for us to work with other Republican mayors and penetrate Democratic resistance.

Other local officials, members of the National Association of Counties (NACo) and the National Association of Towns and Townships (NATaT), while sharing some of the bigger city mayors' concerns, faced somewhat different problems, were generally more conservative, and willing to give the new Republican President

---

57/ In 1984, Mayor Hance served as Co-Chairman of the National Reagan-Bush Re-Election Committee.

support.58/   NATAT, which had been ignored by prior Administrations, and NACo, which desperately wanted to be a "player" with rather than an obstructionist against the new Administration, proved invaluable in letting us avoid a confrontation with united opposition from local officials. Commissioner Roy Orr, of Dallas County, Texas, a Democrat and President of NACo, provided us invaluable bipartisan support.59/

After many meetings with local officials in efforts to gain their support, the Administration did propose one substantive change in CDBG. It was that the remaining 30 percent, or approximately $1.09 billion, would be transferred to the states for their administration and allocation to cities of less than 50,000 in population.60/

By the time of the congressional vote, however, the mood of most big city mayors had changed. It was a result of our education efforts, and the realization by local officials that we understood their concerns. Mayor Margaret Hance of Phoenix said on the nationally televised "MacNeil-Lehrer Report":

> "We have no problem with the block grants [of 1981] ... We are more concerned about those block grants which are going to come down the line ... [and], we have been assured that before even any option papers are presented to the President we will have a great deal of input to the White House, and we're grateful for this."61/

The coalition of state and local officials was thus completed. Both personally and through his emissaries, Reagan lobbied and negotiated with Congress. As Democratic Speaker Tip O'Neill remarked ruefully, the problem with negotiating with Reagan was

---

58/   George E. Hale and Marion Lief Palley, The Politics of Federal Grants (Congressional Quarterly Press, Washington, D.C., 1981), pp. 143-163.

59/   Later, Roy Orr switched from the Democratic to the Republican party.

60/   For a more detailed discussion, see Richard S. Williamson, "Community Development Block Grants," Urban Lawyer, December, 1981.

61/   Honorable Margaret Hance, Mayor of Phoenix, remarks on the "MacNeil-Lehrer Report", "New Federalism," Educational Broadcasting Corporation, July 9, 1981.

that "every time you compromise with the President, the President gets 80 percent of what he wants." Reagan's response when he heard about O'Neill's quip was, "I'll take 80 percent every time, and I'll go back the next year for the additional 20 percent."62/

The Economic Recovery Program of 1981 -- and along with it the most sweeping block grants in the history of federal-state-local relations -- passed the Congress by six votes.63/ The new Block Grants were: Alcohol, Drug Abuse and Mental Health;64/ Preventive Health and Health Services;65/ Maternal and Child Health Services;66/ Primary Care;67/ Social Services;68/

62/ Jack Nelson, "The Reagan Legacy," in ed. Paul Duke, Beyond Reagan: The Politics of Upheaval (Warner Books, New York, 1986), pp. 83, 105.

63/ The Congress did water down the President's proposals. Some categoricals escaped consolidation, and some block grants were encumbered with earmarks. However, the President had no flexibility to veto any of the block grants individually because they were all incorporated as a part of the crucial Budget Reconciliation bill which had passed the House of Representatives by only six votes. The President's choice was either to sign all of the bill or veto all of the bill. This being no real choice at all, he signed the bill. But the situation provided an instructive example of how the Administration had inherited a budget so badly hemorrhaged that reining in excessive spending by necessity superseded and dominated all other aspects of its domestic policy-making machinery.

64/ The Alcohol Drug Abuse and Mental Health Block Grant covers drug abuse community services; alcoholism treatment and rehabilitation; alcohol formula grants; alcohol project grants; drug abuse formula grants; drug abuse project grants; and grants to community mental health centers.

65/ The Preventive Health and Health Services Block Grant covers health incentive grants; rape crisis centers; urban rat control; fluoridation; home education and risk reduction; emergency medical services; home health services; and hypertension.

66/ The Maternal and Child Health Services Block Grant covers crippled children's services; disabled children
(Cont'd)

Community Services;69/ Low Income Home Energy Assistance;70/ Elementary and Secondary Education;71/ and Community Development.72/ The first wave of them became effective on October 1, 1981.

* * * * *

While the states were fully equiped to handle their new responsibilities, the magnitude of nine new block grants -- nearly twice as many as had been promulgated in the entire preceding two decades -- forced them to drastically alter grant administration strategies. Although there was little time between congressional

---

(SSI); sudden infant death syndrome grants; hemophilia centers; lead-based paint poisoning; genetic diseases; and adolescent pregnancy.

67/ The Primary Care Block Grant converts the Community Health Center Program from a direct federal-local program into a state-administered program.

68/ The Social Services Block Grant covers Title XX social services; Title XX day care; and Title XX state and local training.

69/ The Community Services Block Grant replaces the Community Services Administration program.

70/ The Low Income Home Energy Assistance Block Grant converts the Low Income Energy Assistance Program into a state-administered block grant.

71/ The Elementary and Secondary Education Block Grant consolidates 42 federal activities and programs into a single block grant including, the Emergency School Aid Act; school libraries and instructional resources; career education; Follow Through; teacher corps; and teacher centers.

72/ The Community Development Block Grant replaces Community Development Block Grant for small cities and rural areas.

enactment and their effective dates, the states moved quickly and made significant progress in the transition.73/

For the Administration's part, we established an Implementation Task Force.74/ In addition to my office, the Task Force included representatives from HHS, HUD, the Department of Education, and OMB. The implementation agenda included a series of eight regional briefings between August and mid-September. They were attended by hundreds of state and local officials from across the country. In the words of the Director of the Division of Health from the Georgia Department of Health: "We were given a good orientation from Washington to begin the preparation for block grants."75/ The briefings were unprecedented and they reflected President Reagan's desire to treat state and local officials as true partners in the intergovernmental system. Also, local officials were brought together with state officials, forcing them to realize that they were going to have to start working more closely with each other. Many officials expressed surprise during the briefings at how many decisions on grant administration would be left to them under the new blocks. Because of these preparatory sessions, the actual block grant implementation process was highly successful.

While states could continue programs as categoricals, most readily accepted the new block grants. For example, 37 states participated in HUD's Community Development Block Grant in Fiscal Year 1982, and 48 participated in FY '83. The primary reason for nonparticipation were problems of timing, which were later resolved.76/ All 50 states accepted the five HHS Block Grants when

---

73/ The implementation process went smoothly for most states because they followed the allocation patterns that were already in place from previous grants. Thus, relatively few organizational changes were needed. See Nathan, "The Reagan Presidency in Domestic Affairs," op. cit., p. 32.

74/ According to a General Accounting Office report, Early Observations on Block Grant Implementation, a number of states mentioned the usefulness of such things as the HHS Secretary's letter to governors explaining the transition process.

75/ Phone conversation with Jocelyn White of my staff on October 16, 1982.

76/ Department of Housing and Urban Development (HUD), "Block Grants - One Year Later," Washington, D.C., August, 1982, p. 1.

they became effective in 1981, and 48 accepted a sixth HHS Block Grant which became available on October 1, 1982.77/ When the Education block grant became available in July, 1982, 48 states applied in the first week, and applications from the remaining two were received shortly thereafter.

So with a demonstrated willingness on the part of state and local officials to accept their new responsibilities, and with strong evidence that block grants were having desirable results, President Reagan pushed forward with new proposals for program consolidation.78/ In 1982, he proposed seven new block grants,79/ and the expansion of three existing block grants to include more programmatic areas.80/ These ten proposals were designed to replace 46 categoricals.81/ However, the quantum leap in the number of block grants in 1981 was not duplicated thereafter.

Two new block grants were enacted in 1982. The Job Training Partnership Act was signed by the President on September 30,

---

77/ HHS also moved rapidly to issue interim final rules. On October 1, 1981, just six weeks after enactment of the block grant legislation, the regulations were published. To ensure consistency among the blocks and flexibility for the states, a single rule was prepared for all seven block grants.

78/ In an address to the Annual Meeting of the National Conference of State Legislatures on July 30, 1981, the President had promised to "go back and back and back" to the Congress to get the flexibility that state and local governments need and deserve.

79/ The proposals for new block grants were: Child Welfare; Combined Welfare Administration; Rehabilitation Services; Vocational and Adult Education; Education for the Handicapped; Dental Rehabilitation Grants; and Job Training.

80/ The existing block grants to be expanded were: Primary Care; Maternal and Child Health; and Energy and Emergency Assistance.

81/ Office of Management and Budget (OMB), "Information on Block Grants and Program Consolidations in the FY 83 Budget," Washington, D.C., February 18, 1982, p. 156.

1982.82/ Replacing the Comprehensive Employment and Training Act, it was called "the most significant federalism achievement of 1982" by National Governors' Association Chairman Scott Matheson of Utah.83/ It transferred to states several job training prerogatives that had been controlled by the federal government.84/ The legislation was designed to enhance long-term employment prospects, not just provide temporary "make-work." Unlike CETA, where only 18 cents of every dollar went to actual training, the new block grant guaranteed 70 percent of the funds would be spent on that effort.85/ And, on January 6, 1983, the President signed the Surface Transportation Assistance Act of 1982.86/ Part of this legislation was a block grant to state and local governments to refurbish roads, bridges, and mass transit systems.

* * * * *

82/ White House Office of Policy Information, The Job Training Partnership Act of 1982, Issue Alert, No. 6, White House, Washington, D.C., October 19, 1982.

83/ Governor Scott Matheson, American Enterprise Institute, Seminar on "The Deeper Dimensions of the New Federalism," Mayflower Hotel, Washington, D.C., December 7, 1982.

84/ Department of Labor, New Federalism Aspects of the Job Training Partnership Act, Memorandum from Don Shasteen, Department of Labor, to Jocelyn White, White House, October 20, 1982, p. 1.

85/ On September 23, 1982, the President said of the Job Training bill:

"Several principles which I consider absolutely essential are the core of this proposal. The delivery system for job training incorporates the block grant funding approach of our New Federalism."

86/ P.L. 97-424.

In 1983, President Reagan proposed four mega-block grants, which sought to consolidate 34 programs, with a proposed total fiscal year 1984 funding level of approximately $21 billion. They provided for level funding for each of five fiscal years from 1984 through 1988.

State Block Grant. A grant to states combining 22 health, social services, education, and community development programs, involving approximately $11 billion annually.

Local Block Grant. A grant to localities combining the General Revenue Sharing program and the entitlement portion of the Community Development Block Grant, involving approximately $7 billion annually.

Transportation Block Grant. A ground transportation grant to states consolidating six highway programs, covering urban and secondary systems, bridges (other than primary), and safety activities, involving some $2 billion annually.

Rural Housing Block Grant. A grant to states consolidating four programs for low-income rural housing construction and repair, involving $850 million annually.

Unfortunately, the continuing huge federal budget deficits and the consequent battles over budget cuts crowded out serious congressional consideration of non-budgetary domestic initiatives in 1983 and 1984. The President's mega-block grants were among the victims of this phenomenon. Nonetheless, President Reagan's commitment to block grants as a federalist tool continued with a 1985 proposal for a science and education block grant and expanding the Primary Care Block Grant. Also, in 1986 the White House was busy evaluating a possible welfare block grant.

In his 1986 State of the Union address, President Reagan again renewed his commitment to this vehicle for devolution.

"Through block grants, we have been able to cut through federal red tape and allow state and local officials to design and administer programs that make sense to them and their taxpayers. Accordingly, the budget I submitted contains proposals for new block grants, and maintains healthy funding levels for the ones already in place."87/

* * * * *

In describing the spirit of President Nixon's "New Federalism" -- much of which consisted of block grant proposals -- then Secretary of Labor George Shultz (now Secretary of State) used the analogy of the "Hawthorne Effect."88/ This is named after the Hawthorne Works of the Western Electric Company. Hawthorne was conducting experiments on the effect of different physical variables on productivity, one of which was the intensity of lighting. The workers were told that the light level would be raised to see if productivity increased. It did. This received much attention by the workers involved, so again they were told that the light level would be increased. Again, productivity went up. Then the workers were told that the lighting would be lowered to its original level and, surprisingly enough, productivity still rose. This experience led to identification of the so-called "Hawthorne Effect." The level of lighting wasn't nearly as important as the active participation and sense of importance of the workers involved.

The point, Shultz said, was that by involving people in government we can "replace the deadening 'Washington Effect' with a constructive 'Hawthorne Effect.' The very fact of our effort to try a new approach, a new experiment in government, involving the people in this experiment, should have a stimulating effect of its own and help make that experiment succeed."

To embellish on Secretary Shultz's analogy, the "Hawthorne Effect" demonstrates the virtues of federalism. By involving

---

87/ Ronald Reagan, "America's Agenda for the Future," State of the Union Address to Congress, Washington, D.C., February 6, 1986. See also, Executive Office of the President and Office of Management and Budget, "General Purpose and Broad-based Grants," Special Analysis Budget of the United States Government, Fiscal Year 1989, pp. H-22-23.

88/ Shultz, George P., "The New Federalism," The 1970 Executive Program Lecture, Graduate School of Business, The University of Chicago.

people in government, we promote civic responsibility, foster social harmony, secure individual rights, and achieve efficiency. All these goals are advanced by block grants.

As a result of the 1981 block grants, for example, about two-thirds of the governors established task forces or similar groups to study implementation options and the impact of federal budget reductions on state programs.89/ The governors of several states employed strategies that included holding public hearings and preparing analyses of issues for their state legislatures.90/ This process greatly increased citizen participation in these programs compared to that which existed with the prior federal administration.91/

The law enacting the block grants required a forum for public comments on intended use, distribution of funds, and arrangements for independent audits of expenditures. Most of the states published advertisements in one or more major newspapers noting the locations where copies of the reports were available. In a few states, toll-free telephone numbers were provided and public service announcements were made.92/

Under the HHS block grants, the governors and state legislatures became directly involved in block grant implementation. The governors' offices were more heavily involved in the planning and resource allocation of the block grants than they were in most federal categorical programs. Because the governors, as well as other state and local officials, had active participation in designing the discharge of responsibilities, they had a vested interest in making the block grants succeed.

By recognizing the legitimacy of diversity, the block grants achieved greater accountability. A General Accounting Office (GAO) report documented that states made substantial progress in becoming more accountable to their citizens during the implemen-

---

89/ Department of Health and Human Services (HHS), "Block Grant Report," Memorandum from Secretary of HHS to Director, Office of Cabinet Affairs, August 27, 1982, p. 5.

90/ Ibid.

91/ Vash, Edgar, Why Block Grants Work, A New Federalism Task Force Report, Heritage Foundation, No. 228, Washington, D.C., November 24, 1982, p. 11.

92/ HHS, "Block Grant Report," op. cit., p. 6.

tation process.93/   For example, a systematic study of public participation and planning process under the Social Services Block Grant showed that most states exceeded federal requirements for participation.94/   The Assistant Secretary of the North Carolina Human Resources Council stated that: "We have been able to target services more carefully and have really taken advantage of the flexibility. We are now able to help some of the 41 area mental health centers that were given less money. Block grants allow for this kind of discretion."95/   As noted in a November 1982 report by the Heritage Foundation entitled Why Block Grants Work, even with reduced federal funding, "there has been an increase in new, previously uncovered recipients -- a change directly attributed to the reassignment of priorities within the blocks."96/

The ability to transfer funds gave states the flexibility to be innovative in meeting the needs of their communities. For example, some states made shifts within the energy block grant to better target resources to explicit needs -- such as imminent power shut-off due to problems in paying a bill.97/ Shifts were also made out of the energy block into social services by states with warm climates who did not consider energy assistance a primary necessity.98/

Flexibility allowed more creativity in targeting funds. For example, the Commonwealth of Virginia used a larger "needs" test under the Small Cities Community Development Block Grant than the Department of Housing and Urban Development (HUD) for the CDBG

93/   U.S. General Accounting Office (GAO), Early Observations on Block Grant Implementation, U.S.G.A.O., Washington, D.C., August 24, 1982, p. 30.

94/   Robert Agranoff, "SSBG Planning and Participation Process," Publius, Vol. 17, No. 3, Summer, 1987, p. 111.

95/   Telephone conversation between Ted Parrish, Assistant Secretary, North Carolina Department of Human Resources, and my staff assistant, Jocelyn White, October 15, 1982.

96/   Vash, Why Block Grants Work, op. cit., p. 4.

97/   National Governors' Association, Guide to Block Grant Implementation, op. cit., p. 7.

98/   Ibid., p. 7.

funds.99/ HUD's test was relatively unsophisticated, while Virginia's test is detailed and very comprehensive.100/ Noting that many states were taking advantage of the flexibility of the block grants, Dr. Robert Rubin of HHS said in May, 1982:

> "So far, 36 states have taken advantage of the transfer or are planning on doing so. Thirty-three states are transferring funds from the Energy block to other blocks, primarily the Social Services block. Four other states have transferred funds to Maternal and Child Health Care from two other health block grants. From the Community Services block, three states are transferring funds to the Older Americans Act and one state to the Head Start Program."101/

There were many examples of increased efficiency. Block grant consolidations in the Department of Education enabled the Secretary to eliminate 118 pages of regulations in the Federal Register, 200,000 pages of grant applications, 7,000 pages of financial reports and 20,000 pages of programmatic reports. This represented a savings of over $1.5 million.102/

The Heritage Foundation found in its report on block grants that states expected to spend at least 40 percent less on conducting audits and compliance reports than in fiscal year 1981.103/ The

---

99/ U.S. Department of Housing and Urban Development, Memorandum from Clark Judge of HUD to Jocelyn White of the White House on HUD's Standard for Awarding Community Development Block Grants vs. Virginia's Standards for Awarding Community Improvement Grants, December 1, 1982.

100/ The HUD test asked what number of people and what proportion of people in an area live below the poverty line. The Virginia test compared average income levels, population changes, unemployment levels and relative tax effort and ability. In addition, Virginia gave "need" more weight than does HUD.

101/ Rubin, Robert J., Statement before the Subcommittee on Intergovernmental Relations, May 11, 1982, p. 7.

102/ Department of Education, "Block Grant Report," Memorandum from Secretary of Education to Director, Office of Cabinet Affairs, August, 1982, p. 2.

103/ Vash, Why Block Grants Work, op. cit., p. 16.

GAO, in its block grant status report, also noted management improvements in developing and reporting requirements. In the GAO report, a Massachusetts official found that the preparation of their Low-Income Energy Assistance Block Grant only took three days compared to the 22 days needed under the prior categorical programs.104/

Through the President's block grants, the intergovernmental system was clearly functioning better.

* * * * *

The President's federalism agenda in general, and block grants in particular, faced increasingly strong opposition as his tenure progressed.105/ Several factors caused this, and they had surfaced even during the first round of block grant proposals in 1981.

For one thing, the friction between local governments and states continued to exist.106/ Some local officials continue to be concerned about state administration of federal block grants and

---

104/ GAO, Block Grant Implementation, op. cit., p. 27.

105/ See Governor Michael N. Castle (DE), "To Provide Efficient Service Delivery," Restoring the Balance: State Leadership for America's Future (National Governors' Association, Washington, D.C., 1988), pp. 37-44.

106/ According to a survey by the U.S. Conference of Mayors:
"Most [city human services officials] indicated that their cities had not been adequately involved in either the state block grant planning process or the state resource allocation process. They indicated, in addition, that state block grant funds had not been passed through to their cities in an adequate manner."

See U.S. Conference of Mayors, Human Services in FY 82: Shrinking Resources in Troubled Times, Washington, D.C., October, 1982, p. 15.

funding allocation.107/   This had been summed up well by Columbus, Ohio Mayor Tom Moody (R). At a February 1981 hearing of the Senate Subcommittee on Intergovernmental Affairs he said:

> "But we in home-rule cities prefer to deal directly with the federal government because the state is in the way and does not add much in the way of real contributions."108/

Secondly, the "iron triangle" was resourceful in derailing federalism proposals. For example, Congressman John Ashbrook (R-Ohio) was the ranking Republican on the House Education and Labor Committee to which the 1981 Education Block Grant was referred.   Under normal circumstances, Ashbrook would have been an ardent supporter of the President's goals. He had been a founder and past Chairman of the American Conservative Union. However, he also was running for the U.S. Senate, and he hoped to neutralize the National Education Association.   In an effort to halt their probable opposition to his candidacy, he acquiesced to certain restrictions and mandates in the block grant.109/

The Ashbrook example was repeated dozens of times throughout Congress by both Republicans and Democrats. This greatly contributed to the ability of the vested special interest groups, some turf conscious Congressmen, and some members of Congress who sincerely had little faith in state and local officials, to water down the President's proposals.

Perhaps most importantly, block grants often became stuck in the quagmire of the budget battle. This problem deepened with the recession and intensified after the President announced his major Federalism Initiative.   The block grant proposal of 1981 represented an aggregate 25% reduction in funding levels. While state

---

107/ See, for example, Edward T. Jennings, Jr., Dale Krane, Alex N. Pattakos, and B.J. Reed, From Nation to States: The Small Cities Community Development (State University of New York Press, Albany, 1986).

108/ Senate Subcommittee on Intergovernmental Relations, Intergovernmental Relations in the 1980's, Hearings, 97th Congress, 1st session, U.S.G.P.O., February 25 and 26, 1981, p. 11.

109/ On April 24, 1982, John Ashbrook died in Newark, Ohio while campaigning for the Republican nomination for the Senate seat held by Senator Howard Metzenbaum (D-Ohio).

officials had said they could do with less money if they had more flexibility, they were thinking more in line with a 10% reduction. Some saw the funding reductions, coupled with the block grants, as a retreat from social programs by the federal government.

Even though reductions in funding levels of grants-in-aid would have occurred in any event (because of the realities of budget constraints), some state and local officials and liberal constituency groups saw the defeat of block grants as a way to sandbag the President's efforts to get domestic spending under control.

The Federalism Initiative first announced by the President in his 1982 State of the Union message escalated and heightened the debate of our intergovernmental system. The Initiative was a philosophical framework designed to transcend the battle of the budget over who gets how many tens for a five. It was meant to get the federal government out of the money changing business and return actual tax sources to states and localities. But another interim step was to be taken, and it was taken concurrently with enactment of block grants -- regulatory relief.

Along with reducing taxes and cutting the rate of growth of federal spending, the President had promised in 1980 to provide regulatory relief to all segments of society. A major part of that effort was directed at those regulations tying the hands of state and local officials, and thus was a major part of his federalism agenda.

CHAPTER 5

REGULATORY RELIEF

"If a bureaucrat had been writing the Ten Commandments, a simple rock slab would not have been near enough room.

Those simple rules would have read: 'Thou shalt not, unless you feel strongly to the contrary, or for the following stated exceptions, see paragraphs 1-10, subsection #A.'"

-Ronald Reagan1/

During the 1960's and 1970's the increasingly incomprehensible mandates of Washington spawned a mighty army of new professionals. They are the code breakers -- the consultants and communicators paid handsomely by clients (including state and local governments) to traverse the labyrinth of federal rules and regulations. Their Washington nickname is "Beltway Bandits," after the highway that girdles the city where their office buildings stand.

They do nothing illegal or devious. But their existence is an indictment of a federal establishment grown estranged from the people it serves. Washington's over-regulation created a huge industry -- a shadow government -- that acts as a buffer between elected officials and the citizens. The expense of these regulations drains our economic vitality, stifles our creativity, suffocates state and local governments and, at the time Ronald Reagan assumed the Presidency, was costing every person in the country $500 annually.2/

Over the years, Ronald Reagan made well known his concerns about Washington's over-regulation. As governor of California, he had experienced first hand the damaging effect of federal over-regulation. He had, after all, promised "to make the state an effective bulwark for the people on an ever-encroaching federal

---

1/ Ronald Reagan, Speech, June 6, 1974, in ed. Joseph R. Holmes, The Quotable Ronald Reagan (JRH & Associates, Inc., San Diego, CA, 1974), p. 23.

2/ Weidenbaum, Murray L., Costs of Regulation and Benefits of Reform, Center for the Study of American Business, Washington University, St. Louis (Publication Number 35, November 1980), p. 11.

government."3/   While Governor he quipped, "If the Interstate Commerce Commission had been in business during the pioneer days, the 49ers would still be trying to find out what the rules are for crossing the Mississippi River."4/

Attacking federal over-regulation is good, accepted Republican rhetoric. But for Reagan, the call for deregulation had a special urgency. Excessive federal regulation challenged his free market economic views. It choked initiative and distorted the market place.5/ The enormous bureaucratic machinery to dream up, write down and enforce these regulations offended his anti-government bias. It was counter-productive and wasteful. And the federal government, through its extravagant regulatory zeal, abused, contorted and distorted the federal system. It forced upon the states national norms that failed to consider state or local individual circumstances (desires or needs). It gave faceless bureaucrats in Washington enormous power over the duly elected local and state leaders. It moved the state and local officials to become clerks and enforcement officers for often foolish federal mandates.

At the same time, Reagan's anti-government deregulation instincts were tempered by a recognition of the need for regulations to "protect the health and safety of workers, and consumers, and the quality of our environment." While governor of California Reagan signed bills creating a state Occupational Safety and Health Administration, establishing state control over the location of power plants, requiring environmental impact statements for major construction projects, and creating the California Air Resources Board.6/ Nonetheless, it is clear that Ronald Reagan has a presumption against government regulations. It is a rebuttable presumption. But the burden is on champions of any particular

---

3/   Governor Ronald Reagan, Address to the California Republican Assembly, April 1, 1967, Long Beach, California.

4/   Ibid., p. 103.

5/   See Paul W. MacAvoy, "The Existing Condition of Regulation and Regulatory Reform," in Regulating Business: The Search for an Optimum (Institute for Contemporary Studies, San Francisco, 1978), pp. 3-16.

6/   James C. Miller, III and Jeffrey A. Eisenach, "Regulatory Reform under Ronald Reagan" in ed. Wayne Vallis, The Future Under President Reagan (Arlington House Publishers, Westport, Connecticut, 1981), p. 89.

regulation to demonstrate its compelling need and that its benefit exceeds its cost.

Not surprisingly, regulatory relief was a consistent theme in his presidential campaign.7/ In a speech in Youngstown, Ohio on October 8, 1980, he presented these principles for controlling regulatory growth: (1) implementation of sunset legislation to automatically discontinue regulations which become outdated; (2) required cost-benefit analysis for proposed regulations; and (3) flexibility for state and local governments, as well as businesses, in complying with regulations.8/

During the campaign Reagan established a task force on government regulation to provide him analysis on the severity of the problem and to begin to chart out a course for reform. Many members of this task force would go on to hold prominent positions in the Reagan Administration. It was chaired by economist Murray L. Weidenbaum, director of the Center for the Study of American Business. A pioneer in the study of government regulation, Weidenbaum was Reagan's first Chairman of the Council of Economic Advisors. Weidenbaum is a friendly man; loyal and trusting. In later White House in-fighting, he was to learn that his admirable qualities of loyalty and trust were not always the best armor to protect him. But despite whatever bruises he absorbed in other administration economic battles, on the regulatory relief agenda he was an important leader. Also on the task force was William Niskanen, former chief economist for Ford Motor Company, who would go on to serve as a member of Reagan's Council of Economic Advisors; Antonin Scalia, professor at Stanford Law School, who went on to become a Reagan judicial appointee on the D.C. Court of Appeals and then the U.S. Supreme Court; Robert Bork, professor of law at Yale University, who went on to be a Reagan judicial appointee on the D.C. Court of Appeals; Charles Fried, professor of law at Harvard Law School and later Reagan's Solicitor General; Jim Miller, economist at the American Enterprise Institute, who went on to be Reagan's Federal Trade Commission Chairman and OMB Director; and James M. Buchanan, director of the Center for the Study of Public Choice at Virginia Polytechnic Institute and State University, who was a close ad-

---

7/ Candidate Ronald Reagan, Address to the Chicago Economics Club, October, 1980. Therein, candidate Reagan outlined his economic recovery program and identified regulatory relief as one of the four pillars of that program.

8/ Candidate Ronald Reagan, Youngstown, Ohio, October 8, 1980.

visor to many senior Reagan Administration officials and won the 1986 Nobel Prize in Economics. In short, it was a highly distinguished list of experts whose voices were heard in the campaign, during the transition, and on into the Reagan Administration.

Regulatory relief was integrally tied to Reagan's promise to devolve decision making authority to states and localities. The Administration's view of how federal over-regulation had distorted American federalism was perhaps best expressed by Weidenbaum:

> "[I]n the past decade we have seen a boom in federal social regulation with devastating consequences for the federal system ... the federal government, through many of its regulatory actions, had reduced the autonomy of state governments and centralized the responsibilities for many important social, economic, and regulatory programs. This loss of autonomy has weakened the states and reduced their independence, while the centralization of responsibilities better handled at state and local levels has limited the effectiveness of the federal government."9/

During the transition, Jim Miller emerged as the man who would take the lead in the deregulation effort. Dave Stockman knew Miller from the American Enterprise Institute and wanted him to be his Assistant Director running the OMB Office of Information and Regulatory Affairs. Miller is a high energy, enthusiastic, very ambitious economist who has a booming voice that seldom quiets to a normal conversational tone. He is a take charge guy who knew his way around from earlier stints in the Nixon and Ford Administrations.

During the transition, Miller had written that "the key to reforming social regulation is to create laws, implement procedures, and appoint administrators so that agencies will be encouraged to take into account all of the effects of their actions, including those outside their narrowly conceived missions."10/ Once Reagan took office, Miller proved the perfect man to successfully launch the regulatory reform effort.

9/   Weidenbaum, Murray L., "Strengthening Our Federal System," Journal of Contemporary Studies 4 (Fall, 1981), pp. 71-72.

10/ James C. Miller, III and Jeffrey A. Eisenach, "Regulatory Reform Under Ronald Reagan," in ed. Wayne Vallis, The Future Under President Reagan (Arlington House Publishers, Westport, CT, 1981), pp. 89, 93.

In office, President Reagan moved swiftly to make the necessary institutional arrangements for long-range success in regulatory relief. The day after the Inaugural, he established a Cabinet-level Task Force on Regulatory Relief and asked Vice President Bush to chair it.11/ The next week he sent a memorandum to the heads of eleven Cabinet departments and the Environmental Protection Agency, asking them to delay for sixty days the effective date of all final rules that had not yet taken effect. And on February 17, 1981, he issued an executive order to establish a strong centralized mechanism for Presidential management of agency rulemaking that would use cost-benefit analysis in reviewing proposed regulations.12/

These actions led to an easing of the staggering costs of federal dictates, a reversal of the patronizing attitude of big brother in Washington, and a more decentralized regulatory process better able to respond to local needs.

* * * * *

Federal regulation of business can be traced to the establishment of the Interstate Commerce Commission in 1887. New regulatory agencies arose during the early twentieth century -- most notably the Federal Trade Commission in 1914 -- and proliferated during the New Deal era. Examples include the Federal Communications Commission (1934), the Securities and Exchange Commission (1934), the Federal Maritime Commission (1936), and the Civil Aeronautics Board (1938). These agencies were established to regulate market behavior of business. The 1960's and 1970's gave rise to new kinds of regulatory bodies designed to achieve social reform -- e.g., the Equal Employment Opportunity Commission (1964), the Environmental Protection Agency (1970), the Occupational Safety and Health Administration (1970), and the Consumer Product Safety Commission (1972).

11/ Other members appointed by the President were: Treasury Secretary Donald Regan, Commerce Secretary Malcolm Baldridge, Labor Secretary Raymond Donovan, Attorney General William French Smith, Office of Management and Budget Director David Stockman, Council of Economic Advisors Chairman Murray Weidenbaum, and Assistant to the President for Policy Development Martin Anderson.

12/ Executive Order 12291, 46 FR 13193, February 19, 1981.

While state and local governments had long been accustomed to quasi-regulations through "strings" attached to grants-in-aid, direct federal mandates on them are a more recent phenomenon. This, too, was an outgrowth of the social reform of the 1960's and 1970's. Some of the federal controls were directly aimed at states and localities; others were intended for private concerns, but were to be implemented at the state and local level.

In a sense, subdivisions of the national government were being conscripted into the infantry of social reform. Washington's high command was issuing directives and assigning the unpopular task of carrying them out to other political jurisdictions. In an effort to create a monolithic regulatory system, the federal government overused its power in the pursuit of unattainable goals, and showed a callousness toward the burdens it was placing on states and localities.13/ As New York City Mayor Ed Koch wrote in 1980, "The federal government... has shown no reluctance in ordering sweeping changes, the impact of which it will never have to face since it does not hold the final service-delivery responsibilities... [and the] statutory commands are rarely accompanied by adequate financial assistance."14/

Well over 1,200 new federal regulations affecting state and local governments were promulgated during the 1960's and 1970's. They were both programmatic, specifying actions, goals or functions expected of a jurisdiction, and procedural, focusing on how a task must be accomplished. Over 1,000 of the new regulations were added during the 70's alone, paralleling the explosive growth in federal grant-in-aid programs to state and local governments. Again, Koch wrote, "By the close of the 1970's, the cities found themselves under the guns of dozens of federal laws imposing increasingly draconian mandates."15/

13/ For a discussion of local officials' concerns about federal regulatory mandates and federal intrusions into local affairs see, for example, Lewis B. Kaden, Barry Friedman, and Robin J.H. Maxwell, How Can Cities Be Protected Under the U.S. Constitution (National League of Cities, Washington, D.C., 1986).

14/ Edward I. Koch, "The Mandate Millstone," The Public Interest 61 (Fall 1980), pp. 42-43.

15/ Ibid.

Eighty percent of the new regulations accompanied the new grants-in-aid, and therefore were conditional.16/ They could be imposed only on the condition that a jurisdiction accepted the grant. This was Washington's "carrot" approach to regulation. In exchange for states and localities fulfilling the desires of the national government, they were rewarded with largess from the federal treasury. As already established, the reality of fiscal pressures forced them to comply. It was either take the federal money and suffer the restrictions, or have no program at all. Even if they could get out of certain programs, other, less benign, regulations still would force compliance. These were Washington's stick. As opposed to conditional, they were direct orders.

Some direct orders told state and local governments what to do internally. The Equal Employment Opportunity Act of 1972, for instance, barred job discrimination by state and local governments on the basis of race, color, sex or national origin.17/ This was a legal dictate extending the requirements imposed on private employers in 1964. In other cases, the dictates overlapped or superseded regulations imposed as a condition of aid. The Civil Rights Act of 1964 barred discrimination on the basis of race, color, creed or national origin "under any program (emphasis added) receiving federal financial assistance."18/

A second classification of direct orders told states and localities how to regulate business. The Clean Air Act, for example, set national standards but required states to devise plans for their implementation.19/ The Occupational Safety and Health Act allowed state control of the workplace, but only if their standards were "at least as effective" as federal ones.20/ These regulations also come under the category of "partial preemption." The federal government established basic policies,

---

16/ For a general discussion of the overloading and congestion of the federal system, see "A Crisis of Confidence and Competence," The Federal Role in the Federal System: The Dynamics of Growth (Advisory Commission on Intergovernmental Relations, A-77, 1980).

17/ 86 Stat. 103.

18/ 78 Stat. 241 et seq.

19/ 77 Stat. 392 et seq.

20/ 84 Stat. 1590.

while delegating responsibility for implementation to other jurisdictions -- but, they were required to meet minimum nation-
ally-determined standards. States and localities had no say in
where the minimum should be set, or if there should have been any
standard at all.

Another important distinction is between "vertical" mandates and
"horizontal" mandates. When regulations affect only a single
department or function, they are referred to as vertical. When
they are generally applicable to all federal programs or agencies, they are called horizontal.

A hybrid between the two and perhaps the most troubling aspect of
growing federal regulations on state and local governments is the
crossover regulation. This imposes a requirement on one program
to influence state and local policy in other areas. Failure to
comply with these dictates can cause loss of funds in an unrelated or semi-related federal assistance program.

True horizontal mandates are called crosscutting. One of the
first and most important was the 1964 Civil Rights Act mentioned
earlier, barring racial discrimination under any federal assistance program.21/ By 1980 there were 59 of these regulations
which cut across all grants-in-aid.22/ They were expanded in the
civil rights area to include the handicapped, women, and the
elderly.23/ In environmental protection they included air and
water pollution,24/ historic preservation,25/ endangered

21/ Applicable provision of the 1964 Civil Rights Act
(P.L. 88-352, July 2, 1964) is Title VI.

22/ For a general discussion, see U.S. Office of
Management and Budget, Managing Federal Assistance in
the 1980's: A Report to the Congress of the United
States Pursuant to the Federal Grant and Cooperative
Agreement Act of 1977 (P.L. 95-224), (Washington,
D.C.: U.S. Government Printing Office, March, 1980).

23/ Examples include the Age Discrimination Act of 1975
(42 U.S.C. 6101); Title IX of the Education Act
Amendments of 1972, as amended by P.L. 93-568, 88
Stat. 1855 (20 U.S.C. 1681 et seq.); and the
Architectural Barriers Act of 1968, as amended, P.L.
90-480 (42 U.S.C. 4151 et seq.).

24/ Examples include the National Environmental Policy Act
of 1969, as amended, P.L. 91-190 (42 U.S.C. 4321 et
seq.); Sec. 508 of the Federal Water Pollution Control
(Cont'd)

species26/ and land management.27/ The Davis-Bacon Act,28/ Anti-Kickback (Copeland) Act,29/ and Contract Work Hours and Safety Standards Act30/ engendered crosscutting rules in labor standards. Health, welfare, and worker safety had crosscutting protections,31/ as did the Freedom of Information Act.32/

Crosscutting requirements are particularly menacing to state and local officials because they are imposed without regard to how

Act Amendments of 1972, P.L. 92-500 (33 U.S.C. 1251 et seq.); and Conformity of Federal Activities with state implementation plans under the Clean Air Act Amendments of 1977, Title I, Sec. 129(b).

25/   Examples include Sec. 106 of the National Historical Preservation Act of 1966, P.L. 89-665 as amended (16 U.S.C. 470), 84 Stat. 204 (1970), 87 Stat. 139 (1973), 90 Stat. 1320 (1976), 92 Stat. 3467 (1978); Procedures for the Protection of Historic and Cultural Properties (36 CFR 800); and Executive Order 11593, May 31, 1971, Protection and Enhancement of the Cultural Environment (36 FR 8921, 16 U.S.C. 470).

26/   For example, the Endangered Species Act of 1973, P.L. 93-205 (16 U.S.C. 1531 et seq.), as amended by P.L. 95-632.

27/   Examples include Executive Orders 11988 and 11990, May 24, 1977, Floodplain Management and Protection of Wetlands, respectively; the Wild and Scenic Rivers Act of 1968, p. 1. 90-542, as amended (16 U.S.C. 1271 et seq.); and Secs. 307(c) and (d) of the Coastal Zone Management Act of 1972, as amended (16 U.S.C. 1451 et seq.).

28/   40 U.S.C. 276a-276a-7 and 27 CFR Pt. 1, 46 Stat. 1494, Appendix A.

29/   18 U.S.C. 874; 40 U.S.C. 276c.

30/   40 U.S.C. 327-332.

31/   Examples include the Comprehensive Alcohol Abuse and Alcoholism Prevention, Treatment, and Rehabilitation Act of 1970, P.L. 91-616 (42 U.S.C. 4581); Lead-Based Paint Poisoning Prohibition (42 U.S.C. 4831(b)); and the Animal Welfare Act of 1966 (7 U.S.C. 2131-2147).

32/   5 U.S.C. 552.

they affect specific programs or how they collectively alter the efficiency of government. As concluded in a 1980 study by the Office of Management and Budget:

"Individually, each crosscutting requirement may be sound. But cumulatively the conditions may be extra-ordinarily burdensome... They can distort the alloca-tion of resources, as the conditions are frequently imposed with minimal judgment as to relative costs and benefits in any given transition. Frequently, the recipients must absorb substantial portions of the costs."33/

One analyst has written, "One person's 'red tape' may be another's treasured procedural safeguard."34/ But clearly, by 1981 things had gotten out of control.

Regulation is a dynamic political process. As President Carter's White House Counsel has written, regulation presents "choices between competing social and economic values and competing alter-natives for government action."35/ The political process and elected representatives of the people should not lose control of regulation. And the duly elected local and state officials should not become mere enforcers for federal bureaucrats.

Members of the iron triangle in Washington have had inordinate influence over the federal regulatory process. As Professor Donald Kettl has written, "The regulatory era that began in the 1960's and reached its peak in the 1970's... marked the growth of horizontal power in Washington at the expense of vertical rela-tionships."36/ The key players directing the rule-making were Washington-based special interest groups, congressional committee members and staff, and federal bureaucrats in the departments and agencies. "They used that power to reach deeply into the deci-

---

33/ U.S. Office of Management and Budget, op. cit., p. 20.

34/ Herbert Kaufman, Red Tape: Its Origins, Uses and Abuses (Washington, D.C., 1977), p. 4.

35/ Lloyd N. Cutler and David R. Johnson, "Regulation and the Political Process," Yale Law Journal, LXXXIV (1975), 1399.

36/ Donald F. Kettl, The Regulation of American Federalism (Louisiana State University Press, Baton Rouge, LA, 1983), p. 157.

sions local officials made."37/ Over-regulation was shifting power from state and local governments to a Washington-based network. Where was the input and perspective of elected state and local officials who were required to deliver services? Where was the latitude and flexibility to accommodate local needs and desires? Where was the room for innovation? Where was the accountability?

In 1980, Mayor Koch wrote:

> "Throughout its history, this nation has encouraged local independence and diversity. We cannot allow the powerful diversity of spirit that is a basic characteristic of our federal system to be crushed under the grim conformity that will be the most enduring legacy of the mandate millstone."38/

* * * * *

The mass of federal rulemaking led to delays, overlap, and patently absurd requirements. Costs inflicted on businesses were much discussed in the media and other public forums, and generated volumes of "horror" stories. The hamburger, for instance -- a staple of the quick, inexpensive meal -- was cited as the subject of 41,000 federal and state regulations, adding an estimated 8 to 11 cents per pound to the cost of ground meat.39/ An Oregon businessman was required to pay his 70 employees biweekly instead of monthly to accommodate Internal Revenue Service forms. This added $200 per month to bookkeeping charges.40/

Regulatory excess of business is, of course, paid for in the marketplace in the form of higher prices.41/ Equally as costly

---

37/ Ibid.

38/ Edward I. Koch, "The Mandate Millstone," The Public Interest, 61 (Fall, 1980) 42.

39/ The Presidential Task Force on Regulatory Relief, Internal Memorandum, July 16, 1982.

40/ Ibid.

41/ For a general discussion, see Weidenbaum, Murray L., (Cont'd)

to Americans are regulations on state and local governments. These show up on the tax bill, and again there are "horror" stories.

Archaeological investigations stymied construction of a Phoenix, Arizona highway for many months, adding $6 million per month to the ultimate cost.42/ An Urban Institute study of six federal regulatory programs in seven U.S. cities concluded that compliance with rules costs these governments an average $24 per capita -- $96 for a family of four.43/ A 1981 Washington Post series entitled "Appleton: A Regulated City" reported that the Wisconsin town of about 60,000 people was regulated by over 100 federal agencies. For example, a local university was forced to install a $4,000 wheelchair lift that was used once in three years.44/

With the taxpayers' revolts beginning in the late 1970's, states and localities faced shrinking resources. Regulations were diverting funds from needed local services. The alarm of state and local officials due to over-regulation crossed partisan and ideological lines. Said a New York Times editorial in August 1980:

> "Each new day seems to bring some new directive from Congress, the courts or bureaucrats ... The mandates are piling up so fast that liberal governors and mayors are enrolling in a cause once pressed only by arch-conservatives."45/

Many also felt that if Washington wanted these social reforms enacted, it should be willing to pay for them.

Beyond the absolute costs, state and local officials were disturbed by the inflexibility of bureaucratic rulemaking.

Costs of Regulation and Benefits of Reform, op. cit.

42/ Mayor Margaret T. Hance, Policy Position Paper -- Papago Freeway Inner Loop, February 25, 1981.

43/ Cited in Murray L. Weidenbaum, "Strengthening our Federal System," American Federalism: A New Partnership for the Republic (Institute for Contemporary Studies, San Francisco, 1982), pp. 90-91.

44/ "Appleton: A Regulated City," The Washington Post, April 7, 8, 9 and 10, 1981.

45/ "Fighting Federal Mandates," The New York Times, August 16, 1980.

Washington not only told them what to do, but how to do it. Only one solution was recognized, and creative problem-solving was precluded. The Carter Administration's proposed bilingual education rules were a good example.

In a 1974 case brought to the Supreme Court by Chinese-American parents, the Court held that the 1964 Civil Rights Act required school districts to give special instruction to non-English speaking students.46/ The decision stated that:

> "Teaching English to the students of Chinese ancestry
> is one choice. Giving instructions to this group in
> Chinese is another. There may be others."47/

Instead of taking the Court's lead by allowing for flexibility under differing circumstances, the Department of Health, Education and Welfare mandated subject-matter courses in native languages.48/ Failure to comply would result in a cutoff of funds and alternative approaches were generally prohibited. It didn't matter whether the school district included many students speaking the same foreign language (such as Spanish in the Southwest), or students speaking many differing languages (such as in the metropolitan Washington area).

Regulations not only intruded in program areas of traditional state-local responsibility, they also directed the structure of their governments. The National Health Planning and Resources Development Act of 1974, for example, required each state to designate a State Health Planning and Development Agency.49/ State and local elected officials were thus being reduced from chief operating officers of their jurisdictions to shop foremen, taking orders from company headquarters in Washington.

Because the regulations were being planned in federal agency conference rooms -- on paper rather than on site -- they were inefficient, and often impractical. Legislation to accommodate the handicapped, for instance, was interpreted by the Department

---

46/ Lau v. Nichols, 414 U.S. 563 (1974).

47/ Ibid., p. 565.

48/ For a general discussion see Stanfield, Rochelle L., "Are the Federal Bilingual Rules A Foot in the Schoolhouse Door?" National Journal, October 18, 1980, p. 1736.

49/ 88 Stat. 2225.

of Transportation to apply to existing transit systems.50/ This would have required retrofitting 90 year old subway systems -- such as those in New York and Chicago -- at an astronomical cost. Similarly, there were proposals to require all buses to be equipped with wheelchair lifts. The Congressional Budget Office estimated that it would cost $38 per trip to provide full wheel- chair access to mass transportation.51/ And, because different federal agencies were pursuing conflicting goals, state and local officials were often faced with inconsistent standards and proce- dures in complying with all the crosscutting mandates.

All of this led to a deterioration of the democratic process and scapegoating. Citizens didn't know whom to blame for excessive costs and poor services. Was it the Congress for legislating simplistic solutions to complex problems? Was it the courts going beyond the bounds of congressional intent? Was it the bureaucracy for abusing legislative license?

Back in 1974, Ronald Reagan had said:

> "There is only one way to make government bite the bullet on inflation, on high taxes, on all those things that should be a matter of concern. And that is to hold all elected officials accountable. Match their performance with their promises, and if you find some who don't measure up, vote them out of office."52/

50/ Clark, Timothy B., "Regulations Gone Amok: How Many Billions for Wheelchair Transit?" Regulation, March/ April 1980, p. 49.

51/ Congressional Budget Office, Urban Transportation for Handicapped Persons: Alternative Federal Approaches (Washington, D.C.: U.S. Government Printing Office, 1979).

52/ Ronald Reagan, Speech, Oct. 15, 1974, in Joseph R. Holmes, The Quotable Ronald Reagan (JRH & Associates, Inc., San Diego, CA, 1974), p. 125. See also, Governor Edward DiPrete (R.I.), "To Instill Accountability" in Restoring the Balance: State Leadership for America's Future (National Governors' Association, Washington, D.C., 1988), pp. 55-64.

One harmful result of the growing maze of complex statutory and administrative regulations was a break-down of that accountability necessary in a representative government.

* * * * *

Reagan's regulatory relief program did not start at ground zero. It built on a process of deregulation that began under Presidents Ford and Carter. Both had taken steps to bring more control of the federal regulatory process into the White House. And both had taken tentative steps toward applying some cost-benefit analysis to regulations.

Soon after taking office, on November 27, 1974, Ford issued Executive Order 11821 requiring all federal agencies to review the inflationary impact of proposed regulations. Later he revised the order to require a full economic study of proposed regulations that carried compliance costs of over $100 million. Ford created the Council on Wage and Price Stability to review agency studies and selectively conduct its own analysis. On March 23, 1978, Carter issued Executive Order 12044 creating a semiannual calendar of proposed regulations. It was intended to provide an early warning system for proposed regulations. Also, this executive order proposed greater time for public comment on proposed rules. It required cabinet members to review the regulations their agencies published in order to seek consistency with agency policy. And, it required agencies to do a "regulatory analysis" of the costs of proposed regulations. Carter created a Regulatory Analysis Review Group which, along with the Council on Wage and Price Stability, supervised the new guidelines.53/

While Ford and Carter tentatively had addressed over-regulation, they primarily dealt with private sector rules such as airline deregulation and workplace safety. Very seldom did they venture into public sector rules. Reagan built on the foundation left by his predecessors, but pushed harder. And, importantly for the

---

53/ Donald F. Kettl, "The Uncertain Brides: Regulatory Reform in Reagan's New Federalism," Publius: Annual Review of American Federalism: 1981, pp. 19, 21-2.

efforts to decentralize government, he made federalism an important element of his regulatory reform efforts.54/

* * * * *

During the transition there had been substantial deliberation on
exactly how to implement Reagan's regulatory reform program. It
was understood well that to get the sort of dramatic results the
President-elect expected, cabinet members had to ramrod their
departments. And while Jim Miller would have day-to-day leadership, it was unrealistic to expect that an Assistant Director of
OMB could compel the issue to the top of cabinet members' agendas
or that he could force cabinet members to override their own
bureaucracies on disputed deregulation issues. At one point,
there was consideration of an idea advanced by Miller that in
addition to his title as an Assistant Director of OMB, he be
given the title of Special Assistant to the President. While
this would give him the indicia of greater authority, Jim Baker
wasn't anxious to have that title given out to someone not on his
staff. An alternative suggestion was to have the President create a Regulatory Relief Task Force chaired by Vice President
Bush.

After the President's personal involvement in the management of
the regulatory relief effort, an impossibility due to his many
other obligations, there could be no more effective person than
Bush. His close involvement would be symbolic to the world, both
inside and outside the Administration, of the regulatory reform
effort's importance. And he could force resolution of issues.
Early in the Administration, Bush once quipped to me that one of
the nice things about his job was that everyone returned his
calls. Well, that's exactly what would be needed as regulatory
issues competed for the time of busy cabinet members.

Those that later charged that George Bush was a passive Vice
President, just a cheerleader who didn't do anything, are
wrong. From close personal experience, I know Bush was deeply
involved in the important regulatory relief process. He took a

---

54/ See Timothy J. Conlan, "Ambivalent Federalism:
     Intergovernmental Policy in the Reagan
     Administration," in Lewis G. Bender and James A.
     Stever, Administering the New Federalism (Westview
     Press, Boulder, 1986), pp. 15-40.

strong personal interest and worked hard to make it achieve real results. While always a consummate gentleman, Bush did lean on cabinet members from time to time when necessary. He broke up log jams. He kept things moving. At the end of the first year, Bush said, "We can't say that we've done everything we set out to do. But we've started -- and made a good start."55/ And that simply would not have happened without Bush's active leadership.

Of course, Bush also demonstrated leadership in many other areas such as crisis management and the terrorism task force. I, however, did not deal with him in those activities. But in regulatory reform I do know that he proved an indispensable involved chairman.

As soon as Reagan took office, the Task Force on Regulatory Relief chaired by Vice President Bush set out to get control of this regulatory machine gone haywire. The executive order signed by the President on February 17, 1981 put teeth into the effort. It required that the federal government not regulate unless there was a demonstrated need, that the benefits exceed the cost, and where it was impossible to quantify benefits, that the most cost-effective solution be chosen (including targeting the best and most responsive unit of government to regulate).56/ To contrast to the Ford and Carter initiatives, Reagan made cost-benefit analysis mandatory for rules with an anticipated cost of $100 million or more. And OMB had a procedure to review proposed regulations before their publication in the Federal Register as proposed rules. OMB had the power to force the agencies to do a better job. It was a new ball game.

I had the chance to work actively on this effort. Under the Vice President's chairmanship, the day to day regulatory relief effort was run by OMB Assistant Director Jim Miller and the Vice

---

55/ Caroline E. Mayer, "Bush: Rules Reform Has Long Way to Go," Washington Post, Dec. 9, 1981.

56/ Executive Order 12291, op. cit.

President's Counsel Boyden Gray.57/ To ensure that the White House Senior Staff fully participated in the process, Vice President Bush asked me to serve as Associate Director of the Task Force. Consequently, I met weekly for breakfast with Miller and Gray to review all staff activity and help where possible. All three of us met every couple of weeks with Vice President Bush. He was well briefed and willing to force the process along against the often entrenched bureaucracies. Also his political instincts and clout on a number of occasions proved invaluable with Capitol Hill.

In addition to everything else, this post gave me an added avenue to push the President's federalism agenda. For a number of reasons, including the need to foster the best possible relations with the White House Senior Staff, both Miller and Gray provided strong support to help ease over-regulations on state and local governments. Vice President Bush shared President Reagan's commitment to regulatory relief and fully appreciated the political benefits of easing the unfair burdens on state and local governments. The Vice President met with scores of elected officials both carrying the President's message about regulatory relief to them and, more importantly, hearing their stories of Washington over-regulation and abuse.

The Task Force was charged with three major responsibilities:

- to review major proposals by Executive Branch regulatory agencies, especially those proposals with overlapping jurisdiction among agencies;

- to assess major Executive Branch regulations already on the books, especially those which analysts determined to be particularly burdensome to the economy;

- to oversee the development of legislation, where necessary, in the regulatory area.

57/ Jim Miller served as Director of the President's Regulatory Relief Task Force and his staff at OMB did most of the leg work. Later in the Administration, Miller served as Chairman of the Federal Trade Commission and then returned to OMB as Director. Boyden Gray served as Counsel to the Task Force and provided daily briefings to the Vice President regarding ongoing activities. For an excellent overview of Reagan's regulatory relief efforts in this area, see C. Boyden Gray, "Regulation and Federalism," Yale Journal on Regulation, Vol. 1, No. 1, 1983, p. 93.

It began its work by enlisting the help of business, labor, state and local officials, and others to identify objectionable regulatory burdens. Over 1,000 state and local governments sent in detailed documents outlining their major problems with Washington over-regulation. In reviewing these regulations, the Task Force developed four major principles for streamlining the regulatory process.

A first was to harness market incentives. A regulatory program can benefit in many ways from incentives based on market performance. Instead of getting compliance details from Washington, it is more efficient to set performance standards and let the affected industry determine the most competitive way to comply. Similarly, it is more useful to encourage self-regulation of well-managed firms, concentrating limited enforcement resources on more serious problems.

The second principle required by the President's Executive Order was to modify regulations where costs exceed benefits. The law of diminishing returns is that if it costs X to achieve 95% of a regulatory goal, 10X to achieve 97%, and 100X to achieve 99%, the best use of resources may be to aim for only the 95-96% level.

The third principle was the streamlining of regulatory procedures. Statutes frequently required firms to obtain government permits or approvals before undertaking certain activities. When the approval process was lengthy, uncertain or bureaucratic, the result was costly delays in introducing beneficial new products or sometimes cancellation of important development projects. The Task Force placed heavy emphasis on making federal permit programs more prompt, predictable and efficient.

Last, but perhaps most important, was the goal to reduce burdens on state and local governments. The Task Force sought to strengthen the authority of state and local elected officials over federal financing and development activities in their jurisdictions.

These initiatives could be judged both by direct monetary rewards and how they fulfilled the goals of the virtues of federalism. As Vice President Bush said in issuing an August 1982 _Progress Report_ on the Task Force's accomplishments:

> "Cost savings are a good benchmark for measuring our progress ... Other benefits of regulatory relief --

such as elimination of bureaucratic harassment -- do not carry a price tag."58/

Later, more detailed Regulatory Policy Guidelines were developed by the Office of Management and Budget to apply the economic principles of Executive Order 12291 to the most frequently encountered issues of regulatory policy so as to "guide agencies in the administration of regulatory programs, to the extent permitted by law." One reads:

"Federal regulations should not preempt state laws or regulations, except to guarantee rights of national citizenship or to avoid significant burdens on interstate commerce."59/

In other words, the administration sought fewer overall regulations as well as greater respect for (and in many cases deference to) alternative governmental sources of rules.60/

The August 1982 Progress Report showed that the review of federal regulations achieved a savings of $9 to $11 billion in one-time investment costs, and $6 billion in annual recurring costs. Paperwork was cut by 200 million man-hours, new regulations were cut in half, and the pages in the Federal Register were reduced by one-third.61/ Because of this greater efficiency, more funds could be put to productive job-creating uses, easing inflationary

---

58/ Statement of Vice President George Bush, August 4, 1982.

59/ President's Task Force on Regulatory Relief, "Reagan Administration Regulatory Achievements," August 11, 1983, pp. 17, 19. Also see, statement of Christopher Demuth, Administrator for Information and Regulatory Affairs, Office of Management and Budget, before the Subcommittee on Administrative Law and Governmental Relations, Committee on Judicism, U.S. House of Representatives, on H.R. 2327, The Regulatory Reform Act of 1983, July 28, 1983.

60/ See Eads, George C., and Fix, Michael, "Regulatory Policy," The Reagan Experiment, eds. Palmer, John L. and Sawhill, Isabel V. (Washington, D.C.: The Urban Institute Press, 1982), pp. 129-153.

61/ Presidential Task Force on Regulatory Relief, Reagan Administration Achievements in Regulatory Relief: A Progress Report, August 1982.

pressures, reducing the burden on taxpayers, and relieving the strain on state and local budgets.

Of the 119 reviews undertaken, 24 related directly to states and localities so that elected officials could be held more accountable for regulatory actions.62/ The Office of Management and Budget estimated that these initial actions deregulating state and local governments alone saved between $4 and $6 billion in total investment costs, and $2 billion in annual recurring costs. OMB estimated these actions reduced paperwork reporting requirements by almost 11.8 million work hours per year for state and local government employees. These covered a broad range of federal programs, and were directed at diverse operating functions of government.

A great deal of this regulatory relief was achieved through quick implementation of the administration's block grant legislation, which dramatically reduced federal interference in grant-in-aid programs administered by state and local governments. For example, by combining 28 categorical grants into a single block grant, the Department of Education was able to issue a single set of regulations reducing the governing rules from 667 pages in the Federal Register to 20 pages. OMB estimates that the paperwork requirements reduced thereby were 83 percent in FY 1982 (5.4 million hours) and further reduced in FY 1983 for a cumulative reduction of 91 percent (5.9 million hours). The Department of Health and Human Services' new block grants were estimated to save states $52 million in paperwork costs. The small-cities portion of the new Community Development Block Grant program also had vastly reduced regulations.

The eased paperwork burden on states and localities under the block grants was vividly demonstrated by the President in an October 1, 1982 news conference. At the issues luncheon with the President that day, I had come with a prop. During these luncheons, it was normal practice for the Assistants to the President to both raise upcoming issues and to provide status reports on pending matters. When it was my turn, I lifted onto the Cabinet

---

62/ Presidential Task Force on Regulatory Relief, Reagan Administration Achievements in Regulatory Relief for State and Local Governments: A Progress Report, August 1982. For a more conceptual review of the first year's accomplishments in regulatory relief see Kettl, Donald F., "The Uncertain Bridges: Regulations Reform in Reagan's New Federalism," Ed. Schecter, Stephen L., Publius: Annual Review of American Federalism 1981, p. 19.

table a 318 page stack of paper. These were the sections from the _Federal Register_ detailing regulations for the HHS categorical programs prior to their consolidation into block grants. I then showed the President the six pages of regulations for the new block grants. I then explained how the block grants had reduced paperwork burdens by 5.4 million man-hours (83%) during their first year (FY '82).

The President asked a few questions. Then the agenda went on to other issues. When the luncheon was finished, however, the President asked me for the 318 pages of former HHS regulations and the mere six pages that had replaced them.

Later that day at his press conference, the President pulled out these props to emphasize his Administration's progress on regulatory relief and to reiterate his commitment to decentralize decision making.63/

The administration's regulatory relief effort for state and local governments went far beyond block grants, covering a broad range of federal programs directed at diverse operating functions of government. In education, for example, the proposed Bilingual Education rules were rescinded.64/ This saved school systems $900 - $2,950 million in investment costs, and $70 - $155 million in annual costs. A Department of Education regulation prohibiting discrimination in dress codes on the basis of sex was rescinded.65/ A sterling example of federal overreaching, this rule prohibited schools from requiring boys to wear ties or girls to wear skirts unless the same requirements were imposed on the opposite sex. Also, school systems were given flexibility in accounting requirements for the school lunch program, reducing by 11.7 million hours the time spent filling out forms each year.66/ More decisions could thus be made through civic participation and under the responsibility of local school boards.

63/ President Ronald Reagan, _Compilation of Presidential Documents_, p. 106.

64/ ED/Bilingual Education (Law Rules) (45 FR 52052). Proposed regulations withdrawn February 3, 1981.

65/ ED/Personal Appearance Codes (34 CFR 106). Rule rescinded July 8, 1982.

66/ USDA/National School Lunch Program -- Cost Accounting (7 CFR 210). Final rule published July 20, 1982.

In health care, states received greater flexibility in revising reimbursement levels, making eligibility determinations, and deciding which services to offer in what setting.67/

In the area of transportation, the Federal Highway Administration determined that it was asking for more statistical data than it was using, and reduced reporting requirements by 50 percent.68/ Based on comments from state officials, this resulted in a $300,000 annual savings. New rules were issued to permit states to design their own procedures and criteria for highway mainte-nance.69/

The volatile, vocal mayor of New York City, Ed Koch was vigorous in seeking relief from the handicapped-access for transit sys-tems. Regulations had been promulgated during the Carter Administration in response to Section 504 of the Rehabilitation Act of 1973. The Carter Department of Transportation regulations set as a mandate, total accessibility for the handicapped to transit systems. The argument Koch made, as did many other may-ors, was that the regulations dealt with transportation systems, instead of dealing with the function, which was mobility. "No one would argue that we need not commit funds to make transit systems and buildings accessible to the handicapped," said Koch. "But one also has to deal with the limitations -- both financial and physical -- that exist in the real world beyond the printed pages of the _Federal Register_."70/

From conversations with a number of mayors soon after our arrival at the White House, I had been made fully aware of the priority many placed on revising the Section 504 regulations. Within weeks a complete review of the situation was going on under the direction of Drew Lewis, Reagan's initial Secretary of Transportation, one of the most able, smooth and certainly the most politically skillful of all the early cabinet members. Therefore, I was well prepared to brief the President on the

---

67/ HHS/Health Care Financing Administration Rules (42 CFR 431, 435, 436, 440, 441, 447, 456). Final Rules pub-lished September 30, October 1, and December 3, 1981.

68/ DOT/Guide to Reporting Highway Statistics. Reduced paperwork requirements cleared by OMB May 5, 1982.

69/ DOT/Highway Geometric Design Standards for 3R Projects (23 CFR 625). Final rule published June 10, 1982.

70/ Edward Koch, "The Mandate Millstone," _The Public Interest_ 61 (Fall, 1980), pp. 42, 45.

issue as we helicoptered to the West 30th Street heliport in New York City in mid-March, 1981. The President was going to New York for a variety of matters, including a media event luncheon with Senator Al D'Amato in a restaurant on Mulberry Street in Little Italy, an evening at the ballet to see his son Ron perform, and a meeting with Koch in his suite at the Waldorf Hotel. I felt confident Koch would raise the Section 504 regulations.

When Koch arrived, there were the ritualistic photographs before business began in the sitting room. When the media had left, Koch proceded to raise a number of matters dealing with the budget and the 504 regulations. He said to Reagan that "where ever I go, I always say, 'The President came into office by the largest sweep in the country since F.D.R. beat Hoover in 1932, and he is entitled to put his plans into effect.'"71/ Koch went on to briefly outline some of his ideas and asked if he might meet with Dave Stockman to review these ideas in detail. Reagan turned to me to ask for it to be arranged.

Then Koch turned to details about the Section 504 regulations. He told about past failed efforts under Carter to get modest exemptions and waivers. He said alternatives were available:

"Given the numbers of handicapped people affected -- some 22,800 in wheelchairs and 110,000 semi-ambulatory for a system that carries about 5.3 million on a week-day -- a more reasonable approach can be formulated to meet the transportation needs of the disabled. The City of New York has proposed making its buses accessible and providing a paratransit system for the most severely disabled. Paratransit will provide door-to-door service and can make the difference between a handicapped person being a prisoner in his or her home or a mobile member of the community."72/

Koch was singing Reagan's song.

Koch said:

"The regulations appear to demand accessibility in 53 percent of our subway stations within 30 years, at a

---

71/ Edward I. Koch, Mayor (Simon and Schuester, New York, 1984), p. 298.

72/ Edward Koch, "The Mandate Millstone," The Public Interest 61 (Fall 1980) pp. 42, 45.

cost in today's dollars of some $1.3 billion. Added to this will be at least $50 million in recurring annual operating expenses."

Koch referenced a 1979 Congressional Budget Office estimate that the cost of implementing these regulations for wheelchair users and severely disabled passengers would be $38 per trip. In contrast, Koch noted, "transit trips by the general public cost, on the average, about 85 cents."

Reagan said that while the absolute dollar figures weren't as large, he knew that other towns and cities faced proportionally and equally serious problem with the current 504 regulations. These regulations, he said, were distorting transit systems and usurping power properly left to the people and their elected local officials. Reagan said that he was aware of similar paratransit plans in other cities and that his task force on regulatory relief already was working on the problem.

Reagan and Koch continued to sally back and forth until it was time to finish the meeting. Koch is full of energy, sassy, outrageous and very clever. A practical politician, he had driven the Carter people crazy with his "shoot from the hip" style and his personal coolness toward the Georgian President. As Republicans, of course, we had much lower expectations for our relations with Koch. But generally, these were quite good under the circumstances. He repeatedly attacked our proposed budget cuts, but he never got personal and he gave Reagan credit for both good intentions and some good results.

In fact, after the meeting in the President's suite at the Waldorf, the President's Press Secretary Jim Brady, Dave Gergen and I accompanied Koch down to the first floor where he was scheduled to have a press conference. On the way down he asked us what we'd like him to say. Brady's reply was to just say that the meeting went well and Ronald Reagan's a terrific guy. Well, during his opening remarks, Koch said in part, "I am not here to defend Ronald Reagan. But I'll tell you, I like him. He's a man of character."[73] And as he said it, his eyes weren't on the television cameras nor scanning the reporters. His eyes were focused directely on Brady, Gergen and me standing together at the back of the room. After his colorful repartee with the reporters, he stopped by us to say good-bye. And he smiled a big infectious smile and said, "Well, how am I doing? Did I say what you wanted me to?"

73/ Edward I. Koch, Mayor (Simon and Schuester, New York, 1984), p. 300.

A follow-up meeting for Koch with Stockman did occur the next week. Koch came to my office in the West Wing of the White House and together we walked accross West Executive Avenue to the OMB Director's large ornate office in the Old Executive Office Building. Koch began the meeting by reminding Stockman that as a Congressman, his office had been near the congressional staff offices where Stockman had worked as an aide to Congressman John Anderson in the early 1970's. Koch said that while he didn't actually know Stockman then, he was aware of him because Stockman was the only person on the entire floor who regularly got to the office earlier than Koch and often left later. Stockman, a prodigious worker who took pride in his well publicized disciplined workaholic practices -- excessive even by Washington standards -- said how his current job was even tougher. His hours were crushing, the burdens enormous and the assignment, at times, overwhelming. Instead of the sympathy Stockman expected, Koch laughed and said sometimes he felt the same way. "But," he said, "you and I know we have the best jobs in America."

Anyway, the Section 504 handicapped accommodation requirements for public transit were revised by the Regulatory Relief Task Force. Koch, as well as many other mayors, was delighted. Alternative means to provide transportation for the handicapped became allowable. And the estimated savings was over $2.2 billion.74/

The Department of Housing and Urban Development was an arena of some deregulation controversy which demonstrated that congressional committees and special interest groups, critical parts of the iron triangle, often were effective in resisting the sort of vigorous decentralization sought by the Reagan Administration. Soon after Reagan took office, the new political appointees in HUD criticized the Carter Administration's management of the community development program:

> "Over the past few years, HUD has imposed additional administrative requirements which have tended to reduce the freedom of localities to decide which activities to fund and have increased administrative costs."75/

74/ DOT/Section 504 of the Rehabilitation Act (49 CFR 27). Interim final rule published July 20, 1981.

75/ U.S. Department of Housing and Urban Development, Community Planning and Development Notice 81-5, May 15, 1981.

Soon HUD, under the leadership of Sam Pierce, said it would move to ease the regulatory burden on cities. It would presume that local governments' information submitted to HUD was accurate. It would more readily grant waivers to nonstatutory regulation. Also, it would seek to stop putting extra conditions on grants. It revised rules to speed up environmental impact evaluations and allow greater local autonomy under the Community Development Block Grant program.76/ Another HUD rule revision streamlined the application process, and liberalized the governing rules under the Modernization of Public Housing program.77/ These regulatory reform initiatives were generally welcomed. But when HUD moved to allow states to determine their own CDBG administrative requirements and to relieve states of burdensome reporting,78/ local public interest groups in Washington and some members of Congress fought us.

Part of Reagan's block grant proposals that Congress adopted turned administration of the small cities program over to the states.79/ This, of course, was consistent with Reagan's overall strategy to decentralize government. In late November, 1981, HUD proposed brief general regulations for the program that were consistent with the Administration's block grant guidelines. Among other things, states would be free to determine which local communities received funding from the program, how much they got, what they could use the money for, and what review standards would be applied. Performance reports could be "in such form and contain such information... as the state shall deem appropriate" and, HUD said, it would give "maximum feasible deference to the State's interpretation of the statutory requirements."80/

76/ HUD/Environmental Policies (24 CFR 58). Interim final rule published April 12, 1982.

77/ HUD/Modernization of Public Housing Projects (24 CFR 868). Final rule published May 21, 1982.

78/ HUD/Community Development (24 CFR 570, Subpart F). Final rules published February 23 and April 8, 1982.

79/ For an excellent, more detailed discussion of this issue, see Donald Kettl, The Regulation of American Federalism (Louisiana State University Press, Baton Rouge, Louisiana, 1983), pp. 142-146.

80/ 46 Federal Register 57256 (Nov. 20, 1981).

Not surprisingly, the nation's governors were in total support for the HUD regulations allowing states maximum flexibility.81/ Local governments, however, were deeply suspicious of their state capitals and consequently did not support so much power devolving from the federal to the state governments. Their Washington-based interest group, the National League of Cities, filed comments raising many concerns.82/ But it was the Washington special interest groups that most violently objected. The Working Group for Community Development Reform submitted comments charging HUD's proposed rules were "seriously defective." They wrote, "It is inconceivable that HUD would permit States to choose themselves what to report on, given the fact that there is national legislation, with a national objective and specific eligible activities, as well as mandates in civil rights and environmental impact, among others."83/ Other Washington special interest groups such as the National Housing Law Project echoed these challenges to the Administration's efforts to decentralize government.84/ These groups were located in Washington, D.C. Their staff had existing working relationships with HUD personnel and congressional committee staff. Therefore, a priori, it is in Washington, where they felt they could have maximum impact, that decisions should be made. To decentralize decision-making, to get it closer to the people, diluted the role they could play.

Some powerful members of Congress had similar concerns. Congressman Henry B. Gonzalez (D-TX) was chairman of the Housing Subcommittee of the House Committee on Banking, Finance and Urban Affairs. He called a subcommittee hearing on this matter in which he forcefully presented his views. He said:

81/   Letter from Governors Christopher S. Bond (R-MO) and William F. Winter (D-MS), January 19, 1982, HUD Docket File 81-940 on rules proposed Nov. 20, 1981.

82/   Letter from Alan Beals, Executive Director, National League of Cities, Jan. 19, 1982, HUD Docket File 81-940 on rules proposed Nov. 20, 1981.

83/   Letter from Paul Bloyd, project director, Working Group for Community Development Reform, Jan. 19, 1982, HUD Docket File 81-940 on rules proposed Nov. 20, 1981.

84/   Letter from Frances E. Weiner, staff attorney, National Housing Law Project, Jan. 8, 1982, HUD Docket File 81-940 on rules proposed Nov. 20, 1981. In this submission, it charged that HUD's "present interpretation fails utterly to carry out Congress' purposes and intent."

"I view these regulations as an attempt to do by administrative fiat what the Administration could not
achieve through the legislative process.

We are concerned that the regulations... have the
likely result of making the small cities' community
development block grant programs ineffective in reach-
ing its purposes, subject to endless abuse, and reduce
it to a general revenue sharing program. ...Under
this absense of guidelines, a partisan-minded governor
could literally turn the program into a slush fund to
reward the loyal and punish the opposition. ...If ever
there were a more open invitation to fraud, waste and
abuse than this, I have not seen it.

...The lack of any meaningful program guidelines and
the absence of any accounting standard simply means
that this program will break down in administrative
chaos."85/

At that hearing, Gonzalez threatened HUD with a resolution of
disapproval on the regulations unless HUD revised them. Eventually there were discussions and negotiations. I even enlisted
Chief of Staff Jim Baker to help. The results were revised HUD
regulations, somewhat less flexible than those we originally
sought but certainly far more open and flexible than the
Washington-based special interest groups or some members of
Congress had hoped. Fortunately the fears of Congressman
Gonzalez have not been realized. The states have done a superb
job in administering the program with no reports of political
"slush fund" abuse by governors nor the predicted increases of
fraud and waste. This was the philosophic divide. The
Washington establishment simply did not trust the competence,
capacity nor compassion of state and local governments. Nor did
they want to dilute their own power, whereas the Reagan
Administration had confidence in those elected officials and the
people who voted them into office. The Reagan Administration
wanted to curb the excessive power in Washington and return it
closer to the people.

85/ The witnesses to whom Chairman Gonzalez made this
     speech were HUD Assistant Secretary Stephen J.
     Bollinger and HUD General Counsel John J. Knapp. U.S.
     House of Representatives, Committee on Banking,
     Finance and Urban Affairs, Subcommittee on Housing and
     Community Development, Community Development Block
     Grant -- Small Cities Regulations, hearing, 97th
     Congress, 1st Session, 1981, pp. 1-2.

-128-

At the Environmental Protection Agency, review procedures for air quality rules were relaxed to eliminate a backlog.86/ This allowed clean air goals to be achieved faster, more efficiently and at a lower cost. Similarly, regulations governing sewage treatment plants were changed to permit jurisdictions receiving grants to choose the most cost effective processes.87/

The most sweeping change made in federal government philosophy and procedures in regulating the intergovernmental system came on July 14, 1982, when President Reagan signed Executive Order 12372, "Intergovernmental Review of Federal Programs."88/ This allowed elected state and local officials to decide which federal grant and development programs to review and how.

Two Great Society programs had resulted in OMB circular A-95 that required governments applying for federal aid to submit their applications to area-wide clearinghouses. Section 204 of the Demonstration Cities and Metropolitan Development Act (Model Cities) of 1966 stipulated that applications from local governments in metropolitan areas must first have been screened by an area-wide comprehensive planning agency. Then the Intergovernmental Cooperation Act (ICA) of 1968 had three more coordination requirements. Title IV directed that evaluation and review procedures be established for grant requests. Section 401(b) called for policy development to consider all national, state, regional, and local viewpoints. And section 401(c) said the goal should be maximum congruence between national program objectives and the objectives of state, regional and local planning. While at first glance, some coordination would be helpful, predictably A-95 became just one more layer of red tape with which to comply. Critics charged that while the clearinghouse studies were time

---

86/   EPA/Emissions Trading Policy. Statement released April 7, 1982. EPA/State Implementation Plans (40 CFR 51). Policy announced June 23, 1982.

87/   EPA/Construction Grant Regulations (40 CFR 35). Interim final rule published May 12, 1982. Note that local officials have continued to be concerned by costly state mandates in the area of environmental protection, as well as personnel and finance. See National League of Cities, State Mandates on Municipal Governments: A Municipal Government Perspective (NLC, Washington, D.C., 1986).

88/   OMB/Local Clearinghouses (Circular A-95). Executive Order 12372 signed July 14, 1982. See also, OMB, Fiscal Year 1985: Special Analysis, p. H-22.

consuming and costly, the results were not particularly helpful. One OMB official said, the process "is detailed and descriptive and requires a lot of paperwork, with no distinction between important and unimportant subjects. It is so weighty that state and local governments were not able to get good comments in, and the federal government agencies were not paying that much attention."89/ A-95 was a perfect example of a quip Ronald Reagan once made, "The federal government goes to press more often than the New York Times."90/

Soon after Reagan entered the White House, I began hearing complaints about A-95 from mayors. Assistant Director of OMB Hal Steinberg, and from my staff Special Assistant to the President Steve Rhodes, worked on getting consensus for a revision of A-95. The result, executive order 12372, greatly simplified the requirements. The Order required federal agencies to accommodate the recommendations of state and local officials where possible. Federal agencies were ordered to allow states to simplify and consolidate federally required state plans and to discourage continuation of special purpose, federally-dominated state planning agencies. These changes were to foster intergovernmental and social harmony through consideration of state and local priorities in the administration of federal programs. Concurrently, the Administration rescinded OMB Circular A-95.91/ On June 24, 1983, final regulations and notices implementing the order were published simultaneously in the _Federal Register_ by 28 federal agencies.92/

In October 1986, the National Governors' Association further advanced the federalism regulatory relief effort. In behalf of the NGA, New Hampshire Governor John Sununu presented President Reagan with 80 recommendations for alleviating federal regulatory

---

89/ Quoted by Douglas B. Feaver, "Another Great Society Milepost Falls," _Washington Post_, May 27, 1982, p. A25.

90/ Ronald Reagan, "Torrents of Government Paper," radio address, 8/9/78 quoted in Ronnie Dugger, _On Reagan: The Man and His Presidency_ (McGraw Hill, New York, 1983), p. 485.

91/ OMB/Local Clearinghouse (Circular A-195), Executive Order signed July 14, 1982.

92/ _Op. cit._ RR 5/2, p. 83.

and administrative burdens on state and local governments.93/ In February, 1988, the NGA list had grown to over 160 new proposals for federal regulatory relief. Over the next few months, OMB and the White House Intergovernmental Affairs Office worked to implement many of those recommendations. For example:

- Buses in Alabama which had been used exclusively to transport Head Start children under a state interpretation that the vehicles could not be used for other programs, following a clarification of federal policy, began to be used to transport elderly people participating in federally assisted programs.

- Virginia's State Medicaid agency no longer had to submit voluminous, time-consuming documents to the governor every time his certification was needed in order to demonstrate compliance with federal requirements.

- New Hampshire and other affected states no longer were required to review all subcontract agreements supported with federal highway funds, thereby increasing the efficiency of the state's highway program and reducing costs to contractors and, ultimately, taxpayers.94/

In addition to these and other specific responses, President Reagan kept pressure on the executive branch throughout the fall of 1988 to expand state administrative flexibility by revising government-wide cost principles and standards for administering federal grants and cooperative agreements by state and local governments, improve federal-state cash management practices, and cut federal red tape and provide more state decision-making au-

---

93/ John Sununu, first elected Governor of New Hampshire in 1982, is enormously intelligent, energetic and forceful. His deep commitment to federalism was manifest further in 1987-88 when, as chairman of NGA, he made the "Spirit of Federalism" the centerpiece of his tenure.

94/ Executive Office of the President, Office of Management and Budget, OMB Release 88-16, August 7, 1988.

thority in historic preservation issues.95/ So to the very end of his administration, Ronald Reagan sought to advance federalism through active regulatory relief.

Decentralization of rulemaking recognizes the advantages of diversity and experimentation. The costs and benefits of regulatory strategies can vary enormously from place to place. Differing factors such as typography, climate, demographics, local industry, economic conditions and citizen preferences dictate that state and local officials are in a better position to choose a strategy or make a trade-off that is responsive to local needs. One state can learn from another, and a single failure will not jeopardize the entire national economy. People and businesses can also adjust to local policies. It is only reasonable to allow businesses to flourish where they are welcome, and citizens to live where they can get the job they want, the air and water quality they want, and the government policies they want.

* * * * *

Surely there is a place for reasonable regulations. In many instances there is an overriding concern for public health and safety. But, as in most aspects of life, there is a need for moderation in government. Too frequently Washington automatically assumes that if some is good, more must be better. This has been the case in rulemaking procedures.

The federal government too often has been thoughtless or arbitrary in compelling universal requirements without sufficient consideration of the real world constraints on localities and without an appreciation of the historical independence of states and localities: an independence which has allowed the powerful diversity of spirit and innovation to flourish in our federal system. Reagan's regulatory reform program built on the tentative steps taken by the Ford and Carter Administrations. But

---

95/ Ibid. See also White Office of Intergovernmental Affairs and Office of Management and Budget, The Administration's Final Report on the National Governors' Association's Federal Assistance Review Project Recommendations, February, 1988; and Gwendolyn S. King, "View From the Commission," Intergovernmental Perspective, Spring, 1988, p. 2.

Reagan, by making it a pillar of his economic recovery program, put deregulation center stage. By enlisting Vice President Bush to chair his efforts, he gave it added prestige and authority. By fully exploiting the coordination and review process of OMB, he gave his efforts teeth.96/ And Ronald Reagan was the first President to make federalism a significant goal of his regulatory reform program. Reagan did curb the flow of over-regulation.97/ Reagan created a new regulatory climate in Washington and thereby gave further life to decentralized government.

The Federalism Initiative announced by the President in his January 1982 State of the Union Message was designed to overcome the Washington elitist mind-set that elected officials of non-federal jurisdictions are subservient to the national government. By devolving program responsibilities from Washington to states and localities, the "iron triangle" could be muted permanently. And, because there would be a curtailment of federal grant involvement -- and a return of optional tax sources -- a certain amount of deregulation would be automatic. In other words, the strings, the federal umbilical cord, would be cut.

96/ See George C. Eads, "White House Oversight of Executive Branch Regulation," in ed. Eugene Bardach and Robert A. Kagan, Social Regulation: Strategies for Reform (Institute for Contemporary Studies, San Francisco, CA, 1982), pp. 177-97.

97/ One measure of the decline in regulations under Reagan was the pages of the Federal Register which totaled 63,353 in 1981, a decline of more than 23,000 pages from the year before.

CHAPTER 6

STATE OF THE UNION INITIATIVE

By the fall of 1981, it was readily apparent that the President had made significant strides in achieving his federalism agenda, due in large part to the active, bipartisan support of state and local officials.

Nine new block grants had been enacted, consolidating fifty-seven categorical grant-in-aid programs;1/ dozens of relief actions were taken to reduce the regulatory burden on state and local governments;2/ and the President and his Cabinet secretaries had made it clear through hundreds of different actions that they were treating state and local officials as true partners in our intergovernmental system.3/

Throughout 1981, President Reagan held many meetings at the White House in which he consulted with over 1,700 state and local officials on a broad range of state-local issues. The ideas and concerns expressed during those meetings emphasized that much work remained to be done to rebalance our federal system. They provided an impetus for more dramatic action.

In addition, the President had established the Advisory Committee on Federalism, which was charged with formulating long-range federalism goals. The committee consisted of members of the U.S. Senate and House of Representatives, as well as state and local

---

1/ The block grants were as follows: Alcohol, Drug Abuse and Mental Health; Preventive Health and Health Services Grant; Maternal and Child Health Services; Primary Care; Social Services; Community Services; Low Income Home Energy Assistance; Elementary and Secondary Education; and Community Development. See Chapter Four for a detailed discussion.

2/ See: Presidential Task Force on Regulatory Relief, Reagan Administration Achievements in Regulatory Relief for State and Local Governments, A Progress Report, August, 1982. See Chapter Five for a detailed discussion.

3/ See: Executive Office of the President, Federalism, The First Ten Months, A Report from the President, November, 1981.

officials and private citizens.4/   The committee was chaired by
Nevada Senator Paul Laxalt.   Laxalt, a former county official and
a former governor, shared Reagan's commitment to federalism.5/
As the committee's work progressed, Laxalt's clout insured White
House attention and, eventually, helped in pushing Presidential
action.   It was instrumental to the development of the New
Federalism Initiative, both by providing a forum to develop ideas
and by keeping Congress informed and involved in the process.6/

4/   Members of the President's Advisory Committee on
Federalism were: U.S. Senators Paul Laxalt (R-NV),
William V. Roth, Jr. (R-DE), David Durenberger (R-MN),
Pete V. Domenici (R-NM), David L. Boren (D-OK), and
Ernest F. Hollings (D-SC);   U.S. Representatives
Richard T. Schulze (R-PA), Richard Bolling (D-MO),
L.H. Fountain (D-NC), Clarence Brown (R-OH), Frank
Horton (R-NY), and Jack Brooks (D-TX);   Governors
George Busbee (D-GA), Scott Matheson (D-UT), Lamar
Alexander (R-TN), James R. Thompson (R-IL), Pierre S.
duPont, IV (R-DE), and Richard A. Snelling (R-VT);
State Legislators T.W. Stivers (R-ID), Chuck Hardwick
(R-NJ), Anne Lindeman (R-AZ), Benjamin L. Cardin
(D-MD), Dean Rhodes (R-NV), and John Hainkel (D-LA);
Mayors Margaret Hance (R-Phoenix, AZ), Tom Moody (R-
Columbus, OH), Johnny Ford (D-Tuskeege, AL), Henry
Cisneros (D-San Antonio, TX), Edward I. Koch (D-New
York, NY), William H. Hudnut (R-Indianapolis, IN), and
Ferd Harrison (D-Scotland Neck, NC); County Officials
Roy Orr (D-Dallas County, TX), Virgil E. Brown (R-
Cuyahoga County, OH), William Murphy (R-Rensselaer
County, NY), Bruce Nestande (R-Orange County, CA),
Sandra Smoley (R-Sacramento County, CA), and Donald L.
Smith (R-Anchorage Municipality, AK);   and private
citizens F. Clifton White, Robert B. Hawkins, C.D.
Ward, Clifford Hansen, Otis Bowen, and William T.
Coleman.

5/   For a statement of Senator Laxalt's commitment to
decentralization,   see   Paul   Laxalt,   "Reagan
Federalism," in American Federalism; A New Partnership
For The Republic, ed. Robert Hawkins (Institute for
Contemporary Studies, Washington, D.C., 1982), pp.
79-89.

6/   For example, during meetings of the Advisory Committee
on Federalism, members of Congress provided practical
advice from the legislative perspective. Senator Dave
Durenberger (R-MN) said that our twelve-year experi-
(Cont'd)

The issue the administration faced as we began planning for 1982 was whether the administration should continue its federalism efforts along the same lines as 1981 -- more regulatory relief, more block grants, etc. -- or whether we should propose a major, bold initiative, one which would focus national attention and energies in this area.

In early September 1981, while both David Stockman and I were at the Midwest Governors' Conference in Milwaukee, I raised with him the possibility of a major federalism initiative in 1982. Stockman asked me what the concept of a "swap" was that he had heard governors raise at the Conference.7/ As we discussed it, he became intrigued with the possibilities. Along with the federalism goals of sorting out and devolution, Stockman quickly grasped the budgetary advantages of defusing special interests to the 50 state capitals.

In late November, a small group of senior White House officials8/ began meeting several times a week on the framework of a major federalism initiative. From the outset, Dave Stockman and I took the point in promoting a large-scale federalism effort. Ed Meese and I shared the same perspective, we were eager to see an expansion of the President's federalism agenda. The attacks by state and local officials on the President's proposed budget cuts had become intense and I felt it was important that they not lose

---

ence with revenue sharing showed that this is an efficient way to get dollars to local officials. Also, Senator Durenberger suggested that the federal government cease collecting excise taxes (10-22-81). Congressman Bud Brown (R-OH) said we should devise a legislative package which follows familiar practice, citing specifically the revenue sharing program (10-22-81). And, Senator Pete Domenici (R-NM) encouraged the President to seek a concrete proposal with consolidation of programs whereby states could have more control of delivery of services. Further, Senator Domenici suggested that a larger revenue sharing program (similar to the turnback program) be proposed (10-29-81).

7/ Governors Lamar Alexander (TN) and Bruce Babbitt (AZ) had been campaigning a swap of all education responsibilities to the states in exchange for federalizing all Medicaid.

8/ The participants in those sessions included Edwin Meese, III, James A. Baker, III, David Stockman, Dick Darman, Craig Fuller, and myself.

sight of the President's commitment to rebalancing the federal system. Also, having spent so much political capital on the 1981 budget and tax cuts, I feared further business-as-usual trench warfare on block grants and regulatory relief would be very difficult. A large bold move might capture media and political attention and, with the President's leadership, succeed.

The OMB perspective was somewhat different. Dave Stockman had two problems. First, he faced enormous projected budget deficits if no tax increases or major spending cuts were passed by Congress. Second, Stockman had only several weeks earlier been the first member of the President's cabinet to be invited to the "woodshed" for his harmful comments in the December 1981 issue of the Atlantic Monthly magazine.9/ He was anxious for a major new enterprise which would divert attention from the hemorrhaging budget and his own indiscretions.

White House Chief of Staff Baker was very concerned about the political problems for the Administration in Stockman's budget numbers, especially in an election year. He saw the damaging impact of months of press coverage on the enormous deficit and

---

9/   See William Greider, The Education of David Stockman
      and Other Americans (E.P. Dutton, Inc., New York,
      1982). In contrast to Dave Stockman's cynicism about
      supply-side economics, see Martin Anderson, Revolution
      (Harcourt Brace Jovanovich, New York, 1988), Paul
      Craig Roberts, The Supply-Side Revolution (Harvard
      University Press, Cambridge, 1984), and Bruce
      Bartlett, Reagonomics: Supply-Side Economics in
      Action (Arlington House, Westport, Connecticut, 1981).

      A condominium of interest had developed between
      Stockman and Jim Baker. Stockman was very bright,
      knew Congress and was an indefatigable worker. Baker
      had the "political/implementation" side of the White
      House, Ed Meese had the policy development side.
      Early on, Baker's Deputy Dick Darman grasped the need
      for Baker to have his own independent policy shop so
      that he was not dependent on Meese, who they felt was
      too ideological, disorganized and independent. OMB
      became the Baker policy staff. Darman and Stockman
      are both bright, intense men who neither suffer from a
      low opinion of their own skills nor suffer fools glad-
      ly. They became fast friends. When the Atlantic
      Monthly firestorm broke, Baker and Darman were the
      fire-fighters inside who helped Stockman successfully
      survive the blaze.

the probable gridlock between the White House and Congress. An extremely astute legislative strategist, Baker also understood that just such a gridlock would enhance White House leverage on the budget by mid to late 1982. In a federalism initiative, Baker saw a bold move that would further Reagan's overall domestic agenda and create another major arena for congressional and media attention.

The first concept paper on the large scale Federalism Initiative, which was prepared under Dave Stockman's direction on December 8, 1981, listed the following objectives:

1) Serve the administration's conservative domestic policy agenda;

2) Measurably ease the budget gap over FY '83-86;

3) Splinter and realign the anti-spending-cut constituency forces which were coalescing against the Administration;

4) Offer a major affirmative legislative package for 1982 to help relieve the fiscal retrenchment theme that inevitably would characterize much of the FY '83 budget program.

The proposal originally called for a $45-60 billion transfer of tax revenues and federal programs to state and local governments.

The transfer of programs originally envisioned included governmental functions that involve decentralized delivery systems or programs traditionally performed at the state and local level, such as education, health, social services, public assistance and local infrastructure.

The revenues transferred would have two characteristics:

1) Currently levied jointly so that the transferred revenues could integrate with existing state tax systems (gasoline, alcohol and tobacco, for example);

2)   Revenues which would be capable of being levied
      in all states with somewhat equivalent per capita
      yield.10/

The attraction to Dave Stockman was a potential reduction in the budget deficit of approximately $45 billion in FY '83. This came from $30 billion in projected revenue increases and $15 billion in spending reductions.

On the revenue side, the original plan called for a tripling of existing excise taxes on gasoline, alcohol, tobacco and telephones. In addition, a ten percent luxury tax would have been imposed. These excise tax changes would have resulted in an increase of federal revenues of approximately $30 billion per year.

On the spending side, in transferring the current federal programs to state and local governments, the Initiative would employ the general fiscal principle reflected in the block grants of 1981 -- transferring $3 in revenues for every $4 of program activity, accompanied by the opportunity for substantially greater flexibility in administering these programs. The rationale was that the states could absorb the 25 percent cuts because of the increased flexibility and reduced federal red tape. Thus, $45 billion in federal revenues would be sufficient to fund $60 billion in programs to be returned to the states under this approach.

This basic fiscal design would have the following effects on federal and state fiscal ledgers:

State Fiscal Ledger

      Revenues Transferred .... $+45 billion
      Federal programs transferred measured
         from base line status quo .... -60 billion
      Net Change .... -15 billion

10/ The December 21, 1981 OMB concept paper included the following parenthetical phrase: "(The tobacco excise tax would satisfy this condition while the oil windfall profits tax would not.)" Later in the process it would become necessary to use the oil windfall profits tax as a revenue source, even though it did not satisfy this second characteristic.

Federal Fiscal Ledger

```
Federal programs transferred ........... $+60 billion
Existing federal revenues transferred ..  -15 billion
Net Change ..............................  +45 billion
```

As development of the Federalism Initiative continued, much to
Stockman's outrage, the budget savings which he had counted on
evaporated. First, the decision was made to provide a dollar-
for-dollar budget exchange with the state and local sector.
State Medicaid savings and excise tax revenues to be turned back
would be equal to the cost of federal programs taken over by
state and local governments. Thus, the 25 percent budget savings
($15 billion) in this area was omitted from the package.

Second, during a Cabinet Room meeting with the President in early
January, the proposal for an increase in excise taxes was the
subject of heated debate. During that session, Stockman argued
forcefully for the increase in excise taxes. He advanced some
very legitimate budget considerations. Ed Meese and others of us
argued for revenue neutrality. Lyn Nofziger, a permanently rum-
pled political pro's pro, also entered the debate. Nofziger had
been with Reagan since the first campaign for governor of
California in 1966 and for the first year of the Reagan White
House years served as Assistant to the President for Political
Affairs. He is gruff, outspoken and often outrageous. He was
something of an oddity in the Reagan White House. Neither a
Brooks Brothers pin stripe suit Washington insider, nor a laid
back congenial Californian, he loved being the conservative attack dog of the Reagan team. Nofziger turns dishevelment into
high fashion. He is balding and the hair he does have is in
constant turmoil and revolt. By the White House years he had
grown a goatee. If the man owns a suit, he never evidenced it at
the White House. His attire was sports coat, appropriately wrin-
kled and never buttoned, a Mickey Mouse tie and a speaking style
with similar decorum. The man has enormous affection for Ronald
Reagan and had only one agenda, helping his old friend. A seasoned political operative who relished the rough and tumble of
political horseplay, he is fiercely loyal to friends, is strongly
anti-government, and is even more strongly partisan. Nofziger
did not often sit in on policy discussions. That wasn't his
thing. But he did sit in on this discussion about the Federalism
Initiative and whether or not Reagan should have some assorted
tax increases in the package. Near the end of the deliberations,
he spoke up. It surprised everyone for this was neither the
forum nor the sort of issue in which Nofziger often joined. He
said something to the effect, "Mr. President, I haven't been
involved in this thing. I don't really understand a lot of
what's been said. But I do know that you didn't come here to
raise taxes. I urge you, don't do it." It was obvious that

Reagan's old friend had cut to the heart of the matter from the President's perspective. Personally, I felt Nofziger's comments were invaluable in sealing the deal. In the end, Reagan rejected any tax increases and the federalism package was revenue neutral.11/

This Presidential decision, made just days before the State of the Union Address, threw the accounting off. Suddenly, we needed to come up with approximately $17 billion in revenues which could be turned back to the states. The oil windfall profits tax, which was already scheduled to be phased out between FY '87 and FY '91, seemed to be a logical candidate, and was incorporated into the package.

With these fundamental decisions made, we proceeded with the final details of the proposal.

It was only at this late stage in the process that the relevant cabinet and agency heads were brought into the process. On the Saturday morning before the State of the Union Address was to be delivered, most of the cabinet members12/ and senior White House staff met in the Roosevelt Room, across from the Oval Office. A couple of cabinet members who were out of town joined the briefing by means of a teleconference phone hook-up. At this session, Stockman and I briefed them on the President's federalism plan.

11/ From leaks to the press it was widely known that some tax increases were under consideration. Many conservative political groups and business groups weighed in against any tax increase. For example, Reagan met with the Board of Directors of the U.S. Chamber of Commerce and they made perfectly clear their unwavering opposition to tax increases. This input also reinforced Reagan's own presumptions against any tax increase.

12/ This included cabinet members for domestic departments. Secretaries Schultz and Weinberger, CIA Director Casey and United Nations Ambassador Jeanne Kirkpatrick did not participate in this or subsequent meetings. See Bradley H. Patterson, Jr., The Ring of Power: The White House Staff and Its Expanding Role In Government (Basic Books, Inc., New York, 1988), pp. 220-228.

Description of Initiative

On January 26, 1982, in his State of the Union address, the President unveiled a $47 billion program to return programs and revenue sources to the state and local level during an eight-year transition period.

The basic framework of the Initiative is shown in Chart I which indicates the programs which would be returned to state and local governments and the revenue sources which would finance them.

On the income maintenance side, the proposal called for the federal government to assume full responsibility for Medicaid in exchange for state takeover of food stamps and AFDC. There would be a net fiscal gain for the states in the first year. Since there is a pattern of greater growth in Medicaid than for Food Stamps and AFDC, the fiscal gain for the states would continue to increase.

In FY '84, states' assumption of AFDC and Food Stamp programs would cost them $16.5 billion. The federal government would spend $19.1 billion to assume what had been the state share of Medicaid. By the end of FY '87, the cost of AFDC and Food Stamps would have grown by $1.1 billion and Medicaid by $6 billion. It is readily apparent that the federal government would be assuming the greater risk and financial responsibility.

Throughout the development of the Initiative in 1982, federalization of Medicaid proved to be the "carrot" that kept state and local officials interested in the package. Governors in particular had experienced the great difficulty of keeping the costs of Medicaid under control. They were anxious to shift the full responsibility for this program to the federal level.

From the Administration's perspective, we were taking a gamble on Medicaid. As expressed by David Stockman, we were betting on the fact that "only [through] an integrated cost containment and reform program"[13]/ could we hope to slow the risk in costs of Medicaid and Medicare which were projected to rise to over $100 billion by FY '84. The OMB Federalism Concept Paper (Draft #2) assumed Medicaid reform savings of $6 billion in FY '84, growing to $10 billion in savings by FY '87.

13/ White House Fact Sheet, "Federalism Initiative," January 27, 1982.

In addition, the package included the turnback of more than 40 federal education, transportation, community development and social services programs to the states along with the resources to fund them. Certain law enforcement and civil rights programs dealing with the handicapped and minorities would remain at the federal level because of the national interest in those programs.

The programs proposed for turnback would be funded by a $28 billion federalism "trust fund" created from current excise taxes and the windfall profits tax. The trust fund would have a separate account for each of the 50 states, with each state's share based on that state's historic percentage of federal funds for the programs turned back.

During Stage I from FY '84 to FY '86, states would have two choices. They could continue to have the programs administered directly from Washington, D.C., or they could opt-out of any or all programs completely, using the money for other purposes.

In other words, they would be free to fashion their own block grants without federal rules and regulations. Beginning in FY '87, the federal turnback programs would be repealed, thus giving the states almost total flexibility in administering these programs.

Establishment of the trust fund and transition period would allow for certainty of funding and opportunity for planning by state and local governments. It is important to note that the trust fund would be financed through existing excise taxes and other tax receipts.

State legislatures and governors would control the use of the trust fund, but the President's program had built-in protections for pass-through of money to local units of government. As the President said in several different meetings with local officials, "I guarantee that one feature of my plan will be a mandatory, pass-through of funds to local governments."14/

The trust fund guaranteed that there would be no winners or losers among the states. If a state were a loser in the swap of Medicaid for AFDC and Food Stamps, that state's trust fund account would be increased by an equal amount.

For example, in FY '84 when the swap was scheduled to take effect, it would cost Alabama $350 million to assume AFDC and Food

---

14/ Ronald Reagan, meeting with Republican mayors in the White House, January 28, 1982.

Stamps. By taking over Alabama's responsibility for Medicaid, the federal government would save Alabama $140 million. The net difference would be a $210 million loss to Alabama. However, Alabama would receive a $713 million allocation from the trust fund. The federal programs turned back to Alabama would cost $503 million. The net difference would be a gain for Alabama of $210 million. Therefore, Alabama's net balance would be zero. No gain or loss. The same principle would apply to every other state. Table I shows the manner in which this principle would apply to each state nationwide.

During the second stage, FY '87-91, the amount of federal excise tax receipts in the trust fund would decrease annually by 25 percent. By 1991, both the taxes and the fund would expire, allowing states to control both the administration and funding of each program. A two-cent tax on gasoline would remain at the federal level to maintain the interstate highways.

There were many other aspects to the proposal, but suffice it to say that it was a revolutionary initiative which would drastically alter the present makeup of federal-state-local relations. Out of approximately $81 billion in grants-in-aid to state and local governments, $19.1 billion would become a full federal responsibility (Medicaid), $46.7 billion in programs would be returned to the states (AFDC, Food Stamps, and other programs), leaving approximately $25 billion in grants which would continue under the present system.

If anything, we erred on the side of producing a proposal which was too all-encompassing to be achievable. As Governor Richard Snelling (R-VT) told me when I briefed him by telephone just hours before the President delivered his State of the Union address, "the President's program is too ambitious."

But to a very significant extent, the package reflected the input we had received from state and local officials throughout 1981.

- For example, governors and state legislators had often called for a sorting out of government responsibilities, which included federalization of health and welfare programs. The President's proposal met them halfway by including federal takeover of the burgeoning Medicaid program.

- The National Conference of State Legislatures and the National Governors' Association Chairman, Dick Snelling, urged us not to raise excise taxes. The program not only rejected an increase in federal excise taxes, it also eliminated them by 1991.

- Mayor Bill Hudnut of Indianapolis, Senate Budget Committee Chairman Pete Domenici of New Mexico, and the National Association of Towns and Townships had called for a giant revenue sharing program. The President's proposal included a super revenue sharing component of $28 billion, and also assumed continued funding of the general revenue sharing program at a cost of $4.6 billion per year through FY '87.

- State and local officials had recommended the need for a transition period. The package included an eight-year transition.

- State and local officials had also expressed a strong desire for certainty in funding levels. The President's proposal met this objective by pledging to take whatever budget figures were enacted for FY '83 and locking them in through FY '87.

- One of the themes heard throughout the meetings in 1981 was the need to return revenue sources to the state and local level. The package accomplished that objective through the return of excise taxes to the states.

- Finally, local governments were protected by a mandatory pass-through formula which required that 100% of the funds of local programs be passed-through the states to local units of government.

Two other guiding principles which became hallmarks of the package during its development in the spring of 1982 were: (1) that there be no winners or losers among the states, and (2) that the package not be a vehicle for a budgetary savings -- on either side.

The Initial Response

State and local officials had been saying for a decade that they wanted more authority and responsibility returned to them. At the meeting of the National Governors' Association in Denver, Colorado during the middle of the 1980 Presidential campaign, the restiveness of the governors was increasing. During their meeting, they went public with their demand for a "sorting out" of responsibility between the federal and state governments. As noted by columnist David Broder:

"The governors of the once sovereign states are working up a fine head of steam about their treatment in Washington, and with help from the state legislators may maneuver themselves into a position where they can do more than complain about it. The National Governors' Association meeting in Denver, held just before the Democratic National Convention, echoed with the sharpest bipartisan rhetoric about the excesses of Washington that I have heard in the last 18 years I've been covering them."15/

Increasingly sophisticated state bureaucracies provided a base from which the governors felt they could better provide effective services to their constituents. An activist group of governors was not convinced that Washington had a better answer. As Broder noted, they were prepared to take on the system, restructure it, and bear the responsibility for whatever resulted.

The governors passed a resolution titled, "Agenda for Restoring Balance to the Federal System." The governors noted that,

> "The federal system has reached a crossroads. The role of the states has been eroded to the point that the authors of the Constitution would not recognize the intergovernmental relationships they crafted so carefully in 1789.

> Accordingly, the governors have developed the following reform agenda which is designed to capture the interest and attention of Congress, the President, and the federal bureaucracy because it responds to the real concerns of the American people. It is grounded on the belief that reform will reduce federal spending; that reform will make government more responsive to the people because the governmental action is closer to them and is therefore easier to understand; and that reform will make the federal system truly consistent."

Their call fell on sympathetic ears. Ronald Reagan had made many of the same comments during his years in public life.

While the President was receptive to the views of state and local officials, most of them were equally receptive to the general concept of the President's Federalism Initiative. Bernie Hillenbrand, the highly-respected Executive Director of the National Association of Counties, said following a briefing of state and local officials on January 26, 1982, "You've succeeded in making souffle where the Carter Administration could only make

---

15/ The Washington Post, August 6, 1980, p. A1.

-146-

scrambled eggs." Governor Snelling, then Chairman of the National Governors' Association, said the President "deserves enormous praise for putting the subject on the table."16/ Governor Bruce Babbitt (D-AZ) called the proposal "elegant and imaginative."17/ Lamar Alexander, Governor of Tennessee, said of President Reagan's New Federalism, "if it ever hits Main Street, the changes will make more difference to the ability of Americans to control every day community decisions than anything Congress has done in half a century."18/ Steve Farber, Executive Director of the National Governors' Association and among the very brightest and most able students of politics and the intergovernmental system, said, "This could be the most exciting opportunity for the states in decades." And Kansas State Senator Ross Doyen, then President of the National Conference of State Legislatures, said the President's plan "is a genuine effort to sort out what level of government can respond to program needs."19/

The attitude of most state and local officials was summed up by the comments of Governor Richard Thornburgh (R-PA) on the ABC "Nightline" program following the President's speech on January 26, 1982. Governor Thornburgh said:

> "The vast majority of the Governors, both Democratic and Republican, across the nation have long had an agenda that very closely jibes with what the President committed himself to this evening. And I think we look forward to a partnership, a real consultation about the sorting out of powers and about the return of revenues to the States in order to bring government closer to the people and make it more effective."

Ed Meese, who was strongly committed to this effort, had stated the Administration view in comments to state and local officials

---

16/ "Two State Leaders Respond to Reagan's Plan," State Government News, March 1982, p. 14.

17/ Bruce Babbitt, "His Plan Deserves a Chance," The Washington Post, January 28, 1982, p. A25.

18/ Senator William Roth, Opening Statement, President's Federalism Initiative, Hearings before the Committee on Governmental Affairs, U.S. Senate, 97th Congress, 2nd Session, February 4, 1982, p. 1.

19/ Broder, David S. and Denton, Herbert H., "Huge 'Sorting Out' of Federal Role," The Washington Post, January 27, 1982, p. 1, col. 6.

at a meeting in the White House Roosevelt Room on January 25, 1982. He said that when President Reagan had been governor of California (and Ed Meese was his Executive Assistant and Chief of Staff), his Administration used to spend a great deal of time fighting with the federal government. The thrust of the President's Federalism Initiative was "to try to take some of the fight out of that relationship."

At the same time, from the outset there were words of warning. Then Governor Hugh Carey (D-NY) called the proposal "hastily conceived and poorly designed."20/ Texas Governor Bill Clements said, "I ain't going to buy a pig in a poke."21/ Marion J. Woods, the California Director of the Department of Social Services under Democratic Governor Jerry Brown said, "It looks like he [Reagan] has abandoned the thrust of the last 50 years in federal efforts to establish minimum floors for welfare programs. It's a radical departure from a 50 year movement of these programs toward equity, uniformity and consistency under both Republican and Democratic presidents."22/

Even more important, key members of Congress made clear that however bold or necessary the President's federalism proposal might be, it would not take precedence over the budget. House Republican Leader Robert M. Michel of Illinois said, "This is right in line with Republican dogma, but my enthusiasm has to be muted a bit because it doesn't create one new job now. It's a partial answer to the long-range problem but it does not do anything for the immediate problem."23/ Senate Budget Committee Chairman Pete Domenici (D-NM) said, "It can't take the place of fiscal policy issues."24/ Senator Robert Dole (R-KS), Chairman

---

20/ Carey, Hugh, "New Federalism Yes, But Reagan's Proposal Needs Major Revision," The New York Times, March 14, 1982, p. E23.

21/ Broder, David S. and Denton, Herbert H., op. cit., p. 1, col. 6.

22/ Shuit, Douglas, "Reagan's Proposals Get Mixed Reviews," Los Angeles Times, January 28, 1982, p. 3, col. 5. In California, the Director of the Department of Social Services administers the Food Stamps and Aid to Families with Dependent Children programs.

23/ Smith, Hedrick, "Reagan's Risk-Taking in Election Year," The New York Times, January 27, 1982, p. A1, col. 3.

24/ Senator William Roth, op. cit., p. 3.

of the Finance Committee, said "Every President wants to find something to get out front with, but the economy can't be subordinated and he knows that."25/ And the powerful Chairman of the Senate Appropriations Committee, Mark Hatfield (R-OR) said, "Success in achieving this remarkable program will ultimately hinge on an economic rebirth in the coming year. A looming specter of increasing federal deficits and high interest rates simply cannot be ignored."26/

Perhaps, the mood of Republicans in Congress was best expressed by Senate Majority Leader Howard Baker. Days before the State of the Union Address, Chief of Staff Jim Baker, who wanted this thing to work and was ever mindful of the courtesies properly due Capitol Hill, asked House Republican leader Bob Michel and Howard Baker to his office for a briefing. Congressional liaison director Ken Duberstein and I were there to outline the Federalism Initiative. When we had finished Howard Baker smiled and said that he was enthusiastic about what we were trying to do and, of course, he'd help in any way that he could. But, he added, the situation reminded him of an old story he had heard back home in the hills of eastern Tennessee:

> Moses had led the Israelites out from the bondage of the Pharaoh in Egypt and was moving them eastward in the desert. He came up to the banks of the Red Sea and just then he could hear the hoofs and see the cloud of dust from the approaching Pharaoh's army. The only escape from slaughter was across the sea.
>
> First, Moses asked his top general what he should do. His general said, "We could arm every man, woman and child, then stand up and fight. But the approaching army would destroy us quickly." So, Moses dismissed him.
>
> Second, Moses called his chief engineer and asked him what he should do. The engineer studied a moment and then said they could construct an enormous bridge across the sea, but it would take years to build. And, of course, in minutes the Pharaoh and his army would arrive and slaughter them all. So, Moses dismissed his engineer.

25/ Ibid.

26/ Ibid.

Then, in desperation, Moses turned to his public relations man and asked him what he should do. His public
relations man said, "Go up on that large rock. Put
your arms up to the heavens. Ask God to part the seas
and the seas will part. Then lead the Israelites to
the other side through the parted sea. Then, when we
are on the other side, again go and stand atop a large
rock. Raise your arms to heaven. By then the Pharaoh
and his army will be crossing the parted sea. Ask God
to close the sea. It will close, killing the Pharaoh
and his army."

Moses was ecstatic. He said, "That's a terrific
idea. Do you think it will work?"

His public relations man said, "No. But if it does, I
promise you two books in the old testament."

Obviously, Senator Baker understood full well how difficult it
would be for us to advance the President's conceptual framework
for a federalism initiative into law. And he was right.

Instead of economic rebirth, in 1982 the United States slid into
even deeper recession. Instead of shrinking deficits, in 1982
the federal deficit would hit record levels and its looming specter would darken, and eventually cloud the entire political landscape.

Nonetheless, immediately after the President's State of the Union
message outlining his Federalism Initiative, a majority of the
members of Congress adopted a "wait and see" attitude.
Congressman Barber Conable (R-NY) was his usual sage self when he
said:

"If the package is not good enough for the states, it
will never succeed [because it will be opposed by
state and local officials]; if it is too good a deal
for the states it will never succeed [because many
members of Congress will oppose the resulting increase
in the budget deficit]."27/

_____

27/ Broder, David S. and Denton, Herbert H., op. cit., p.
1., col. 6. In 1982, Barber Conable was the senior
Republican on the House of Representatives Ways and
Means Committee. In 1986 he became President of the
World Bank.

We recognized that by proposing the turnback of almost $50 billion in federal programs to the states, we were asking the Congress to commit a politically unnatural act, i.e., giving up power.

Our efforts also were not helped by the fact that David Stockman was the principal administration spokesman, and his credibility with Congress has been severely tarnished by the furor over his remarks in the <u>Atlantic Monthly</u> interview.<u>28</u>/ For example, the headline in the <u>Washington Post</u> which followed his testimony before the Senate Governmental Affairs Committee on February 5, 1982 said: "Congress Gives Stockman Chills on New Federalism." Senator John Glenn (D-OH) told Stockman during those hearings:

> "We trusted you last year, the public trusted you last year, and we were deceived, deliberately deceived."<u>29</u>/

The Development Process

As outlined in the State of the Union address, the President's initiative was not a detailed plan, but rather a conceptual

---

<u>28</u>/   See Greider, William, <u>The Education of David Stockman and Other Americans</u> (E.P. Dutton, Inc., New York), 1982.

<u>29</u>/   Senator John Glenn, (D-OH), Opening Statement, President's Federalism Initiative, Hearings before the Committee on Governmental Affairs, U.S. Senate, 97th Congress, 2nd Session, February 4, 1982, p. 20. More fully, Senator Glenn said, "Trust is the most important single element in government. Mr. Stockman, we trusted you last year and the public trusted you and we were deceived -- deliberately deceived. I don't know whether your trip to the woodshed has led you into giving us straight figures this year, unaltered figures, but we believed you last year and this Congress went along with all the figures that you gave us and we voted the programs in. One of the results of that breach of faith is the 1983 budget deficit of nearly $100 billion, interest rates over 16 percent, more business bankruptcies than any other year since 1933 and 5.5 million Americans unemployed ... I hope this year, Mr. Stockman, we can have the straight figures, unaltered which we did not get last year."

framework.30/   It was structured that way deliberately, in order to permit the details to be worked out through extensive consultations with state and local officials.   As the President said: "We need their consensus and support."31/

The negotiation process really began on February 1, 1982 at a meeting in the Cabinet Room in the White House which was attended by the President, David Stockman, Edwin Meese, myself and members of Congress, governors, and state legislators.32/   The governors requested that future sessions be considered "negotiations" rather than "consultations," and Meese assured them that we considered ourselves to be in a state of negotiation.

The process continued at the mid-winter meetings of the National Conference of State Legislatures (NCSL), the National Governors' Association (NGA), the National League of Cities (NLC), and the National Association of Counties (NACo).

The state legislators met first.   Stockman and I appeared jointly before a meeting of the NCSL Executive Committee on Sunday, February 21, 1982.   After extensive discussions, the committee adopted a resolution later that day welcoming the administra-

---

30/   The President had promised the consultations in his State of the Union Message, saying: "I will shortly send this Congress a message describing [the initiative].   I want to emphasize, however, that its full details will have been worked out only after close consultations with congressional, state and local officials."

31/   Meeting with President Ronald Reagan, December 23, 1981.

32/   Four days earlier, on January 28, 1982, the President had met the the National Conference of Republican Mayors and Municipal Officials.   The organization's president, Mayor Margaret Hance of Phoenix, issued a statement that: "Speaking for myself and the great majority of Republican elected local officials, I applaud the President for his initiative and look forward to working with him during the refinement and detailed development stages of the concept."

tion's New Federalism Initiative.33/ I was somewhat disappointed that the resolution continued the state legislators' call for federalization of all income security programs, including AFDC and Food Stamps. However, State Senator Ross Doyen of Kansas, the President of NCSL, issued a statement that the group's action signified "support of the Administration's Federalism Initiative." The story in the Washington Post the next day ran with the headlines, "State Leaders Agree to Negotiate on 'New Federalism' but Fight Cuts."

The meeting of the National Governors' Association, which started the same day, was dominated by two factors: (1) the President's Federalism Initiative and (2) the new Chairman of NGA, Governor Richard Snelling (R-VT).

The Federalism Initiative had galvanized the governors. It clearly placed them at center stage -- a position agreeable to Governor Snelling. An attempt was made by the new Chairman of the Democratic Governors Conference, Jerry Brown (D-CA), to divert the discussion of federalism in favor of an attack on the Administration for its recently proposed FY '83 budget cuts in state and local grants. Given the continued deterioration of their state fiscal conditions, these Administration proposed cuts were met with near unanimous opposition from state and local officials. There was political mileage for the governors in joining into bash the Reagan budget proposals. Nonetheless, the efforts of Jerry Brown, Governor Hugh Gallen (D-NH), Governor Joseph Brennan (D-ME), and a few others to focus attention on the "unfair" budget cuts failed to materialize. Reagan had asked the governors to respond to his revolutionary proposals. He had called on them as partners in the federal system to work with him for solutions to the mess in the intergovernmental system. The governors felt obligated to respond thoughtfully to the President's Federalism Initiative.

The battle was over how to handle the President's call for a swap of Medicaid to the federal government for state assumption of Food Stamps and AFDC. Stockman and I again appeared jointly, this time before the NGA Executive Committee. A significant percentage of the governors were insisting on a reiteration of the long-standing NGA position which called for the federalization of all welfare programs. This group insisted that a propos-

---

33/ On February 21, 1982, the NCSL Executive Committee passed a resolution stating they "welcomed the steps taken by President Reagan for a new Federalism Initiative by the exchange and devolution of programs along with the revenue sources to pay for them."

ed NGA federalism negotiating team should not be allowed to discuss such a proposed swap.

During the NGA meeting, their immediate past Chairman Governor George Busbee (D-GA) met with me a number of times. A moderate Southerner who was widely respected amongst the gubernatorial fraternity, Busbee had been a critical ally to the Reagan Administration in gaining passage of block grants the year before. Genuinely committed to decentralization, he was willing to play a similar role for the grand Federalism Initiative. He proposed a somewhat pared back mini-swap. Rather than a $50 billion dollar program, Busbee's proposal included a mix of programs reaching about $35 billion. After checking with the President, I gave Busbee a green light to sound out his colleagues on the NGA Executive Committee.

After talking to a number of them, Busbee reported most were willing to follow his lead, however, Snelling was not. Snelling felt that as Chairman it was his role to develop any compromise and that "cutting a deal" now was premature. Busbee and I had long talks on whether or not to force the issue. We both felt we had a majority of governors who supported the "Busbee compromise," but we were unsure as to whether we had enough for a two-thirds majority, which was necessary for NGA to take an official position. If we got the two-thirds majority, it would be a key victory. But invariably long negotiations would follow in which Snelling, as NGA Chairman, would would be a pivotal participant. We were concerned that if we rolled Snelling now, he could thwart us later in the negotiations. We needed him on board. Therefore, in the end, Busbee and I agreed not to push for a firm NGA commitment to the President's framework based on his mini-swap. In the end, perhaps that was a mistake.

The NGA resolution which eventually passed unanimously was drafted by Busbee and several of his colleagues. It did not reflect Snelling's views. The problem over the swap component was finessed by language which indicated that it was "deferred for further negotiations." The Reagan administration took the position that this language meant the swap was on the negotiating table. At the same time the governors were able to argue that this meant all other aspects of the Federalism Initiative were to be taken up first. In the plenary session, Charles Thone (R-NB) specifically asked Snelling whether the income maintenance issue could be placed on the table for the first negotiating session. Governor Snelling responded "yes." Though some governors had spoken against any discussion of state assumption of income maintenance in a proposed "swap," Snelling's comment went unchallenged. The resolution complimented the President for "setting out a bold and specific proposal to realign the federal system to achieve more effective and accountable government at al levels." A negotiating team consisting of six governors was appointed.34/

The spirit of the governors was perhaps best reflected by the toast made by Governor Snelling to the President at the conclusion of the state dinner at the White House in the State Dining Room on February 23, 1982. He said:

> "The Governors of the United States appreciate the fact that you, who have been one of us, have fully appreciated that sense of urgency with which the American people wish to see government come back home. And we want to salute you for not only appreciating that urge, but for acting upon it and for putting before us and putting before Congress and putting before the people of the United States an agenda in which the recognition of the constitutional rights and obligations of the states and of local government has a very high priority. And in that spirit, the governors of the states and territories have responded by making specific suggestions to you and by accepting your offer to work with them. And so, we want to salute you for being the kind of leader who recognizes not only what is important to the people of this country, but who also takes the kind of actions which makes it clear that he believes in what he says. I think your offer to negotiate with us these matters and to meet with us and to provide some give and some take is very, very much appreciated by everyone in this room, because you've not just offered, you have demonstrated that you will treat the federal partners as partners. And for that, Mr. President, we applaud you."

Immediately following the meeting with the governors and state legislators, the Administration began working with state and local officials to develop the details of the Administration's federalism package.35/ Despite whatever differences we had, we

---

34/ The NGA negotiating team included Governors Richard Snelling (R-VT), Scott Matheson (D-UT), Bruce Babbitt (D-AZ), James R. Thompson (R-IL), and Lamar Alexander (R-TN).

35/ In addition to the Governors already listed, the following state and local officials were included: State legislators were represented by Assemblyman William F. Passannante (D-NY), Senator Cap Ferry (R-
(Cont'd)

agreed to agree -- to work out those differences through candid give and take.

In a similar vein, the National Association of Counties created a Task Force on Federalism. It was created to bypass the cumbersome NACo policy process so as to allow swift action in responding to the President's proposal. The National League of Cities deferred action on March 1, scheduling a special meeting for mid-April specifically to take action on the Federalism Initiative.

In early February, administration officials began working with state and local officials to develop the details of the President's federalism package.36/ We agreed to work out our differences through candid give and take. The negotiation process proceeded on two tracks. (1) There were frequent meetings with the principals, and (2) there were dozens of meetings be-

---

UT), Representative John Bragg (D-TN), Senator Ross Doyen (R-KS), Representative Richard Hodes (D-FL) and Senator Dave Nething (R-ND). Local officials were represented by Mayor Margaret Hance (R-Phoenix, AZ), Mayor George Voinovich (R-Cleveland, OH), Mayor Coleman Young (D-Detroit, MI), Mayor Patience Latting (D-Oklahoma City, OK), Mayor Ferd Harrison (D-Scotland Neck, NC), County Executive Bill Murphy (R-Rensselaer County, NY), County Commissioner Richard Conder (D-Richmond County, NC) and B. Kenneth Greider (Executive Director, Pennsylvania State Association-National Association of Towns & Townships). The official Administration representatives were James A. Baker, III, Edwin Meese, III, David A. Stockman, Edwin Harper and myself.

36/ Members of the state legislators' negotiating team were Senator Ross Doyen (R-KS), Representative Richard Hodes (D-FL), Assemblyman William Passannante (D-NY), Senator Dave Nething (R-SD), Senator Miles Ferry (R-UT), and Representative John Bragg (D-TN). Members of the local officials negotiating team were: Mayor Richard Carver (R-Peoria, IL), Mayor George Voinovich (R-Cleveland, OH), Mayor Margaret Hance (R-Phoenix, AZ), Mayor Patience Latting (D-Oklahoma City, OK), Mayor Helen Boosalis (D-Lincoln, NB), Mayor Coleman Young (D-Detroit, MI), County Executive William Murphy (R-Rensselaer County, NY), Commissioner Richard Conder (D-Richmond County, NC), Mayor Ferd Harrison (D-Scotland Neck, NC), Commissioner Virgil Brown (R-Cuyahoga County, OH), and township official George Miller (R-Astoria, IL).

-156-

tween the staffs of the various state/local public interest organizations and Alan Holmer, my deputy, and others on the White House Intergovernmental Affairs staff (as follows).37/

CHRONOLOGY OF SIGNIFICANT MEETINGS DURING THE NEW FEDERALISM

Pre-State of the Union Address

Throughout 1981	Eight meetings of the President's Advisory Committee on Federalism and its subcommittees, two of them with the President.
December 1981 and January 1982	Informal meetings with key governors, and Mayors Margaret Hance and Ferd Harrison, briefing them on the draft proposal to be set out by the President in the State of the Union Address.
January 25, 1982	Briefing in Roosevelt Room for selected state and local officials.

During Negotiations

January 26, 1982	President announces New Federalism Initiative in his State of the Union Address.
January 27, 1982	Meeting with the President's Advisory Committee on Federalism.
February 1, 1982	President meets with selected members of Congress, governors, state legislators, mayors and county officials.
February 8, 1982	Briefing of state budget officers by White House staff.

37/ Alan Holmer later served the Reagan Administration as General Counsel of the United States Trade Representatives office and then Deputy USTR. A superb public servant, his diligence and patience throughout this process was critical in keeping it on track.

February 9, 1982	President addresses joint sessions of Iowa and Indiana state legislatures.
February 21 – February 23, 1982	Winter meeting of the National Governors' Association.
February 21, 1982	Meeting of the Executive Committee of the National Conference of State Legislatures.
February 22, 1982	President meets with representatives of the National Association of Counties.
March 1, 1982	President meets with representatives of the National League of Cities.
March 6, 1982	Meeting with state legislators negotiating team.
March 9, 1982	Meeting with local officials negotiating team.
March 15, 1982	President addresses joint sessions of Tennessee and Alabama state legislatures.
March 16, 1982	President addresses joint session of Oklahoma state legislature.
March 17, 1982	Meeting with governors negotiating team.
March 22, 1982	Meeting of the President's Advisory Committee on Federalism.
April 14, 1982	Meeting with the state legislators negotiating team.
April 19, 1982	Meeting with the local officials negotiating team.
April 21, 1982	Meeting with the state legislators negotiating team.
May 5, 1982	Meeting with the state legislators negotiating team.
May 7, 1982	Special meeting between Representative Richard Hodes (representing state legislators) and Dr. Robert Rubin of the Department of Health and Human Services (HHS).

May 21, 1982	Special meeting with Governor Snelling, HHS Secretary Schweiker, and White House staff members James Baker, Edwin Meese III, Richard Williamson, and Alan Holmer.
May 27, 1982	Special meeting between Governor Snelling and Secretary Schweiker.
June 23, 1982	Meeting with governors negotiating team.
June 29, 1982	Meeting with local officials negotiating team.
July 15, 1982	Meeting with the President's Advisory Committee on Federalism.
August 6, 1982	President calls negotiating teams to tell them that he is deferring sending federalism legislation to the Congress until 1983.
September 30, 1982	President meets with all three negotiating teams to determine areas of agreement.

At the same time, frequent meetings were held of a Technical Working Group which reported to Ed Meese, Jim Baker, Dave Stockman and myself. The group was chaired by Don Moran, Senior Associate Director of OMB and comprised of representatives from each of the affected departments and agencies.38/

38/ The members of the technical working group were as follows: Donald W. Moran, Executive Associate OMB Director; Richard Breeden, Executive Assistant to the Labor Undersecretary; June Koch, Deputy Undersecretary for Intergovernmental Relations at the Housing and Urban Development Department; Robert Rubin, Assistant Health and Human Services Secretary for Planning and Evaluation; Gary Jones, Deputy Education Undersecretary for Planning, Budget and Evaluation; Roger W. Mehle, Jr., Assistant Treasury Secretary for Domestic Finance; Mary Clairborne Jarratt, Assistant Agriculture Secretary for Food and Consumer Services; and G. William Hoagland, Special Assistant to Agriculture Secretary John R. Block. White House staff members on the working group besides Moran were
(Cont'd)

In the meetings with the local officials, we were able to accommodate many of their concerns.39/ However, for the majority of local officials, these accommodations were still not enough. They recognized that the Administration's Federalism Initiative dramatically altered the federal government's relationship with local governments. While the President's package included a mandatory pass-through of funds to local units of government, it was readily recognized that this pass-through was only temporary and would begin expiring in fiscal year 1987.

As Mayor Helen Boosalis, (D) of Lincoln, Nebraska, then Chairman of the U.S. Conference of Mayors, testified before Congress, "There should be a much greater role for local officials in the federalism trust fund super grant program. Funds should be given not only to states, but also to local governments directly ... cities stand to lose significantly under any proposal to turn over program funds to the states."40/

Most local officials, particularly big city mayors, had over the years developed grantsmanship into a high art form.41/ They had

---

Robert B. Carleson, Special Assistant to the President for Policy Development; Alan F. Holmer, Deputy Assistant to the President for Intergovernmental Affairs; Jim Medas, Steve Rhodes and Rick Neal, each a Special Assistant to the President for Intergovernmental Affairs; and James F. Kelly, Director of OMB's Intergovernmental Relations Division.

39/ For example, the pass-through formula was amended to make it more acceptable to local officials; Food Stamps was dropped from the proposed swap; windfall profits tax revenues were replaced with general revenues.

40/ Helen Boosalis, Testimony, March 11, 1982, President's Federalism Initiative, Hearings Before the Committee on Governmental Affairs, United States Senate, 97th Congress, 2nd Session, pp. 190, 192. See also, George E. Paterson and Carol W. Lewis, Reagan and the Cities (The Urban Institute Press, Washington, D.C., 1986) for a general analysis of the tensions between the Reagan Administration and the mature cities over policies of devolution.

41/ See Hale, George E., and Palley, Marian Lief, The Politics of Federal Grants (Congressional Quarterly Press, Washington, D.C., 1981).

far more success in getting funding aid directly from Washington, D.C. than from their own state capitols. Local officials, especially those representing large urban areas, believed state governments had been unfair in their distribution of funds. They felt state governments, particularly state legislatures, had historically favored rural areas over urban areas. They believed the federal government had become a valuable ally in correcting this alleged rural bias within state governments.

In addition, mayors and other local officials doubted that state governments had the ability or capacity to handle effectively the new responsibilities which the Administration's budget proposed. As Mayor Charles Royer of Seattle charged, states are "politically, institutionally, and financially ill-equipped to assume added responsibilities of the magnitude contemplated in President Reagan's recovery program."

The bottom line for big city mayors was money. The federal government had become a way by which they could get more and more money without raising taxes themselves. Most big city mayors were so dependent on the federal funding pipeline that the independence, flexibility and autonomy for them promised by Reagan's federalism initiative were little incentive. They did not want to risk the unknown. They were fearful of fending for themselves.

Furthermore, the mayors' public interest groups in Washington, the U.S. Conference of Mayors and the National League of Cities, were effective, entrenched special pleaders on Capitol Hill. The large staffs of these organizations fully understood that the Reagan efforts to decentralize government threatened their organizations' importance and, even, their own job security. The State of the Union initiative to devolve government, they felt, was a direct assault on their well being. These lobbyists worked hard to stop this initiative in any way possible.

The predictability of federal funding, even at diminished levels, and Washington-based special interest group self-preservation were important ingredients in the negotiating mix. Even while many elected local officials favored good faith efforts to work out something, generally their Washington staff did not. It became a tremendous problem because more often than not the elected local officials came to the table to negotiate totally reliant upon the Washington staff for substantive support (and, often, also dependent on these Washington lobbyists for tactical guidance).

All of these factors contributed to the Board of Directors of the National League of Cities passing a Resolution on July 10, 1982, in opposition to the President's federalism package. It stated

-161-

that the NLC _cannot_ support the proposals presently advanced by the administration because they ignore the needs of cities as viable partners in the federal system.

As George Gross, the legislative director of the National League of Cities, told me that summer, "It was inevitable that we would end up in conflict." In part conflict was inevitable because that was what the staffs of the cities' Washington-based special interest groups were committed to.

The reaction of state legislators and governors, however, was more positive. A list of 30 items was released at the July meeting of the National Conference of State Legislatures showing the extent of our progress in addressing the input of this group.

THE NEGOTIATIONS' DISAPPOINTMENT: INCOME MAINTENANCE

While the administration could take great satisfaction in the achievements outlined above, it did not obtain a sorting out of responsibilities in the income maintenance area. The principal reasons were as follows: (1) the gap between the positions of the President and most state and local officials regarding income maintenance responsibilities proved to be too great; (2) many of the issues were too complex to be resolved quickly; and (3) as the year progressed, budget economies and political factors became paramount and crowded out other considerations.

Basic Difference of Opinion

With respect to income maintenance (principally AFDC, Food Stamps, and Medicaid), the President's position had been that all such expenditures should be the responsibility of state and local governments. It is in those arenas that public assistance dollars can best be targeted to those individuals and areas having the greatest needs.42/

Most state and local officials, however, believed that all income maintenance programs are more appropriately the responsibility of the federal government. Arguing that income maintenance costs often are caused by economic factors beyond a state's control, most state and local officials contended that those costs should be a national responsibility.43/

In his Federalism Initiative, the President proposed to meet those concerns halfway by suggesting the federalization of Medicaid in exchange for state assumption of AFDC and Food Stamps. Indeed, early in the negotiations the President compromised even further. Because of the concerns of members of

---

42/ In this respect, the President had been greatly successful in reforming the welfare program in California. He was determined to target funds to those most truly in need, to assure that needs tests were not artificial and manipulative, and that only persons entitled to assistance by genuine need, received it. He instituted work requirements, eliminated the duplication of services, and streamlined administration. The result was that a state welfare system adding a staggering 40,000 people each month was soon able to reduce caseloads by 350,000 while the dollar value of grants for destitute families went up 41 percent. At the same time, forty-two of California's fifty-five counties were able to reduce property taxes. For a discussion of the problems created when eligibility decisions are made by the federal government in Washington, see the paper prepared by David Swoap, the Undersecretary of Health and Human Services, for the President's Federalism Advisory Committee on October 29, 1981.

43/ For instance, a resolution adopted in December 1981 by the policymaking arm of the National Conference of State Legislatures stated: "Individually, state and local governments cannot fully control our national economy and, therefore, cannot fully control certain program costs that fluctuate with it. Programs needed to safeguard the economic condition of our nation and its citizens should be the primary responsibility of the federal government, including: employment programs, anti-poverty programs (including Medicaid), and income security programs."

Congress and state and local officials with respect to state assumption of the Food Stamps program, the President expressed a willingness to take that portion of the package off the table, leaving an exchange of a $19 billion federal Medicaid assumption for a $7 billion state AFDC assumption, plus a sufficient number of categorical and block grant programs to make the exchange equal.44/

Unfortunately, even that compromise was not sufficient to satisfy the governors, state legislators, and local officials. Governors were concerned that if the federal government retained responsibility for Food Stamps and the states assumed responsibility for AFDC, the states would have a disincentive to increase AFDC benefits. For every $1 increase in AFDC benefits, there would be a $0.30 reduction in Food Stamp benefits. This is because AFDC benefits are a factor in determining the level of Food Stamp benefits.

The governors proposed to modify the Food Stamp program so that the Food Stamp benefits would no longer be reduced as state AFDC benefits are increased. The Administration estimated that this would cost the federal government $3.8 billion per year. The states would accept $3.8 billion in categorical grant programs in exchange, or a corresponding reduction in the trust fund. There would be no immediate net cost to the federal government.

The Administration had four major concerns with respect to this proposal:

- It would increase the federal share of income maintenance expenditures.

- It would place persons who receive AFDC income in a more favorable position than those who receive non-AFDC income.

- It might lead to increased reliance on the Food Stamp program for establishing a national minimum level for income maintenance expenditures.

- The Administration would be exchanging $3.8 billion in rising entitlement expenditures for $3.8 billion of less explosive discretionary expenditures.

44/ I first announced that we were looking toward possible removal of Food Stamps from the swap at a meeting with the state legislators' negotiating team on April 14, 1982.

It became clear that the principal result of the governors' proposal to decouple AFDC and Food Stamps would be to take a large step toward further federalization of all income maintenance expenditures. It reflected the views of Governor Matheson who told the President at the meeting in the Cabinet Room on February 1, 1982, "The Governors are unanimously on record as opposing the transfer of income maintenance to the states."

As much as the President wanted to strike a deal with the governors, and walk in step with them to Capitol Hill, the philosophical gap proved to be too wide. To move state and local officials, the President needed a bigger carrot than he felt he could offer in good faith.45/

In my opinion, each side of the negotiating process misjudged its ability to find common ground on income maintenance. Neither side appreciated how firmly committed the other was to its position.46/

45/ In all fairness, it should be noted that not all of the governors were opposed to meeting the President halfway in the income maintenance area. At the National Governors' Association meeting in February 1982, Governor Busbee came up with a proposed "mini-swap" which included the following provisions: (1) food stamps would continue as a federal responsibility; (2) the states would assume full responsibility for all AFDC costs plus Medicaid costs for AFDC; and (3) the federal government would assume responsibility for all other Medicaid expenditures.

We had several useful discussions with Governor Busbee on his mini-swap proposal, and an apparent majority of governors supported such an approach. However, we were never able to reach closure on a mini-swap which would be acceptable to the Administration and a full two-thirds of the governors necessary for official NGA endorsement.

46/ At one point during the process, Governor Snelling was quoted by some of his colleagues as saying that he was convinced that the White House ultimately would come around to the governors' proposal that Medicaid be federalized in exchange for state assumption of categorical grant programs of equal value. He felt that the White House was more desperate for a federalism program than ultimately turned out to be the case.

Complexity of Issues

The second major reason why the negotiations broke down over income maintenance was that the issues were often too complex for early resolution. In large part, this was unavoidable because of the complexities of the programs involved. But the result was that the big issues were often overshadowed in the negotiation process by disagreement over technicalities, and fundamental issues of restructuring the federal system were too often lost in a proliferation of "green eye shade" accounting matters. It was also hard to get and maintain public support for a proposal that was incomprehensible to the vast majority of people.47/ The complexity problem could be seen in particular with respect to federalization of Medicaid and the fiscal disparities of the states.

Medicaid: The task with respect to federalization of Medicaid was to take the $19 billion cost of the states' share of Medicaid and add it to the federal share of $22 billion in Medicaid expenditures. The result was intended to be a federally financed Medicaid program. As such, it would reduce the differences in the Medicaid program from state to state.

Implicit in the proposal was the assumption that some states with lean programs would find a new richer Medicaid package,48/ while states with relatively luxurious programs (California, for example, provides benefits for acupuncture and faith healing) would find certain benefits dropped by the new federal program. Obviously, any proposal which included reductions in benefits or eligible populations contained many political minefields.

47/ In general, Americans supported the thrust of what the President was trying to do. For example, a Harris survey, issued February 15, 1982, showed a 2-to-1 approval for the Initiative. However, it was difficult to transfer this support to specifics. This difficulty was reflected in a February 3, 1982 column in The Washington Post by Meg Greenfield in which she said: "When Proposals reach this point of elaborateness, I conclude that they will probably never happen."

48/ To be fair and make the package attractive to the states, we decided that to the extent a state's Medicaid program becomes more expensive as a result of the new national Medicaid program, the federal government would absorb the difference.

Unfortunately, certain administration officials, whose enthusiasm for the New Federalism Initiative had dissipated, dragged their feet and hindered efforts to produce a federalized Medicaid package. The White House Office of Intergovernmental Affairs was forced to take the lead in developing administration options on federalization of Medicaid. Without the active help of Secretary Richard S. Schweiker and Assistant Secretary Robert Rubin at the Department of Health and Human Services (HHS), often against active resistance from other quarters, specific Medicaid proposals would not have been developed.49/

On June 22, 1982, the Administration produced a tentative decision memorandum which included a proposal to federalize Medicaid. The proposal did not include coverage for the medically needy, and this was a sore point with the governors. The medically needy are individuals who had been covered in the past under optional state programs for low-income families and who do not qualify for cash assistance under AFDC or SSI.50/

49/ On March 4, 1982, the OMB timetable called for HHS to have draft specifications for federalization of Medicaid to OMB by March 16, 1982. By May, however, the OMB attitude with respect to the legislation had changed. On May 11, 1982, a memorandum from a senior OMB official stated that they "could not produce costable, reliable consensus legislation in this area until well toward the end of the summer, if not into the fall period."

50/ Under the medically needy program, states are permitted to establish an income eligibility level of up to 133.5 percent of their state's AFDC payment standard, and provide medical assistance to those whose income falls below this standard. Senior administration officials recognized the very large political fallout which would result from dropping the medically needy from the Medicaid program. Such a course of action would result in media coverage that the Administration had once again turned its back on the poor, denying medical coverage to those who have become poor only as a result of a catastrophic illness.

Thirty-four states and territories have medically needy programs. If the federal government did not cover these individuals, most states would have no choice but to continue coverage at state expense. This would be a significant shift of federal costs to the states and would not be consistent with the federalization of Medicaid.
(Cont'd)

If the Administration had produced, in a timely manner, a Medicaid package acceptable to the governors, it might have provided a sufficient incentive for them to accept state assumption of AFDC. I believe that in five years, when state officials look back at the opportunity they passed up on Medicaid (and see Medicaid costs further skyrocketing out of control), they will regret that they failed to seize the opportunity to federalize this program in exchange for state assumption of AFDC.

Fiscal Disparity: It also proved to be very difficult to deal with the issue of fiscal disparity, which centers on the fact that states have widely varying degrees of unemployment, tax capacity, and social needs. Politically, this issue was enormously difficult to address, for in essence it called for taking existing federal funds from one state and giving them to another. It came into direct conflict with one of the basic principles expressed by the President early in the negotiations -- that there be no winners or losers among the states.

The governors proposed to address this issue by requesting that the administration establish a safety net Supplemental Assistance Fund to assist those states with high poverty, high unemployment, and low fiscal capacity. Assistance from the fund was to be temporary, based on cyclical economic considerations. The fund was estimated to cost between $1 and $3 billion annually, depending on the conditions that would have triggered assistance and on economic and demographic assumptions for FY '84 and thereafter.

The principal administration concern about this proposal was that the projected federal deficits in FY '84 and beyond were so great that the federal government could not afford another $1 to $3 billion in increased expenditures. The governors' proposal thus came into conflict with another of the President's principles -- that the package not be a vehicle for budgetary increases on either side.51/

The concern of some administration officials was that even if the HHS estimates were presumed to be accurate, there would be significant out-year cost exposure. Some felt that adequate cost estimates for this group could not be done because there are no data on the income distribution of the medically needy population.

51/ The Administration requested that the Advisory Commission on Intergovernmental Relations take a leadership role with respect to the fiscal disparity issue. Senator Dave Durenberger (R-MN) also provided helpful guidance and counsel.

Economic/Political Factors

Our difficulty in achieving a consensus with respect to income maintenance was also influenced by three other factors: (1) the recession, (2) the Administration's proposed budget cuts, and (3) the politicization of federalism.

Recession: State and local officials began to feel the pinch of the recession by the fall of 1981. Indeed, five days before President Reagan's 1982 State of the Union Address, the National Conference of State Legislatures issued a news release head-lined: "Fifty State Survey Shows State Budgets in Bad Shape as 1982 Begins."

The poor performance of the economy had placed substantial down-ward pressure on state revenues. By June 30, 1982, the end of most states' fiscal year, the aggregate state revenue surplus had fallen to $2.4 billion from $4.8 billion. As the governors received these projections in the summer of 1982, their concern increased. Many state legislatures were called into special session. Over 20 states adopted hiring limitations and made selected budget cuts. Fifteen states made across-the-board bud-get cuts. Twelve states laid off state workers. Twenty-two states adopted permanent or temporary revenue raising measures to cover fiscal years 1982 and 1983. Since all states but Vermont are required by law to balance their budgets, the governors had to confront these difficult fiscal matters with limited options.

Budget Cuts: The Administration's proposed budget cuts severely poisoned the well for federalism reform. Early in 1981, the governors supported block grants along with 10 percent budget cuts. What we proposed -- and what was generally enacted by the Congress -- was a 25 percent cut. This was followed by the unex-pected announcement in September 1981 that the Administration was seeking an additional 12 percent cut in the FY 1982 budget. This proved to be a tactical blunder. We failed to get those cuts through Congress, yet the damage had been done with state and local officials. Many of them felt that they had cut a deal with the Administration when they supported our original round of budget cuts. Now we were proposing to go much deeper, and many of them believed that we were using state and local programs as a scapegoat for our own budget miscalculations.

The situation was made even worse when we proposed cuts in grants-in-aid to state and local officials from $91 billion in FY 1982 to $81 billion in FY 1983. These cuts were sent to the Congress at the start of the negotiation process. State and local officials had proposed level funding for their programs between FY 1982 and 1983. But by not taking their recommendation (and thereby failing to enlist their support) for level funding, the Administration ended up with $93 billion in outlays for state and local governments for FY 1983, a $2 billion increase.

Political Strains: By mid-summer 1982, political strains had eroded the bipartisan spirit which had characterized the negotiations. With the delays caused by a lack of cooperation by some administration officials, and the relentless attacks on the Administration by its critics, it became clear by the end of July that it was too late in the political season for the Congress to act favorably on our federalism proposal. In separate meetings with me in their offices, Senators Roth (R-DE), Laxalt (R-NE), and Domenici (R-NM) all urged that congressional action on any specific administration proposal be deferred until after the first of the year. The President's Assistant for Legislative Affairs, Kenneth M. Duberstein, checked with the staffs of Senate Majority Leader Howard Baker and House Speaker Thomas P. ("Tip") O'Neill, Jr.; he was advised that the limited number of legislative days remaining precluded meaningful congressional consideration in 1982. Hearings in the House and Senate might have even produced rhetoric which would have tarnished the Administration's chances in 1983.

As a result, on Friday, August 6, 1982, the President called the key state and local officials on the negotiating teams and advised them that, for the reasons discussed above, he would not be sending federalism legislation to the Congress until early 1983. However, the President wanted the development process to continue, and told the state and local officials that he wished to meet with them when he returned from California later that month.

The NGA's summer meeting in Afton, Oklahoma, reflected the political difficulties surrounding the Federalism Initiative. By the time of the Afton meeting, the bipartisan nature of NGA had become strained. Thirty-six of the 50 governorships were up for election in November 1982. Most governors' concern focused on not generating anything controversial which might affect their reelection chances. Their willingness to pursue new federalism was substantially decreased by their desire not to have to return home and explain a specific resolution calling for a sorting out of federal-state governmental roles.

The emerging themes for the 1982 election had a significant impact on politically cautious governors. "Stay the Course" and

"It's not fair, it's Republican"52/ caused many to adopt a wait and see attitude.

Consequently, NGA became more defensive and less willing to pursue any Federalism Initiative vigorously. Governor Snelling, as NGA chairman, sought the authority to break with the President and present a separate Federalism Initiative to Congress. The resolution that ultimately passed at the NGA meeting in Afton rejected Snelling's proposed course of action. It approved development of a governors' plan, but explicitly stated that the governors would go to the White House to seek to work out unresolved differences with the President before going to Congress. Further, there was a call to continue the negotiating process with the White House. Finally, NGA made it clear that nothing should be presented until after the first of the new year (and the 1982 elections).

While discussions with state and local officials continued into the fall, the action by the governors had for all practical purposes precluded any possibility of achieving agreement in the income maintenance area.

With the November elections behind us, and as 1982 came to a close, the Administration concluded that we should put areas of disagreement (income maintenance) aside and attempt to focus on areas of agreement (turnback of programs and revenue sources). We also concluded that we would eliminate the most controversial programs53/ from the package and separate the program into smaller groups. The result was the package of megablock grants which was submitted to the Congress on February 24, 1983.54/

52/ These were the respective campaign slogans of the national Republican and Democratic parties.

53/ For example, the following programs were dropped from the original package: CETA, Child Nutrition, Legal Services, Black Lung, Migrant Health, WIC, Airports, Primary Roads, Primary Bridges, Interstate Transfers, Appalachian Highways, UMTA Construction, UMTA Operating, UDAG, and OSHA State Grants.

54/ See Chapter Five on "Block Grants" for a detailed discussion of the megablock grant proposal.

CHAPTER 7

THE FEDERAL BUDGET AND THE NEW FEDERALISM

A major front in the Reagan Administration's campaign to return authority and revenue to state and local governments was to cut the size of the federal government itself; and to cut the growth of Washington's role in the federal system. President Reagan intended to halt and then reverse the dominance of federal aid and federal interference in state and local governments. He intended to reduce the role of the federal government in domestic life.

As Hugh Heclo and Rudolph Penner wrote about the Reagan Administration's fiscal and political strategy:

"Within the conservative movement two concerns, each identifying something real, had become inextricably linked: the problem of a malfunctioning economy and the problem of a malfunctioning big government. It was an act of political theory to link the latter as the chief cause of the former."1/

Throughout Reagan's Administration, he has struggled to shift the priorities of the federal government. While he expanded military spending, he shrank the federal role in domestic programs.2/ As we sat in the long arduous budget review board meetings with the President and he fashioned his first three budgets, there was never any question to me or my colleagues about his thematic goal to restructure the federal role.

The different participants in those budget review board meetings came to the table with different assignments and differing van-

---

1/ Hugh Heclo and Rudolph G. Penner, "Fiscal and Political Strategy in the Reagan Administration," in Fred I. Greenstein, ed., The Reagan Presidency: An Early Assessment (The Johns Hopkins University Press, Baltimore, 1983), p. 28.

2/ See Hoffman, David, "Reagan Continues Shift of Priorities," The Washington Post, July 6, 1986, p. A1, col. 5. See also, Timothy Conlan, New Federalism: Intergovernmental Reform From Nixon to Reagan (The Brookings Institution, Washington, D.C., 1988), pp. 112-149.

tage points. For example Dave Stockman, whose budgetary bril-
liance and indefatigable energy were invaluable to Reagan's early
budget cutting success, was fanatically focused on cutting, cutting, cutting. His blade was so sharp that he made Caspar
Weinberger, who had been known as "Cap the Knife" when he was OMB
Director in the Nixon Administration, look like he had a butter
knife whereas Stockman had a razor sharp machete. Stockman's
commitment to cutting the budget was so great that for him no
trick was unacceptable for his trade. There's no question he was
critical for Reagan's budget victories in the early years when he
still had political credibility. Ed Meese tried to anticipate
the President's goals and guide the deliberations toward those
ends. Marty Anderson had a libertarian free market analysis he
stamped upon the issues. Jim Baker kept his sharp eyes on
Congress and the media, constantly trying to put a package together that would be "credible" and, hopefully, "saleable" to
those two constituencies. I was there to give the federalism
spin on the items. The relevant cabinet members, invariably,
carried water for their constituencies and their bureaucracies,
and so on. Each of us came to the table with a slightly different perspective, each legitimate and apparently each in its own
way helpful from Reagan's perspective. Reagan encouraged free
and full debate. Sometimes, it became heated. Reagan stood
apart. He let us all have our say. But he made the decisions.
And due to his strong anti-government and strong federalism bias,
he more often than not sided with the cause of trimming budget
items and re-ordering priorities that advanced the goal of decentralizing government.

In all his fiscal plans, Reagan has demonstrated his belief that
support of essentially local activities is not an appropriate
federal role. To quote President Reagan's fiscal year 1987 budget message, his budget proposal "contemplates an end to unwar-
ranted federal intrusion into the state and local sphere and
restoration of a more balanced, constitutionally appropriate
federalism with more clearly defined roles for the various levels
of government."3/ But to achieve his goal of having the federal
government "get out of the business of paying for local sewage
treatment systems, local airports, local law enforcement, subsidies to state maritime schools and local coastal management,"4/
President Reagan has had to reverse an eighty year trend of federal budget domestic spending growth.

3/   Ronald Reagan, Budget Message of the President,
      February 5, 1986, The United States Budget in Brief:
      Fiscal Year 1987, p. 8.

4/   Ibid.

In 1902, the total revenues of all governments were less than eight percent of the gross national product; by 1983, they were almost 31 percent. A similar pattern holds for expenditures.5/ At the same time, there has been a steady trend upward in fiscal responsibilities from the local to the state to the federal levels in government. By 1980, financing responsibility had increasingly concentrated in Washington.6/

The great expansion of federal aid funds to other political jurisdictions began during Franklin D. Roosevelt's presidency. Between 1932 and 1934 federal intergovernmental aid quadrupled.7/ In the 1930's, "the states lost their confidence, and the people lost faith in the states."8/ The attitude of the Roosevelt Administration was perhaps best described by one of its members, Professor Samuel Beer: "I vividly recall our preoccupation with persuading people to look to Washington for the solution to problems, and one sensed what a great change in public attitude this involves."9/

5/   Office of State and Local Finance, Department of the Treasury, Federal-State-Local Fiscal Relations: Report to the President and the Congress, September, 1985, p. viii.

6/   For an excellent discussion of the growth of federal intergovernmental aid, see Richard P. Nathan, Fred C. Doolittle, and Associates, Reagan and the States (Princeton University Press, Princeton, NJ, 1987), Chapter 2, "The Evolution of Federal Aid."

7/   Federal aid funds to other political jurisdictions grew from $232 million in the last year of the Hoover Administration to more than $1 billion in the second year of the Roosevelt Administration.

8/   Sanford, Terry, Storm Over the States, McGraw Hill Book Company, New York, 1967, p. 21.

9/   Wright, Deil S., "New Federalism: Recent Varieties of an Older Species," paper drafted for symposium on federalism in the American Review of Public Administration, July, 1982, p. 4.

During the 1930's, federal domestic spending10/ increased more than six fold -- from 1.2 percent of gross national product to 7.1 percent.11/ Federal aid to state and local governments grew by 1,000 percent in 10 years.12/ Expansion continued after World War II. The Employment Act of 1946 gave permanence to the federal role in public welfare. And, with the 1949 urban renewal program, even broader support for enlarging the federal role in urban affairs.

In 1953, federal aid represented 10 percent of the annual budgets of state and local governments. In 1973, it represented just over 20 percent; and by 1978 federal aid financed 26 percent of state and local spending.13/ Viewed from a different perspective, while the federal share of all government spending has remained fairly constant since 1950 (between 65 and 70 percent), intergovernmental grants have assumed a dramatically increasing proportion of federal spending. In 1950, federal intergovernmental grants were approximately 6 percent of all federal spending; by 1978, they had risen to 17 percent.14/ Government employment figures show that state and local government employment grew by 218 percent from 1950 to 1982, while federal employment grew by 42 percent.15/ This would suggest that growing federal intergovernmental grants allowed Washington to use state and local governments as its administrative agents.

10/ Excludes major national security, international affairs and finance, veterans' services and benefits, and interest on the national debt.

11/ U.S. Bureau of the Census, Historical Statistics of the United States, Colonial Times to 1970 (Washington, D.C., 1975), pp. 225, 1115.

12/ Ibid. p. 1125.

13/ Advisory Commission on Intergovernmental Relations, Recent Trends in Federal and State Aid to Local Governments (July, 1980), Table 5, p. 8. (Note: This declined to 21 percent in 1982.)

14/ Congressional Budget Office, The Federal Government in a Federal System: Current Intergovernmental Programs and Options for Change, August 1983, p. 14. (Note: This declined to 11 percent in 1982.)

15/ Economic Report of the President, 1983, Table B-37, p. 205.

Various arguments are offered to justify intergovernmental grants. They are required to accommodate benefit spillovers. That is, some services benefit residents beyond the boundaries of subnational jurisdictions; whether in neighboring jurisdictions or entire regions. Wastewater treatment is an example of benefit spillovers. Also, intergovernmental grants can be used to reduce fiscal disparities. The fiscal capacity of a government is its ability to raise revenues from its own sources relative to its fiscal responsibilities.16/ Such grants are necessary, it is argued, to enlist the involvement of state and local governments in the delivery of services under a national program. The clearest example is federal aid to states for the administration of the Food Stamp program. In fiscal year 1985, these grants were estimated to be approximately $840 million for the payment of $10.5 billion to recipients.17/ And the fourth argument to justify intergovernmental grants is that they are used to induce states and local governments to deliver minimum, national levels of services.

While all four of these rationales may warrant some federal intergovernmental grants, President Reagan felt that clearly by 1981 things had gone too far. By January 1, 1981, there were 534 federal categorical grant-in-aid programs to state and local governments.18/ And the total expenditure for federal grants-in-aid had risen in fiscal year 1980 to $91.5 billion.19/

16/ Office of Management and Budget, Budget of the United States Government 1986-Appendix (1985, p. 1-E89).

17/ Office of State and Local Finance, Department of the Treasury, op. cit., p. 133-152. For a discussion of reasons to be concerned about fiscal disparities on efficiency grounds, see Buchanan, James M., and Wagner, Richard E., "An Efficiency Basis for Fiscal Equalization," in Margolis, Julius (ed.), The Analysis of Public Output (Columbia University Press for the National Bureau of Economic Research, 1970), pp. 139-158.

18/ On January 1, 1984, there were 392 federal categorical grant-in-aid programs available to state and local governments. This represented a decrease of 142, or about 27% since Reagan had taken office. This was the first decline since ACIR first counted federal categorical grants. Advisory Commission on Intergovernmental Relations, A Catalog of Federal Grant-In-Aid Programs to State and Local Governments: Grants Funded FY 1984, December, 1984, p. 1.
(Cont'd)

President Reagan's first budget proposals demonstrated his commitment to halt this growth of Washington's role in the intergovernmental system. As President Reagan's first Chairman of the
Council of Economic Advisors Murray Weidenbaum said that year,
"The Administration's budget also reflects a shift in federal
priorities to truly national needs. Both national defense and an
adequate social safety net for the truly needy are national priorities and federal responsibilities."20/ Other existing federal
programs, however, were not seen as paramount federal responsibilities. As President Reagan said in addressing the nation's
mayors at the time he sent his first budget to Congress,

> "I know that accepting responsibility, especially for
> cutbacks, is not easy. But this package should be
> looked at by state and local governments as a great
> step toward not only getting America moving again, but
> toward reconstructing the power system which led to
> the economic stagnation and urban deterioration."21/

In fiscal year 1981, the federal government spend $657.2
billion. Within this budget, federal aid to state and local
governments was $91.5 billion in outlays, or 14.4 percent of all
budget expenditures. This total combines payments that were
federally funded but administered by state and local governments

---

19/ Office of State and Local Finance, Department of the
Treasury, op. cit., p. 134. The historical development of the grant-in-aid system is discussed in
Maxwell, James A., and Avonson, J. Richard, Financing
State and Local Governments (Brookings Institution,
1977), pp. 10-30; and in Derthick, Martha, The
Influence of Federal Grants (Harvard University Press,
1970), pp. 3-13. Note that the rapid growth of federal grants to the intergovernmental system began to
curb between fiscal years 1978 and 1981. During these
years, while spending in these areas grew in nominal
terms, run-away inflation converted nominal increases
into a real decline of about six percent.

20/ Weidenbaum, Murray L., "Strengthening Our Federal
System," in American Federalism: A New Partnership
for the Republic, Ed. Robert Hawkins (Institute for
Contemporary Studies) San Francisco (1982), pp. 89,
93. ****Italics added.

21/ President Ronald Reagan, remarks to the National
League of Cities, Washington, D.C., March 2, 1981.

(welfare)22/ and federal grants that do not go to individuals but
to state and local governments for their operations or capital
projects (categorical grants, block grants and General Revenue
Sharing).23/ Since FY 1971, federal aid to (and consequent federal interference in) state and local governments had increased
$66 billion in current dollars, increased $18.2 billion in 1972
constant dollars, and increased 0.5 percent of the GNP.24/
President Reagan sought and in fact did reverse this trend.

The Omnibus Budget Reconciliation Act of 198125/ and consequent
congressional budget actions resulted in a fiscal year 1982 budget authority reduction of $45.1 billion, causing a total outlay
reduction of $44.1 billion from the level they would have reached
if Congress had not adopted President Reagan's new policies.
This reduced budget authority by 5.7 percent and outlays by 6.0
percent.26/ Excluding defense expenditure increases and interest

---

22/ Ellwood, John W., "Controlling the Growth of Federal
Domestic Spending," in Reductions in U.S. Domestic
Spending, Ed. John W. Ellwood (Transaction Books, New
Brunswick, NJ, 1982), pp. 7, 8. This category would
include "Medicaid, Aid to Families with Dependent
Children (AFDC), housing assistance, and child nutrition programs. These grant programs spent $39.9 bil-
lion in Fiscal Year 1981, or 6.1 percent of all budget
outlays."

23/ Ibid. "In Fiscal Year 1981, the federal government
spent $54.8 billion, or 8.3 percent of all budget
outlays, for such grants."

24/ Ibid., p. 9, taken from Office of Management and
Budget, Federal Government Finances: 1983 Budget Data
(Washington: Office of Management and Budget,
February 1982), Tables 10, 11, and 12, pp. 59-78.

25/ Ellwood, John W., "The Size and Distribution of Budget
Reductions," ibid., pp. 33, 39.

26/ Another way to look at these reductions is that
Reagan's March, 1981, budget proposals asked that
budget authority be reduced by $37 billion, or 4.6
percent, compared with what it would have been under
President Carter's proposed budget. See John William
Ellwood, ed., Reductions in U.S. Domestic Spending
(Transaction Books, New Brunswick, NJ, 1982), Chapter
4, for a discussion of alternative ways to calculate
the size of the budget changes.

on the public debt, the cuts were 12.3 percent in budget authority and 9.4 percent in outlays.27/ Of these budget reductions, a
substantial amount came in cuts in federal aid to state and local
governments.

Grant payments funded federally but administered by state and
local governments were reduced $16.350 billion, a 23.5 percent
reduction in 1981, while federal grants to state and local governments for their operations and capital projects were reduced
$19.075 billion, a 37.7 percent reduction, in 1981. All federal
aid to state and local governments bore 54.6 percent of reductions in fiscal year 1982 budget authority. On the average, each
budget account had its budget authority reduced by 29.5 percent
compared with 1981 policy levels.

"In fiscal year 1982, federal aid to states registered its first
decline since the Advisory Commission on Intergovernmental
Relations had been tracking intergovernmental aid flows."28/
From FY 1981 to FY 1982, President Reagan reduced federal aid
from $94.8 billion to $88.8 billion. Major components of this
reduction included: a $2.6 billion decline in the Department of
Labor's employment and training assistance program, a $814.4
million decline in temporary employment assistance, a $1 billion
decline in payments to states from the Highway Trust Fund, a $130
million decrease in Airport and Airway Trust Fund payments, a
$490 million decrease in the child nutrition programs administer-
ed by the Department of Agriculture, a $341 million drop in the
Department of Health Services' maintenance assistance (Aid to
Families with Dependent Children) payments. The net $6 billion
reduction in federal aid to state and local governments was realized despite increases in certain other intergovernmental programs such as a $600 million increase in Medicaid and modest
increases in refugee assistance and preventive health
services.29/

Ronald Reagan's first year in office had been one of dramatic
policy change including a general slowing of growth of the government's domestic programs and the actual reduction of intergovernmental grants-in-aid. It was not easy. As Los Angeles

---

27/ Ibid.

28/ Advisory Commission on Intergovernmental Relations,
     "Federal Aid to States Registers First Decline," News
     Release, Washington, D.C., April 28, 1983.

29/ Ibid. See Department of Treasury, Federal Aid to
     States Fiscal Year 1982, Washington, D.C.

Times bureau chief Jack Nelson wrote, "In curbing the growth of social programs, [Reagan] had waged war against a half century of Democratic philosophy, a philosophy often supported by Republicans."30/ At the end of his first year, Reagan said in a press interview:

> "I believe that we have started government on a different course, different than anything we've done in the last half century and since Roosevelt began with the New Deal, and that is the recognition that there is a limit to government -- must be a limit to government size and power -- and that there has been a distortion of the relationship between the various echelons of government -- federal, state, and local."31/

While the fiscal year 1982 budget provided a 12 percent reduction in constant dollars in federal intergovernmental aid, it was projected that FY 1983 would show a 0.7 percent increase. Generally, intergovernmental aid was held constant for FY 1983, but increased funding for transportation programs under the new Surface Transportation Assistance Act (Public Law 97-424)32/ would increase all federal aid to state and local governments to $93.5 billion.33/ However, in contrast to the historic trend for 50 years, President Reagan had made substantial cuts in domestic spending and trimming in the federal government's role in domestic program areas.34/ The general trend in federal payments to state and local governments was continuous, rapid growth until 1978. Between 1978 and 1983, however, total federal grants adjusted for inflation declined nearly 25 percent. Real grants for purposes other than payments to individuals declined by more than

---

30/ Jack Nelson, "The Reagan Legacy," in ed. Paul Duke, Beyond Reagan: The Politics of Upheaval (Warner Books, New York, 1986), pp. 83, 107.

31/ Ibid.

32/ Surface Transportation Assistance Act (P.L. 97-424).

33/ ACIR, ibid.

34/ For an excellent detailed analysis of these budget trends, see Nathan, Richard P., Doolittle, Fred C., and Associates, The Consequences of Cuts: The Effects of the Reagan Domestic Program on State and Local Governments (Princeton Urban and Regional Research Center, Princeton, NJ), 1983.

40 percent during the same period. Since 1983, federal grants have increased at about the rate of inflation.35/

President Reagan said a week after he sent his first 1981 budget requests to Congress:

> "We are not cutting the budget simply for the sake of sounder financial management. This is only a first step toward returning power to states and communities, only a first step toward reordering the relationship between citizen and government."36/

His budget reflected that reordering of relationships. As political commentator David Broder wrote near the end of Reagan's third year in office:

> "There is no doubt that Reagan has won the first stage in his battle to halt almost 50 years of unbroken growth of Washington's role in the federal system."37/

In his second term, President Reagan continued his efforts to squeeze out excessive federal intergovernmental spending. In fiscal year 1985, state and local governments received $24 from Washington for every $100 they raised on their own, in contrast to the high of $32 reached in 1978. And not considering the impact of Gramm-Rudman-Hollings, this figure is projected to drop to less than $20 by 1987.38/

35/ Office of State and Local Finance, Department of the Treasury, op. cit., p. ix.

36/ President Ronald Reagan, remarks to the Conservative Political Action Committee Conference, Washington, D.C., March 20, 1981.

37/ Broder, David, "States Learn to Live with End of New Deal," The Des Moines Register, p. 9A, November 30, 1983.

38/ Advisory Commission on Intergovernmental Relations, Significant Features of Fiscal Federalism: 1985-86 Edition (Washington, D.C.), February, 1986, p. 3. Note that most of this federal aid is devoted to programs where the national government and state-local governments have shared interests such as poverty and health programs, the interstate highway system and education.

President Reagan's proposed fiscal year 1987 budget continued this trend. The U.S. Conference of Mayors observed that:

"[T]his budget continues the dramatic realignment of spending priorities begun in 1981, with less revenue, a substantial shrinking of much of the domestic budget, and the continued buildup of military spending. ... Total federal grants to state and local governments would be reduced by 33 percent in constant dollars from FY '81-'87. From FY '86 to FY '87 alone, grants-in-aid and, excluding payments to individuals, would drop from $57.8 billion to $50.6 billion."39/

As the National Conference of State Legislatures and the National Governors' Association similarly analyzed the proposed FY '87 budget:

"The President proposes to meet the deficit target by continuing his proposal to reorient national priorities. The President's proposal would decrease federal spending by shifting more responsibilities to the state and local sector, to private industry, and to individuals and families."40/

As a result of his budget proposals, according to liberal news commentator Carl T. Rowan, Reagan "has forced us to revive the centuries-old debate about the purpose and the role of the national government."41/

President Reagan's budget preference to cut back federal funding to state and local governments gained determinant political leverage from the enormity of the federal budget deficits. An important distinction between Reagan's efforts to return significant responsibilities to state and local governments and earlier

---

39/ United States Conference of Mayors, The Federal Budget and the Cities: A Review of the President's Budget for Fiscal Year 1987 (Washington, D.C., February, 1986), p. iii.

40/ National Conference of State Legislatures and National Governors' Association, Impact on the States: The President's 1987 Budget (Washington, D.C., February, 1986), p. 1.

41/ Carl T. Rowan, "Reagan's Budget Forces Us Anew to Debate Federal Role," Chicago Sun-Times, February 10, 1986, p. 29, col. 3.

efforts is that, in the 1950's, 1960's and early 1970's, the general tide and fiscal conditions supported centralization. With today's deficits, the federal fiscal conditions practically compel decentralization. As Professor John Kincaid has written, "Fiscal conflict and rising debt have helped to drive Ronald Reagan's New Federalism."42/

"The changing fiscal fortunes of the national government now stand out," according to John Shannon, former executive director of the Advisory Commission on Intergovernmental Relations, "as the single most important factor reshaping the relationship between Washington and the 50 state-local systems. ...It has transformed the expansive 'Great Society' federalism of the 1960's into the fairly austere and competitive 'fend-for-yourself' federalism of the 1980's."43/ Or as Reagan said during his first year in office, "Spending by government must be limited to those functions which are the proper province of government. We can no longer afford things simply because we think of them."44/

The fiscal crowding of the 1980's compelled tough budget decisions. Reagan constantly used this budget dilemma to decentralize government. As Senator Dan Evans, a former governor and expert on the intergovernmental affairs, has said, "There has been a Reagan revolution during the time of Reagan. There is a change going on, but we are doing all these things not so much because we think they are right but because we have to" under the economic realities of recent years.45/ So even members of Congress not in full accord with Reagan's budget priorities, supported many of his domestic cuts due to the continuing dilemma of enormous federal budget deficits.

42/ John Kincaid, "The State of American Federalism-1986," Publius, Vol. 17, No. 3, Summer, 1987, pp. 1, 8.

43/ John Herbers, "The New Federalism: Unplanned Innovative and Here to Stay" in Governing, Vol. 1, No. 1, pp. 28, 33.

44/ Ronald Reagan, "A Program for Economic Recovery," Address to Joint Session of Congress, Washington, D.C., Feb. 18, 1981.

45/ John Herbers, "The New Federalism: Unplanned, Innovative and Here to Stay" in Governing, Vol. 1, No. 1, pp. 28, 30.

During the Reagan Administration, federal aid as a percentage of total state-local outlays has dropped from 25 percent in 1981 to approximately 14 percent for fiscal year 1987.46/ This reverses the long trend in which federal aid grew faster than state and local own source revenue. In 1987, state and local governments collected over $500 billion from their own sources. As John Shannon has written, this "fend-for-yourself federalism is slowly effecting a 'sorting out' of governments. Federal policymakers are being forced by fiscal and political realities to allocate an increasing share of their resources for strictly national government programs: defense, Social Security, Medicare, and interest on a $2.4 trillion debt."47/

State and local governments no longer automatically expect federal money to be available to solve their problems. They are looking to their own resources.48/ Some attribute this "fend-for-yourself" federalism in large part for the burst of creative state activism in the 1980's and the state-local fiscal resiliency at a time when Congress and the President are unable to agree on a budget balancing strategy.49/

As commentator James J. Kilpatrick, long a champion of federalism, has observed:

> "Twenty years ago, during the reign of Lyndon Johnson, I would have thought it impossible to see a day when there would be less government at the national government level. ... I am not so pessimistic now... For

---

46/ See "Federal Aid to States Lowest Since 1966," The Washington Times, November 18, 1988, p. A2. It should be noted that direct federal aid to localities has fallen off more sharply than has aid to state governments. And, one result of this decreased federal aid has been various fundamental revisions of state and local relations. See Steven D. Gold, State and Local Fiscal Relations in the Early 1980's (The Urban Institute Press, Washington, D.C., 1983).

47/ John Shannon, "The Return to Fend-for-Yourself Federalism: The Reagan Mark," Intergovernmental Perspective, Vol. 13, No. 3/4, Summer/Fall 1987, pp. 34, 36.

48/ John Herbers, "With Federal Cuts, It's Each Locality for Itself," The New York Times, June 14, 1987, p. E4.

49/ John Shannon, op. cit. at 36.

one thing, the federal government is broke. To the demand of states for "revenue sharing," the answer today is that Congress has no revenue to share. Whether by scalpel or by meat ax -- our federal deficits must be trimmed. The day of federal subsidies for sewerage, water plants, libraries, local symphonies, law enforcement, a hundred other desirable programs -- that day is ending."50/

"A program like revenue sharing," a Chicago Tribune editorial declared, "is an unaffordable luxury for a government that is almost $2 trillion in debt."51/ Fiscal retrenchment and persistent deficits forced tough decisions. But Reagan's desire, however advanced by fiscal crises, goes beyond federal budget balancing. Commentator Stephen Chapman more nearly echoes Ronald Reagan's federalism principles when he writes:

> "Better to let those 39,000 cities and towns decide for themselves if the programs they finance by revenue sharing are genuinely crucial. If so, their residents should be willing to pay for them. If not, there is no reason anyone else should."52/

50/ Kilpatrick, James J., "Back to Federalism," The Washington Post, February 11, 1986, p. A17, col. 1.

51/ Editorial, "Good-bye to Revenue Sharing," Chicago Tribune, January 16, 1986, Sec. 1, p. 26, col. 1. The FY 1986 federal budget document observed that: "The Federal Government can no longer afford general revenue sharing. ...[T]ermination is essential in order to achieve the President's goal of reducing the Federal deficit. ...[N]ational priorities must be met first." Office of Management and Budget, Budget of the United States Government, 1986 (1985), pp. 5-151. For a good discussion on the expiration of General Revenue Sharing, see Robert W. Rafuse, Jr., "Fiscal Federalism in 1986: The Spotlight Continues to Swing Toward the State and Local Governments," Publius, Vol. 17, No. 3, Summer, 1987, pp. 35-41. See also, Bernard L. Weinstein and Harold T. Gross, Untying the Federal Knot: An Agenda for State and Local Independence (American Legislative Exchange Council, Washington, D.C., 1986), pp. 10-34.

52/ Chapman, Stephen, "Deficit Sharing, Via Washington," The Washington Times, January 28, 1986, p. 3D, col. 3.

The collective decision-making processes of government are a far cruder vehicle for the expression of individual preferences than the market. Decentralized government, while imperfect, at least fosters efficiency by allowing a close match between public goods and the multiplicity of private preferences. It promotes accountability and equity by clearly linking the benefits of services and their costs. And decentralization is a necessary condition for effective management.

President Reagan's commitment to federalism is not merely a political science philosophy. His budgets are based on economic theory which provides a powerful rationale for structuring decision making and the financing and delivery of public services, to the maximum extent possible, on a decentralized basis. "This predisposition toward decentralization is rooted in considerations of efficiency, accountability, manageability, and equity."53/ And, perhaps, no tool welded by Reagan to achieve his dream of decentralization has proven more effective than his budget proposals.

Throughout the Reagan administration, liberal critics charged that the President's federalism rhetoric was just a smoke screen for radical conservative agenda to dismantle all government. Nowhere in his domestic programs was this charge made with greater vehemence and anger than in attacking Reagan's budget proposals. Our explanations that we wanted to devolve responsibility, sort out functions, and decentralize decision-making were rejected out of hand by critics as, at best, disingenuous. They firmly believed that decentralization and retrenchment went hand in hand. As Professors Nathan and Doolittle have written, "The assumption was that if social program retrenchment occurred at the federal level in combination with devolution, the states, too, would pull back on social programs. The service reductions implied by the federal aid cuts would stick, and perhaps even be compounded by parallel state and local action."54/

In literally scores of meetings with President Reagan where budget decisions were made and strategies outlined, budget review board meetings, cabinet meetings, legislative strategy group meetings and small Oval Office meetings, I never once heard Ronald Reagan talk in those terms. Nor did I ever hear any of

---

53/ Office of State and Local Finance, Department of the Treasury, op. cit., pp. 12-13.

54/ Richard P. Nathan, Fred C. Doolittle, and Associates, Reagan and the States (Princeton University Press, Princeton, NJ 1987), p. 7.

his advisors advance that argument with him. If anything, various participants emphasized the genuine federalism dimension to their proposals in efforts to enlist Ronald Reagan's agreement. There is absolutely no question that Reagan, in making budget and other policy decisions, sincerely believed in his federalism dream of decentralizing government. Indeed, it was the depth and sincerity of his belief in this dream that gave me, perhaps, disproportionate impact on some of those decisions.

In even more frequent White House meetings of senior advisors on budget matters where the President did not participate, very rarely was a cynical argument advanced about retrenchment at the expense of other legitimate considerations, be they federalism or others. And to the extent on rare occasion such cynical arguments were presented, they invariably were advanced only by Dave Stockman and other OMB representatives.

Repeatedly in arguing for the federalism agenda during that time, I said that state and local government would pick up the slack. Perhaps not every social program would survive devolution, but the general commitment to help the needy was central to America's political self-identity. The same people who elected members of Congress vote for governors, state legislators, mayors and county officials.55/ The state and local governments now had the capacity to provide services.56/ They were composed of compassionate officials. And they were more representative of women and minorities than Congress. In short, I argued that Ronald Reagan and his administration believed in the American people and had faith in their duly elected state and local officials. To us, it seemed, that harsh liberal critics had faith in the iron triangle of Washington-based special interest pleaders, not the people. And today, the evidence seems to support our faith in the people not the cynical special pleaders in Washington.

The capacity, competence and compassion of state and local governments has been evidenced by their responses to the Reagan federal aid cuts. Drawing on the most exhaustive case studies conducted anywhere, Professors Nathan and Doolittle have conclud-

---

55/ For a general discussion, see "Citizen Participation in the American Federal System," In Brief (Advisory Commission on Intergovernmental Relations, August, 1979).

56/ For a general discussion on the growing sophistication of state legislatures, for example, see Alan Rosenthal Legislative Life (Harper & Row, New York, 1981), pp. 57, 60.

ed that state and local governments "through replacement funding, through a variety of financial coping and delaying measures, and through administrative reforms -- has produced higher service levels than otherwise would have been the case due to the Reagan cuts. ...[D]uring this period in U.S. history, liberals seeking support for social programs have fared better in many states than they have in the nation's capitol. Social programs have had a larger constituency in many states than expected."57/

In fact, one of the interesting developments resulting from Reagan's efforts to decentralize government has been the growth of special interest lobbying in state capitols.58/ Constituent groups seem to be accepting the futility of trying to place demands on a federal government with no money. They are turning to state capitols and city halls. States and local governments are where the action is.59/ They are fending for themselves in unprecedented and imaginative ways.

Responding to Reagan's decentralization, virtually all states have increased user fees for such services as parks or various kinds of licenses. More than half of the states have increased their personal income or sales taxes. In 1986 alone, 16 states enacted tax increases.60/ In 1987, 40 states revamped their tax codes.61/ Lotteries have grown from a rare exception to 27

57/ Richard P. Nathan, Fred C. Doolittle and Associates, Reagan and the States (Princeton University Press, Princeton, NJ, 1987), p. 7.

58/ Neal R. Peirce, "Conservatives Weep as the States Make Left Turn," National Journal, Oct. 10, 1987, p. 2559; Neal R. Peirce, "New Women's Agenda Makes Waves in State Capitols," Chicago Sun-Times, August 17, 1987, p. 27.

59/ "The Great Society may be over in Washington, but it has just begun in the states," writes Paul Weyrich, a conservative leader in Washington, who is President of the Free Congress Foundation. Paul M. Weyrich, "The Reagan Revolution that Wasn't," Policy Review, No. 41, Summer, 1987, pp. 50, 53.

60/ John Kincaid, "The State of American Federalism-1986," Publius, Vol. 17, No. 3, Summer, 1987, pp. 1, 19.

61/ W. John Moore, "Tax Reform Ripples," National Journal, Sept. 12, 1987, p. 2269; David S. Broder, "The Politics Outside Washington," The Washington Post, Aug. 5, 1987, p. A23.

states and the District of Columbia.62/ Between 1983 and 1986, state tax collections rose by a third to $228 billion. State expenditures in Fiscal Year 1986 increased by 8.9 percent over Fiscal Year 1985. The projected increase for Fiscal Year 1987 is 5.8 percent. The average annual increase from Fiscal Year 1979 through Fiscal Year 1987 was 7.9 percent.63/ States took actions to give local governments more power to collect revenue.64/ In part, as a result, total expenditures by local governments increased during that period by 26 percent, to $332 billion.65/ From 1980 through 1986, total state and local government receipts increased by $230.9 billion. Federal aid provided only seven percent of that increase. Collecting well over one-half trillion dollars from their own resources, it is states and localities that are playing the activist role. It is in state and local governments, not national office, where new political leaders aspiring to power, increasingly seek office. It is in state capitols and city halls, not Washington, where they can work at the cutting edge of public policy.66/ As journalist John Herbers has written:

> "Governors Lamar Alexander of Tennessee, known as a moderate Republican, and Bruce Babbitt of Arizona, known as a liberal Democrat, defined their roles in widely diverse states as stretching tax dollars as far as they could, raising taxes when necessary and delivering an array of improved services from environ-

---

62/ Gross lottery revenues exceeded $11 billion in FY 1986, netting approximately $4.7 billion for the states and the District of Columbia.

63/ John Kincaid, op. cit.

64/ John Herbers, "States Act to Give Localities More Power to Collect Taxes," The New York Times, Feb. 2, 1987, p. 8.

65/ John Herbers, "The New Federalism: Unplanned, Innovative and Here to Stay," Governing, Vol. 1, No. 1, Oct., 1987, pp. 22, 34. See also Joseph F. Zimmerman, State-Local Relations: A Partnership Approach (Praeger Publishers, New York, 1983), p. 49-84.

66/ Nadine Brozan, "Women Advised to Seek State Posts," New York Times, Nov. 22, 1986, p. 17, col. 1; Desda Moss, "Women Take Their Place in USA's Legislatures," USA Today, July 30, 1987, p. 7A.

mental programs to new approaches to education, with the consent and support of broad coalitions of citizens who shared their concern about the future."67/

Capable and concerned, competent and compassionate, and, most important, responsive to their voters, state and local officials have met the challenges of Reagan's efforts to decentralize government.68/ As Professors Nathan and Doolittle, early skeptics of the Reagan cuts, have concluded:

"Reagan's federalism reforms have stimulated and are continuing to stimulate state governments to increase their efforts to meet domestic needs in functional areas in which the national government either was cutting grants-in-aid or threatening to do so."69/

67/　John Herbers, op. cit. 62. See also, Don McLeod, "America's Governors: The New CEOs," Insight, Dec. 22, 1986, p. 3.

68/　For Example, see, Ann O.M. Bowman and Richard C. Kearney, The Resurgence of the States (Prentice-Hall, Englewood Cliffs, New Jersey, 1986), Ilene K. Grossman, Initiatives in State Economic Development (Council of State Governments, Chicago, 1984). See also, Roger Vaughan, Robert Pollard and Barbara Dyer, The Wealth of States: Policies for a Dynamic Economy (CSPA, Washington, D.C., 1985); E.S. Savas, Privatizing the Private Sector (Chatham House Publishers, Inc., Chatham, New Jersey, 1982), and Stuart M. Butler, Enterprise Zones: Greenlining the Inner Cities (Universe Books, New York, 1981).

69/　Richard P. Nathan, Fred C. Doolittle, and Associates, Reagan and the States (Princeton University Press, Princeton, NJ, 1987), p. 7 and case studies ¶115-354. See also George E. Peterson, "Federalism and the States: An Experiment in Decentralization," in John L. Palmer and Isabel V. Sawhill, eds., The Reagan Record (Ballinger, Cambridge, MA, 1984); Research Report prepared by Arizona State University College of Public Programs, Impact of the New Federalism on Arizona (Arizona Academy, Phoenix, Arizona, 1982); see also reports published by the U.S. General Accounting Office in Washington, D.C.: Maternal and Child Health Block Grant: Program Changes Emerging Under State Administration, May 8, 1984; States Fund an Expanded Range of Activities Under Low Income Energy Assistance
(Cont'd)

The critics and prophets of doom over Reagan's redirecting the federal budget toward strictly national government programs have been proven wrong. The adjustments have created some dislocations, but a sea change has occurred. State and local officials no longer focus primarily on federally funded (and federally controlled) programs. They once again look to their own resources. There has been a profound burst of state activism. Diversity and innovation have flourished. There has been a remarkable demonstration of state-local fiscal resiliency.70/ American federalism has been reinvigorated.

Block Grant, June 27, 1984; Public Involvement in Block Grant Decision: Multiple Opportunities Provided but Interest Groups Have Mixed Reactions to State Efforts, December 28, 1984; Block Grants Brought Funding Changes and Adjustments to Program Priorities, February 11, 1985.

70/ John Shannon, "The Return to Fend-for-Yourself Federalism: The Reagan Mark," Intergovernmental Perspective, Vol. 13, No. 3/4, Summer/Fall, 1987, pp. 34, 36.

CHAPTER 8

CONCLUSION

Ronald Reagan has had a consistent vision for realigning America's intergovernmental system. Believing in citizen participation and public accountability, and having faith in the diversity of our federal system, Reagan has had a long-time commitment to decentralizing government.

In a speech to the Chicago Executive Club in September, 1975, he said, "What I propose is nothing less than a systematic transfer of authority and resources to the states -- a program of creative federalism for America's third century."1/

By February, 1976, he had begun to put a structural frame on his philosophical goal. In a White Paper on Federalism, he wrote:

> "The federal programs that I believe should be carefully considered for transfer to the states (along with the federal tax resources to finance them) are those which are essentially local in nature. The broad areas that include the most likely prospects for transfer are welfare, education, housing, food stamps, Medicaid, community and regional development, and revenue sharing. These programs represent approximately one-fourth of the current activities of the federal government."2/

Then in July of 1980, Ronald Reagan received the Republican nomination for President.3/ In his acceptance speech -- the first chance that a presidential nominee has to present his platform to the nation -- he said, "Everything that can be run more efficiently by state and local governments we shall turn over to local governments, along with the funding sources to pay for it."4/

1/ Ronald Reagan, Address to the Chicago Executive Club, Chicago, Illinois, September, 1975.

2/ Ronald Reagan, White Paper on Federalism, February 8, 1976.

3/ First ballot nomination, July 16, 1980, Republican National Convention, Detroit, Michigan.

4/ Ronald Reagan, Acceptance Speech, July 17, 1980, Republican National Convention, Detroit, Michigan.

Above all, he was saying that Washington was taking too many tax dollars. As Reagan once quipped, "Herbert Hoover was the first President to return his entire salary to the government. Now we're all doing it."5/ Not only was the federal government stifling the economy, punishing savings and individual initiative, but resources were being usurped from state and local governments; thereby denying those units of government the capacity to do their jobs if our federal system was to flourish.

On election day in November, Reagan felt the people had voted a mandate for change.6/

In his Inaugural Address, Reagan reaffirmed his commitment to decentralized federalism.

> "It is my intention to curb the size and influence of the federal establishment and to demand recognition of the distinction between the powers granted to the federal government and those reserved to the states or to the people. All of us need to be reminded that the federal government did not create the states; the states created the federal government."7/

Once in the White House, Ronald Reagan was good to his word and constant in his philosophic goal to decentralize government. The preceding chapters set out in some detail how President Reagan and his Administration put action behind his words. Block grants, regulatory relief and, most important, by shifting federal budget priorities during the early 1980's. As Denis Doyle and Terry Hartle of the American Enterprise Institute have written, "The story of de facto New Federalism is the most interesting and important domestic policy change to emerge from the Reagan Presidency."8/

5/ James S. Brady, ed., <u>Ronald Reagan: A Man True to his Word</u> (The National Federation of Republican Women, Washington, D.C., 1984), p. 81.

6/ The election results gave Reagan 489 Electoral College votes to Carter's 49.

7/ Ronald Reagan, Inaugural Address as 40th President of the United States, Washington, D.C., January 20, 1981.

8/ "New Federalism was not adopted as policy, nor was it explicitly funded by Washington, but it has emerged. ...The most visible stimuli were undoubtedly the administration's policy changes and budget axe, but the
(Cont'd)

Throughout the Reagan years, federal aid to state and local governments has continued to grow far more slowly than did state and local own-source revenue. It dropped year after year as a percentage of state-local expenditures. It fell to state and local governments to raise taxes, to cut services or to do both in order that revenues would match expenditures.9/ Fiscal stringency in the federal budget propelled fiscal decentralization.

The pressure to hold the line or cut federal domestic programs has been enormous. This fiscal pressure to curb federal aid to state and local governments coupled with the strong public support for Reagan's conservative and decentralist philosophy brought gradual decentralization.

Devolution is happening in the form of federal retrenchment and state-local ascendancy. As political commentator David Broder wrote in the summer of 1985:

> "[T]he initiative on education, social and most economic environmental issues now rests in state capitols rather than in the U.S. Capitol and the White House. That shift is what Reagan set out to accomplish four years ago, and the extent of his success... truly is revolutionary."10/

The fact is that in many areas where state and local governments used to follow Washington, today they lead. Ronald Reagan has liberated state and local governments. These units of government, closer to the people, have met the challenges of a more decentralized government.

While the federal government has cut back spending for education, most states increased outlays for elementary and secondary schools and public colleges. In the ten years from 1973 to 1983,

---

underlying reason is a dramatic transformation of the quality and competence of state government." Denis P. Doyle and Terry W. Hartle, "De Facto New Federalism," State Legislatures, February, 1986, pp. 21-22.

9/ Kenneth S. Howard, "De Facto New Federalism," Intergovernmental Perspective, Winter, 1984, p. 4, and John Shannon, "1984 - Not a Good Fiscal Year for Big Brother," Intergovernmental Perspective, Winter, 1985, p. 4.

10/ David S. Broder, "Reagan's Ironic Revolution," The Washington Post, August 11, 1985, p. L7.

the state share of education expenditures in Indiana increased from 34 to 63 percent; in Washington it climbed from 52 to 80 percent and in California from 38 to 75 percent. Arkansas passed new competency tests for teachers already in the classroom, and the Texas legislature passed education reforms that included higher salaries and a career ladder for teachers, mandatory competency testing for teachers and students, smaller classes, mandatory pre-kindergarten and mandatory tutoring for students with low grades.11/ Similarly, in 1985, the major legislation in Illinois was a comprehensive education bill. And new state task forces on adult illiteracy, such as the one established in 1987 in Missouri, are having a positive impact.12/

At the same time that the Reagan Administration proposed cuts in Medicaid, states were taking action to make health care more available for millions of people who lack insurance.13/ The new state health care initiatives arise because the traditional system of employer-based health insurance is changing, federal retrenchment, and because the states recognize these expanding programs as an investment in people that will save money in the long run. As the Democratic majority leader of the New York State Assembly James R. Tallon, Jr. has said, the states have become "laboratories for new ideas" in health care policy.14/ "In setting health policy, as in protecting the environment and

---

11/   Dennis Doyle and Terry Hartle, "The States are Leading as Washington Wallows," The Washington Post, September 8, 1985, p. C1. See also, Joe Davidson, "South Carolina Scores High Marks as States Act to Improve Their Educational Standards," Wall Street Journal, June, 10, 1985, p. 48.

12/   For a general discussion of recent state leadership in education see Governor Bob Martinez (R-FL), "To Improve the Quality of Education," in Restoring the Balance: State Leadership for America's Future (National Governors' Association, Washington, D.C., 1988), pp. 65-72.

13/   Robert Pear, "States are Found More Responsive on Social Issues," New York Times, May 19, 1985, p. A1. See also, Neal R. Peirce, "States Are Trying Universal Health Insurance," National Journal, November 7, 1987, p. 2812.

14/   Robert Pear, "States Act to Provide Health Care Benefits to Uninsured People," New York Times, November 22, 1987, p. A1.

encouraging the construction of housing for the poor, many states have seized the initiative from the Federal Government," according to <u>New York Times</u> reporter Robert Pear.<u>15</u>/

In 1987, 24 states expanded Medicaid eligibility to include additional pregnant women and children in response to a new federal law permitting such changes. Fifteen states have created special health insurance pools for high risk individuals who cannot obtain private coverage. Among many other states' initiatives, Michigan and Maine are providing financial incentives to encourage small employers to start providing health insurance. Indiana increased its cigarette tax to finance a new program of maternal and child health services, including prenatal care. New Jersey set up a trust fund to pay hospitals for care provided to people who cannot pay their own bills. And Georgia passed a law directing that proceeds from sale or lease of any publicly owned hospital must be placed in a trust to provide care to indigent people in the hospital's service area. As health policy expert Randolph A. Desonia has said, "There is not one monolithic strategy. Each state is trying a slightly different approach to chip away at the problem of the uninsured. States look at the total uninsured population and develop a separate solution for each segment."<u>16</u>/

In recent years, cities also have become more bold and innovative. In part this is because of the healthier fiscal condition of local governments during the prolonged Reagan economic recovery post-1982. City revenues increased 40 percent between 1980 and 1985, while expenditures during that period rose 34 percent.<u>17</u>/ Annual surplus of revenues over expenditures during that period rose from less than $1 billion to over $7.6 billion.<u>18</u>/ Once-bankrupt New York City had a $600 million surplus in 1987.<u>19</u>/ Also federal tax laws encouraged preservation

---

<u>15</u>/ Ibid.

<u>16</u>/ Ibid. at 16.

<u>17</u>/ U.S. Bureau of the Census, <u>City Government Finances in 1984-5</u> (Washington, D.C., 1986). Note that during the same time, federal revenue to cities declined by 8.8 percent.

<u>18</u>/ Ibid.

<u>19</u>/ Kenneth J. Beirne, "The Rebirth of Urban America" Backgrounder No. 613, The Heritage Foundation, Washington, D.C., 1987, p. 4.

in inner cities. Under these tax incentives an estimated $11 billion was spent by private developers from 1981 to 1987 to renovate some 17,000 historic buildings in 1,800 cities and towns.20/ "Almost every city, down to the third tier-places like Dayton and Toledo -- has done something," according to Northwestern University urbanologist Louis Masotti. "It's not a fad. It's a demographic phenomenon. The 1980's have been the decade of the cities' revival."21/

In the early 1980's increasing attention focused on the severe infrastructure problems in urban America.22/ By 1986 local governments had increased their own debt financing for capital needs, innovative methods were developed for infrastructure rehabilitation, and private business grew up to satisfy local repair needs.23/

20/ Under the federal tax laws, developers who rehabilitate historic buildings can get back 20% of their renovation costs in the form of income tax credits, as long as the buildings are put to commercial use. See "Bringing the City Back to Life," Time Magazine, November 23, 1987, pp. 72-83. See also, Kathleen Teltsch, "Sharp Drop in U.S. Aid for Housing Spurs New Push for Private Support," New York Times, Sept. 21, 1987, p. 10; and Lawrence M. Fisher, "Cities Turn Into Entrepreneurs," New York Times, Apr. 4, 1987, p. Y17.

21/ Ibid. at 74. See also, Neal R. Peirce and Carol F. Steinbach, Corrective Capitalism: The Rise of America's Community Development Corporations (Ford Foundation, New York, 1987); Ford S. Worthy, "Booming American Cities," Fortune, Aug. 17, 1987, p. 30; William E. Schmidt, "U.S. Downtowns: No Longer Downtrodden," New York Times, Oct. 11, 1987, p. 1; and William K. Stevens, "Developers Expanding Role in Social Services," New York Times, Nov. 28, 1987, p. 1.

22/ National League of Cities and the United States Conference of Mayors, Capital Budgeting and Infrastructure in American Cities: An Initial Assessment, April, 1983; U.S. Advisory Commission on Intergovernmental Relations, Public Financing of Physical Infrastructure (Washington, D.C., 1983).

23/ U.S. Department of Housing and Urban Development, The President's National Urban Policy Report 1986 (Washington, D.C.), p. 50.

Most states have developed some economic cooperative ventures,24/ using their universities and small amounts of public money to leverage private funds for new technology-based companies or stepped-up application of new technology and worker-training in old firms.25/ Massachusetts has transformed itself from a dying textile-based economy to a modern high-tech economy with low unemployment because of local-state government cooperation with business, labor and education.26/ The Massachusetts Technology Development Corporation, for example, has invested $7 million in 33 companies in 20 industries.27/ Similarly, Pennsylvania is replacing its declining steel jobs with service and manufacturing employment.28/

24/ National Governors' Association, Making America Work (Washington, D.C., 1987) and Thomas Hardy, "Governors Push Competitive Edge," The Chicago Tribune, July 29, 1987, p. 5. See also, David Osborne, Laboratories of Democracy (Harvard Business School Press, Boston, MA, 1988).

25/ David S. Broder, "Midwesterners Cite Signs of Turnaround," The Washington Post, August 21, 1985, p. A4. See also, Terry Nicholas Clark, "A New Breed of Cost-Conscious Mayors," The Wall Street Journal, June 10, 1985, p. 15; Editorial, "Leadership to the States," The Chicago Tribune, May 11, 1985, p. 24; Thomas J. Lueck, "Colleagues Help to 'Incubate' New Industry," New York Times, Dec. 3, 1984, p. A1; Robert J. Reinshuttle, Economic Development: A Survey of State Activities (Council of State Governments, Lexington, KY, 1983).

26/ See Peter T. Kilborn, "In His State's Success, Dukakis Seeks His Own," New York Times, Aug. 15, 1987, p. 11 and Matthew L. Wald, "Dukakis Role: Cheerleader or Fiscal Miracle Worker," New York Times, Nov. 26, 1987, p. 10. But see also, "A Second Look at an Economic Miracle," Newsweek, Nov. 30, 1987, p. 31.

27/ Dennis Doyle and Terry Hartle, supra Note 9.

28/ David S. Broder, "State of Economic Leadership," The Chicago Tribune, August 5, 1985, p. 12. See also, Governor George Deukmejian, "To Stimulate Economic Development" in Restoring the Balance: State Leadership for America's Future (National Governors' Association, Washington, D.C., 1988), pp. 55-64.

States also have taken major steps in international trade. Virtually all the states operate overseas trade offices, sponsor trade missions, and a few have even created export trading companies.29/ As Delaware Governor Michael Castle said during the summer of 1985, "We're looking to Washington less and less. We're taking our futures into our own hands."30/

States also have taken the lead in housing for the poor. Virtually every state has initiated new activity and expanded their commitments toward helping the poor and those with marginal income to find homes they can afford. New York, New Jersey, Connecticut, Massachusetts and other states have increased their appropriations for housing. California has earmarked money from offshore oil taxes for low-income housing. And less wealthy states have developed various other devices and innovations to provide housing assistance. For example, the Kentucky Housing Corporation has established a housing trust fund that is expected to lend nearly $1 billion at low interest rates to help low-income people buy homes; awarded a $1.24 million grant to help pay the salaries of Vietnam veterans hired by builders of low-income housing; and initiated grants to help low-income elderly homeowners make repairs to save energy.31/

In no area, however, have the governors taken the lead more dramatically than in welfare reform. In the early 80's, with encouragement from the Reagan Administration, the states began to experiment with their state's welfare programs.

29/ Dennis Doyle and Terry Hartle, supra Note 9; John M. Kline, "The Expanding International Agenda for State Governments," State Government, 1984, 57(I):2-6; see also, John M. Kline, State Government Influence in U.S. International Economic Policy (Lexington Books, Lexington, MA, 1983), pp. 53-85.

30/ David Shribman, "Governors Feel Limited by U.S. Deficit but Enjoy Freedom from Washington," The Wall Street Journal, August 6, 1985, p. 62. See also, E.J. Dionne, Jr., "Governors' Search For a New Agenda Leads to Activism," New York Times, July 28, 1987, p. 1 and David S. Broder, "Conservative and Activist Governors," The Washington Post, Feb. 25, 1987, p. A23.

31/ John Herbers, "States Forced Into Lead on Housing for Poor," New York Times, March 24, 1986, p. 1.

The governors sought to redirect welfare from a system designed originally to provide maintenance payments to women and their minor children to a new system designed to help clients move to self-sufficiency and independence. The governors reviewed state actions to see how the planning and allocation of resources could help attack the root causes of welfare dependency. Instead of being just administrators for federal Aid to Families with Dependent Children program, the states began to analyze both the characteristics of AFDC clients and the impact of AFDC on their lives. They experimented with various forms of workfare.

As former U.S. Commissioner of Welfare Robert Carleson said,

> "[Reagan] has proven that, left alone, the states can do the job for developing work programs that work and that remove families from devastating dependency. Without the shield of the federal government, either prohibiting workfare, or controlling it to death, the public pressure on states to require able-bodied recipients to earn their benefits will force those in the Welfare Establishment at the state level to create workfare that works -- or else the public will get someone else to do the job."32/

In February, 1987, the nation's governors, drawing from their various states' experiences, adopted their own welfare reform policy to turn the welfare system into a pathway to self-sufficiency and independence.33/ Their policy supports a strong child support program which enforces the belief that each parent has a responsibility to support the children he or she brought into the world. It supports a flexible employment program with a mix of services ranging from remedial education and training to child care. It supports a contract between welfare client and state agency that clarifies the responsibilities of each. It

---

32/ Robert B. Carleson, "The Welfare Reform Booby Trap," Human Events, Nov. 14, 1987, p. 5. Mr. Carleson also served as director of Social Welfare for California while Reagan was governor and as a White House aide in 19814. See also, Josh Barbanel, "New York Rolls Cut With Job Training Program," New York Times, Aug. 26, 1987, p. 14.

33/ Julie Rovner, "Governors Jump-Start Welfare Reform Drive," Congressional Quarterly, Feb. 28, 1987, p. 376; Neal R. Peirce, "Governors' Breakthrough on Welfare Reform," National Journal, March 14, 1987, p. 637.

supports a revised income assistance program based on state-specific costs of living.

In 1987, the governors' welfare reform policy moved toward congressional action. A new social contract on welfare, already validated in several states, moved toward federal enactment allowing state flexibility. The states are not following Washington, they're leading.34/

Senator Patrick Moynihan (D-NY) said in 1987 that 30 years ago welfare experts such as himself were convinced that they could not trust the state capitols. They had to go to Washington to solve the welfare mess. Today, Senator Moynihan says, he's convinced that it's Washington he can't trust. It's the states that have the answers.

"The states are now more vigorous and vibrant than at any other time since the mid-1800's," according to Professors Bowman and Kearney of the University of South Carolina.35/

Federal government austerity, guided by a president with a deep decentralist philosophy, has brought gradual fiscal federalism in the 1980's. Whether this will prove to be a current or a more lasting tide, only time will tell. Debate on the next steps of this devolution process rages on.36/ Even in the fall of 1987,

---

34/ See, for example, Joseph F. Sullivan, "Jersey Gets U.S. Waivers in Effort to Overhaul Welfare," New York Times, Oct. 25, 1987, p. 1.

35/ Ann O'M. Bowman and Richard C. Kearney, The Resurgence of the States (Prentice-Hall, Englewoods Cliffs, New Jersey, 1986), p. 250.

36/ For example, see Governor John H. Sununu, "Remarks as New NGA Chairman," Traverse City, MI, July 27, 1987; David S. Broder, "Governors' Head to Push States Veto Amendment," The Washington Post, July 28, 1987, p. 4A; William K. Stevens, "Governors Focus on State's Authority," New York Times, July 29, 1987, p. 11. See also, Daniel J. Evans and Charles S. Robb, Chairmen, The Report of the Committee on Federalism and National Purpose, To Form A More Perfect Union (National Conference on Social Welfare, Washington, D.C., 1985), Forrest Chisman and Alan Pifer, Government for the People (W.W. Norton & Co., New York, 1987), and Michael Novak and Associates, The New Consensus on Family and Welfare (American Enterprise Institute for (Cont'd)

deep into his second term, Reagan was taking further steps to strengthen federalism through a new Executive Order setting tougher standards for federal pre-emption of state laws.37/

While Ronald Reagan's most grand new federalism proposals were not adopted by Congress in total, a great deal of his decentralization efforts have successfully emerged. Undeniably, Reagan has had a profound impact on our intergovernmental system. As commentator David Broder has written, "Your mayors and city councils, your legislators and governors face a whole new world."38/ Reagan feels a federal government less intrusive in domestic affairs and state and local governments that are more active, independent and innovative is not only a "new world," but a better one. Ronald Reagan has succeeded, in large part, in achieving his dream of a more decentralized government and a reinvigorated federalism.

Public Policy Research, Washington, D.C., 1987), Bernard L. Weinstein and Harold T. Gross, Untying the Federal Knot: An Agenda for State and Local Independence (American Legislative Exchange Council, Washington, D.C., 1986); Claude E. Burfield, Rethinking Federalism (American Enterprise Institute, Washington, D.C., 1981); and Paul Peterson, Barry Rabe and Kenneth Wong, When Federalism Works (The Brookings Institution, Washington, D.C., 1986).

37/ Executive Order No. 12612, The White House, October 28, 1987. For the full text, see Appendix II. Also see, The White House, Office of Intergovernmental Affairs, "Implementation Status Report, Federalism Executive Order No. 12612," August, 1988.

38/ David S. Broder, "States, Cities Get It In the Neck," Chicago Tribune, February 10, 1986, p. 13.

APPENDIX I

THE HISTORIC EVOLUTION OF FEDERAL/STATE/LOCAL RELATIONS

During his much heralded travels and observations of the American scene in the 1830's, Alexis de Tocqueville predicted that within a century the nation would have a population of 100 million, scattered over 40 states. But of the republic, he said: "The federal government is visibly losing strength, and (its continuance) can only be a fortunate accident."[1]

Certainly, this could be a logical conclusion for an early 19th century observer. It was a time when state and local governments were expanding, while the federal government was contracting.[2]

De Tocqueville did not envision the profound changes that would occur during the next century and a half. Three decades later, the Civil War would end claims to absolute state sovereignty. The Constitution would be amended to curtail state powers, whereas by the 1830's it had only been amended to define or expand the rights of states and individuals. The agrarian society that de Tocqueville observed was fundamentally different from the industrialized nation that would begin to emerge. America grew from a mostly rural population to an urban one, causing a shift in the intergovernmental balance. The federal government would be granted new revenue sources and regulatory authority, and along with them an ability to dictate its prerogatives to states and localities. And, while the Supreme Court, prior to de Tocqueville's visit, had legitimized federal supremacy over the states in certain areas, this had been extremely modest in comparison to the activist courts of the mid-twentieth century, which endeavored to establish national government dominance over most areas of jurisprudence and social policy.

Understandably, de Tocqueville had concluded that under the Constitution, we were "... an incomplete national government,

---

[1] Cited in Paul Studenski and Herman E. Kross, _Financial History of the United States_ (McGraw Hill, New York, 1963), p. 130.

[2] During the period 1800 to 1860, municipal activities expanded tremendously, financed by increased city taxation. _Ibid._, p. 133.

which is neither exactly national, nor exactly federal."3/ This reiterated an argument by James Madison advocating ratification of the Constitution. "The proposed Constitution," he said "[is] neither a national nor a federal constitution; but a composition of both."4/

Even so, with the adoption of the Constitution in 1787, and ratification in the following year,5/ the young nation had become distinctly more national in its governance than it was under the Articles of Confederation.6/ The Articles were a reflection of the American Revolution that spawned them. They vested almost all powers in sovereign states. The purpose for declaring independence, after all, was freedom from a distant and centralized government in London.

Also, the new world was a diverse land. The northern colonists held different social, economic and religious views from the southern colonists. Life on the frontier was a world away from the Atlantic coast. Most importantly, the citizens strongly identified with the traditions of their regions and specific locales. Thus, the Articles created a very weak central government. After passing a law, Congress had no way of forcing states to comply.

By far, the most crippling aspect under the Articles was that the national government had no taxing authority. It had to rely on a system of appropriations from state legislatures. One unit of government was dependent on another for revenues. To a degree, this is true today, only in reverse. Just as states and locali-

---

3/   Alexis de Tocqueville, Democracy in America, edited by Phillips Bradley, Volume 1 (Alfred A. Knopf, New York, 1945), p. 159.

4/   Benjamin Fletcher Wright ed., The Federalist (The Belknap Press and Harvard University Press, Cambridge, Massachusetts, 1961), p. 271.

5/   Nine states were required for ratification but eventually, all thirteen states ratified. Delaware, Pennsylvania and New Jersey in 1787; Georgia, Connecticut, Massachusetts, Maryland, South Carolina, New Hampshire, Virginia and New York in 1788; North Carolina in 1789; and Rhode Island in 1790.

6/   For a general discussion, see Dictionary of American History (Revised Edition), Volume 1 (Charles Scribner's Sons, New York, 1976), pp. 197, 199.

ties in the 20th Century are burdened with unreliable funding levels for federal grants-in-aid, the national government under the Articles of Confederation operated in chronic bankruptcy. The appropriations from the states often went unpaid.7/

The problem was vividly demonstrated during the Revolutionary War years. At Valley Forge, for instance, just a few miles from the national capital of Philadelphia, Washington's troops suffered deaths from starvation and exposure. Many felt this was because the federal government could not force the states to provide promised food, material and money to support the Revolutionary armies.

With war's end came the realization by many that there was a need for a stronger central government to carry out general powers and to control foreign commerce (another power which had been prohibited to the national government under the Articles).8/ For all their differences, the citizens of the new nation had much in common. They shared European heritage and language, and having been bonded by a crisis of war, they shared a common political ideology.9/ Given the alternative of possible recolonization by Britain (or France or Spain), they preferred to share the continent.

Nevertheless, the Constitution of the United States came into being under surreptitious circumstances. Fearing that opponents of a stronger central government would sabotage a new constitution, proponents called for a convention to amend the Articles of Confederation.10/ They met in Philadelphia in 1787. On one hand, there were those, such as Patrick Henry, who felt that a fragmented government was best and favored retaining the Articles. Indeed, Henry did not go to Philadelphia because he

---

7/   Alfred H. Kelly and Winford A. Harbison, The American Constitution: Its   Origins   and   Development   (W.W. Norton and Company, Inc., 1955), pp. 101, 105.

8/   House Committee on Government Operations, The Final Report   of   the   Commission   on   Intergovernmental Relations, Pursuant to Public Law 109, 83rd Congress (GOP, House Document No. 198, 84th Congress, 1st session, Washington, D.C., June 28, 1955), p. 10.

9/   The Encyclopedia Americana, op. cit., p. 412.

10/   Herbert J. Storing, What the Anti-Federalists Were For (The University of Chicago Press, Chicago and London, 1981), p. 7.

said he "smelled a rat."11/ The anti-federalists saw a strong national government as threatening to four cherished values: law, political stability, the principles of the Declaration of Independence, and federalism.12/ Richard Henry Lee of Virginia, a major force behind the movement for independence, wrote that so vast and various a territory as the United States "cannot be governed in freedom" except in a confederation of states.13/

On the other end of the spectrum there were a few, such as Alexander Hamilton, who believed there should be a unitary authority. Hamilton wished to abolish the states as autonomous entities, and appoint governors from the nation's capital.14/ In the end, a new constitution was adopted, and its overriding theme was compromise. Sovereign states had entrusted many more powers to the national government; but they had created a system of checks and balances to disperse power,15/ and they had made it clear

---

11/ "Far from straying from the principles of the American revolution as some of the Federalists accused them of doing, the Anti-Federalists saw themselves as the true defenders of those principles. 'I am fearful,' said Patrick Henry, 'I have lived long enough to become an old fashioned fellow: Perhaps an invincible attachment to the dearest rights of man may, in these refined enlightened days, be deemed old fashioned. If so, I am content to be so: I say, the time has been, when every pore of my heart beat for American liberty, and which, I believed, had a counterpart in the breast of every true American.'" Ibid., p. 8.

12/ Ibid., p. 7.

13/ Ibid., pp. 16-17.

14/ House Committee on Government Operations, Report of the Commission on Intergovernmental Relations, op. cit., p. 10.

15/ John Adams counted eight explicit balancing mechanisms and proudly proclaimed them as evidence of the Constitution's republican virtue. These instances of government branches checking one another were as follows: (1) the states v. the central government, (2) the House v. the Senate, (3) the President v. Congress, (4) the courts v. Congress, (5) the Senate v. the President, (6) the people v. their representatives, (7) the state legislatures v. the Senate (in the original election of senators), and (8) the Electoral College v. the people.

that they were retaining vast areas of authority for ...
selves. It was understood by the delegates that the Constitution
would soon be amended with a Bill of Rights, one of which, the
Tenth Amendment, states: "The powers not delegated to the United
States by the Constitution, nor prohibited by it to the states
are reserved to the states respectively, or to the people."16/

With adoption, the Constitution was sent to the states with no
assurance of ratification. Hamilton conceived the idea of pub-
lishing essays in New York newspapers to champion its virtues,
and solicited James Madison of Virginia, who had been instrumental in drafting the document, and John Jay of New York as collab-
orators. Collectively, these essays become known as The
Federalist Papers,17/ and they endure today as a major work of
political science. Throughout the essays, the Constitution's
characteristics of compromise and dispersal of power were trumpeted. Said Hamilton in Federalist #9:

> The proposed Constitution, far from implying an aboli-
> tion of the state governments ... leaves in their
> possession certain exclusive and very important por-
> tions of sovereign power. This fully corresponds, in
> every rational impart of the terms, with the idea of a
> federal government.18/

Said Madison in #10:

> The federal Constitution forms a happy combination in
> this respect; the great and aggregate interests being
> referred to the national, the local and particular to
> the state legislatures.19/

Surely, this ambiguity must have presented a dilemma for our
early presidents. George Washington had commanded the
Continental Army under proposition that "these united colonies

---

16/ Twelve amendments were adopted by Congress and sent to
     the states on September 25, 1789. Ten were ultimately
     ratified and enacted on December 15, 1791.

17/ Alexander Hamilton, James Madison and John Jay, The
     Federalist Papers (The New Americana Literary, Inc.,
     New York, 1961).

18/ Ibid., p. 71.

19/ Ibid., p. 77.

are, and of right, ought to be free and independent states."20/
Many took that quite literally in 1794.

Yet President Washington did not hesitate to send federal troops
to quiet the Pennsylvania Whiskey Rebellion.21/ His action reinforced the right of the federal government to impose levies -- in
this case on spirits -- and is generally considered the first
effort by the national government to establish its authority
within the states.

Future presidents likewise learned to accept the ambiguities of
the Constitution and base their policies on pragmatism. The
Louisiana Purchase was a major case in point. Having no specific
authority -- yet no specific prohibition either -- Thomas
Jefferson weighed the constitutionality of using federal money to
acquire lands. Faced with the opportunity to double the size of
the nation at very modest cost, Jefferson bought. Further, in
his second inaugural address, Jefferson advocated a
Constitutional amendment specifically permitting the use of federal funds for "internal improvements" within the states.22/

Jefferson's two immediate successors in office, Madison and
Monroe, cited a lack of constitutional authority for federal
funds to be used for internal improvements.23/ But the legisla-

---

20/ Richard Henry Lee of Virginia, Resolution proposed at
the Continental Congress in Philadelphia, June 7,
1776: "Resolved that these united colonies are, and
of right ought to be, free and independent states."

21/ For general discussion on the Whiskey Rebellion, see
Samuel Elliot Morison, Henry Steele Commager and
William E. Leuchtenburg, A Concise History of the
American Republic (New York: Oxford Press, 1977), pp.
138-139.

22/ Jefferson's Second Inaugural Address given March 4,
1805. For full text see Saul K. Padover, The Complete
Jefferson (Duell, Sloan and Pearce, Inc., New York,
1943), pp. 410-415.

23/ James Madison, while in the Virginia legislature, went
so far as to express in legislative language the right
of a state to "impose its sovereignty" between the
laws of the national government and the citizens of
the states. Virginia Commission on Constitutional
Government, We the States: An Anthology of Historic
Documents and Commentaries Thereon Expanding the State
(Cont'd)

tive and judicial branches of the federal government were going in the opposite direction.

As early as 1790, the pattern of assistance to states and localities was developing with Congress decreeing that the federal government assume the Revolutionary War debt.24/ The prime proponent was Alexander Hamilton, who viewed it "as a centralizing force that would focus attention and loyalty on the central government, away from the states."25/ That is undoubtedly why the action did not happen without what Thomas Jefferson called "the most bitter and angry contest ever known in Congress before or since the union of the states."26/

Hamilton's zeal in promoting the national government over the states was understandable. He had been the Receiver of Continental Taxes during the Revolution and it was his frustrating responsibility to finance the war through the unreliable appropriations from state legislatures. But for another man who was to play a monumental role in defining the powers of the new national government, the war experience had been even more vivid. Young John Marshall had been a captain under George Washington during that excruciating winter at Valley Forge. And, some twenty-odd years later, he became the Chief Justice of the United States. Under him, the Supreme Court took major strides in establishing federal jurisdiction over the states.27/

The most encompassing decision over state sovereignty was the 1819 case of McCulloch v. Maryland.28/ The Court ruled unanimously against the authority of the state to regulate or tax a federally chartered corporation. It determined that the central

---

and Federal Relationship, (Byrd Press, Richmond, VA, 1964), pp. 143-156.

24/ August 4, 1790, Statutes at Large, Chapter 31, Vol. 1, p. 138.

25/ Sandia S. Osbourn, "Federalism: Key Episode in the American Federal System," Congressional Research Service, Report No. 82-139 (GPO, Washington, D.C. August 16, 1982), p. 15.

26/ Thomas Jefferson, "The Hamiltonian System," The Annals, Volume 3, p. 419.

27/ Warren E. Burger, remarks to the American Law Institute, op. cit., p. 5.

28/ 4 Wheat 316 (1819).

government was dominant over the states within its allotted sphere. McCulloch also established the supremacy of federal laws and the doctrine of implied powers that Congress had the discretion to pass laws under the "necessary and proper" clause of the Constitution.29/ This was just part of a consistent pattern that was being established by the Marshall Court.

In the 1803 case of Marbury v. Madison,30/ Marshall had promulgated the doctrine of judicial review. He asserted that it was the power and duty of the judiciary to determine what a law means when questions are raised in proper cases. In Fletcher v. Peck,31/ and Dartmouth College v. Woodward,32/ the Marshall Court held that the Constitution forbids a state to impair the obligation of contracts. In Martin v. Hunter's Lessee 33/ and Cohens

---

29/ Article 1, Section 8: "The Congress shall have the power... to make all laws which shall be necessary and proper for conveying into execution the foregoing powers, and all other powers vested by this Constitution in the government of the United States, or in any department or office thereof."

30/ 1 Cranch 138 (1803).

31/ 6 Cranch 61 (1809). (Peck sold Fletcher a piece of land in Georgia. In his deed, Fletcher states that the State was at the time passing an act to preempt their contract and sell the land itself.)

32/ 4 Wheat 519 (1819). (The British Crown granted a charter to Dartmouth College in 1769 which was not dissolved by the Revolution. The New Hampshire State Legislature altered the charter without the consent of Dartmouth, which was considered a private corporation.)

33/ 1 Wheat 304 (1816). (The case involved a long-running dispute over ownership of a large tract of land known as the Northern Neck of Virginia. In 1813, the Court considered the case, deciding in favor of the British claim to the land, rejecting a Virginian's claim. The Virginia courts refused to obey the decision, ruling that the Supreme Court could not constitutionally tell a state court what to do. The Supreme Court overruled the Virginia courts in 1816.)

v. Virginia,34/ it upheld the constitutionality of the Judiciary Act of 1789,35/ under which the Court was empowered to review, and affirm or reverse, the rulings of state courts denying federal claims. In Oshorn v. Bank of the United States,36/ the court upheld the right of the Bank of the United States to sue state officials in federal court -- despite the fact that an eleventh amendment had been added to the Constitution with the purpose of keeping suits between states and their citizens out of federal court.

These court actions were the product of a Constitution that failed to address the tensions between units of government. Neither did the Constitution settle the question of slavery -- a specific and passionate issue under the overall question of state sovereignty. The Civil War, of course, ended slavery. But it also crossed a threshold on the state sovereignty question. That war determined that states were to obey federal laws and could not secede. As Abraham Lincoln said in his first inaugural address, "...no state upon its own mere motion can lawfully get out of the Union... I trust this will not be regarded as a menace, but only as the declared purpose of the Union that it will constitutionally defend and maintain itself."37/

With the questions of slavery and union preservation resolved, however, intergovernmental discord continued. Today it is evidenced by the overloaded system of federal grants and revenue usurpation by the national government. Perhaps coincidentally,

---

34/ 6 Wheat 264 (1821). (Virginia brought suit against P.J. and M.J. Cohens for the sale of the National Lottery tickets, lotteries being illegal in Virginia. The drawing was to be held in the City of Washington in the District of Columbia where lotteries were permissible, but the State alleged that the sale occurred in Norfolk, Virginia and came under state law.)

35/ 1 Stat. 73 (1850).

36/ 9 Wheat 738 (1824). (The Ohio State Legislature passed a law to collect taxes from all banks, individuals, and companies that conducted banking business in Ohio. The State auditor brought suit against the Bank of the United States for not paying taxes according to the state law.)

37/ Whitehall Company, The Presidents ... Their Inaugural Addresses (Whitehall Company, Chicago, 1968), p. 122.

the first traces of these problems appeared during the Civil War period.

The Morrill Act of 1862, providing land grants for states to establish colleges, represented a fundamental change in the philosophy of federal grants.38/ Whereas previous grants had come with few restrictions, the Morrill Act dictated land use, stipulated that curriculum be kept within five broad areas,39/ and had reporting requirements for programs and finances.

Many historians trace the origins of federal grants to 1803 when Congress enacted legislation earmarking three percent of proceeds from the sale of public lands for distribution to Ohio to build roads, and $1.25 million from land sales to Georgia to do with as it pleased.40/ This "no strings attached" attitude remained essentially intact throughout succeeding Congresses leading to the Civil War. In 1836, for example, Arkansas, Michigan and Alabama were awarded five percent from the proceeds of public land sales for their respective legislatures to appropriate as they saw fit for roads and canals.41/

After the Morrill Act, direct federal grant programs began to emerge in the early 1900's. In most cases, they addressed truly national needs, but there was an increasing tendency toward allocating funds for specific purposes. By the 1960's and 1970's, grants would mushroom and come attached with a dizzying array of regulations, mandates, entitlements, and legal requirements on how the money was to be spent.

On the revenue side, the Civil War saw the enactment of the first federal personal income tax.42/ After a confrontation over the

---

38/   July 2, 1862, Chapter 130, Vol. 12, Stat., p. 503.

39/   Subject areas were: Military Tactics, Agriculture, Military Arts, Scientific and Classical studies.

40/   March 3, 1803, Chapter 21, Vol. 2, Stat., pp. 225-226, Section 2; and March 3, 1803, Chapter 26, Vol. 2, Stat., pp. 222, 235, Section 16, respectively.

41/   June 23, 1836, Chapter 120 Vol. 5, Stat., p. 58, Section 3; June 23, 1836, Chapter 121 Vol. 5, Stat., pp. 59-60, Section 5; and July 4, 1836, Chapter 355 Vol. 5, Stat., p. 113, Section 3, respectively.

42/   Edwin R.A. Seligman, The Income Tax (MacMillan Company, New York, 1921), pp. 435, 449.

constitutionality of the federal government collecting this tax, succeeding wars would help in causing its expansion, and it would grow to become, by far, the most important revenue source for the national treasury. The federal government could not have grown so immense today, proliferating grants impinging on traditional areas of state and local governments, had it not been for this new revenue source.

* * * * *

In the post-Civil War period, however, the evolution of the American federal system was most fundamentally altered by Constitutional amendment. The 13th, 14th and 15th amendments of Reconstruction marked the first time that the Constitution was altered to contract the rights of the states.43/ The Bill of Rights was designed to protect individuals and states from actions by the national government, the 11th amendment was in a similar vein,44/ and the 12th amendment was merely procedural regarding the election of President and Vice President.

Of these, the 14th amendment proved to be the most important -- in fact, it could be the most important Constitutional provision ever. To greatly simplify this multifaceted amendment, it had two intents: 1) to politically reconstruct (many would say punish) the South;45/ and 2) to overturn the Supreme Court's Dred

---

43/   The 13th Amendment outlawed slavery and the 15th Amendment gave the freed men the right to vote. See footnote 45 on the 14th Amendment.

44/   The 11th Amendment was designed to keep suits between citizens and states out of federal court. It was ratified on February 7, 1795.

45/   Section 2 of the Amendment provided enumeration of all males over 21 ("excluding Indians not taxed") on an equal basis. This reversed part of Article 1, Section 2 of the Constitution in which slaves were counted as three-fifths of a person for purposes of representation and taxation. Section 3 of the Amendment barred officials of states which had rebelled from holding any public office, unless the disability was removed by two-thirds vote of Congress. Section 4 of the Amendment prohibited the payment by the federal gov-
(Cont'd)

Scott decision and grant citizenship to the freed men.46/ As part of the citizenship provision, Section 1 prohibited the states from abridging "the privileges or immunities of citizens...," denying "equal protection of the laws," or depriving "any person of life, liberty, or property, without due process of law."

Proponents of the 14th Amendment could not have imagined its long-term effects. In the 1940's, 1950's and especially the 1960's, the federal judiciary used it to expand the scope of its authority over a vast array of state affairs that were totally unrelated to the original purpose of the amendment.47/ Even in the short term, the intent of the amendment was grossly distorted. By the late nineteenth and early twentieth centuries, it was revolutionizing the meaning of due process48/ and being used to protect the interests of corporations.49/ In a sense this was consistent with the times. The industrialization of America had begun, and with it would come a convolution of social and econom-

---

ernment or any state of "any debt or obligation incurred in aid of insurrection or rebellion against the United States." This included pensions for Confederate soldiers.

46/ Scott v. Sandford, 19 How. 393 (1857).

47/ See Gideon v. Wainwright, 372 U.S. 335 (1963) (The Court held that the due process clause of the Fourteenth Amendment extended to state as well as federal defendants the Sixth Amendment guarantee that all persons charged with serious crimes will be provided the aid of an attorney). See also Malory v. Hogan, 378 U.S. 1 (1964) (The Court held that the Fifth Amendment provision against self-incrimination is extended to state defendants through the due process clause of the Fourteenth Amendment). See also Pointer v. Texas, 380 U.S. 400 (1965) (The Court held that the Sixth Amendment guarantee of the right to confront and cross-examine witnesses is applied to state defendants by the Fourteenth Amendment's due process clause).

48/ See generally Raoul Berger, Government by the Judiciary: The Transformation of the Fourteenth Amendment (1977).

49/ See San Mateo County v. Southern Pacific R.R., 116 U.S. 138 (1883); and Santa Clara County v. Southern Pacific R.R., 118 U.S. 394 (1886).

ic changes fostering sweeping realignments in intergovernmental balance.

The great corporate empires of the late 1800's outgrew the juris-dictions of their home states, opening the question of national responsibility in interstate commerce.50/   Industrialization encouraged urban growth. As the cities grew, so did city govern-ments. Because city voters heavily influenced state and national elections, urbanization added to the scope and complexity of both national and state responsibilities.51/ Most importantly, the excesses of the Robber Barons of industry -- and the personal fortunes being amassed by the few at the expense of the many -- led to a backlash of social reform52/ and launched the Progressive Era.

The Interstate Commerce Act of 1887 and the Sherman Antitrust Act of 1890 were the beginnings of national regulation. The creation of two new federal departments -- Commerce and Labor -- estab-lished a bureaucracy with muscle to enforce congressional will. And, taxes began to shift from those based on consumption (tar-iff) toward those based on wealth (the income tax).

The income tax imposed during the Civil War, while first ruled constitutional by the Supreme Court,53/ was later declared uncon-stitutional.54/ The basis of contention was the Constitution's clause that "the Congress shall have power to lay and collect taxes, duties, imposts and excise, to pay the debts and provide for the general welfare of the United States; but all duties,

---

50/ House Committee on Government Operations, Report of The Commission on Intergovernmental Relations, op. cit., p. 14.

51/ Ibid., p. 15.

52/ For a general discussion, see Mathew Josephson, The Robber Barons (Harcourt, Brace and Company, New York, 1934).

53/ The tax had been repealed in 1872. It was not until 1880 that the Supreme Court in Springer v. United States unanimously decided that the income tax was not a direct tax and therefore not unconstitutional.

54/ The Wilson-Gorman Act of 1894 established a new income tax, but the Supreme Court declared it unconstitution-al the next year in Pollack v. Farmers Loan and Trust Company.

imposts, and excises shall be uniform throughout the United States." (emphasis added) That meant uniform not on individuals, but on the amount extracted from each state. It was a recognition of the right of each state to control its own resources. An income tax is not uniform. There is a disparity of collections among states because of income distribution. Other clauses in the Constitution likewise supported the contention that a direct tax like that on incomes was reserved to the states.55/

After much court action -- and congressional and national debate -- the issue was finally settled by adoption and ratification of the 16th amendment in 1913.56/ It said: "The Congress shall have power to lay and collect taxes on incomes, from whatever source derived, without apportionment among the several states..."

The final amendment of the era was the 17th. Also an outgrowth of the progressive movement (ratified two months after the 16th), it provided for the popular election of U.S. Senators. Under the Constitution, members of the Upper House were to be elected by state legislatures. While not as important as the 14th and 16th Amendments in its long term effect of shifting powers in the federal system, it did eliminate one of the checks and balances embodies in the Constitution -- the states versus the Congress. Senators were no longer responsible to the institutional structure of state governments.57/

By close of World War I, the federal government was in a position to assert its dominance over the states. The war had catapulted America onto the world scene, and vastly expanded the ranks in Washington. Federal regulatory activity had been legitimized. Constitutional changes had occurred, enabling the federal judiciary to involve itself in state affairs. A demographic shift had made cities entities unto themselves, rather than just creatures of states. Washington was setting national program priorities through a pattern of grants-in-aid and a vast pool of revenue sources had been opened to the federal treasury. With the next

---

55/ See Kelly and Harbison, The American Constitution: Its Origins and Development, op. cit.

56/ For a general discussion, see John D. Buenken, "The Ratification of the Federal Income Tax Amendment," Cato Journal (The Cato Institute, Spring 1981), pp. 161, 182.

57/ See James M. Beck, The Vanishing Rights of the States, (George H. Doran Company, New York, 1926).

crisis, it was inevitable that the national government would claim new responsibilities, powers and authority. The Great Depression would usher in a new era for American federalism.

* * * *

Federal aid funds to other political jurisdictions quadrupled between 1932 and 1934,58/ and not-too-gradually, the welfare of the individual American was perceived to be the concern of the federal government. The steady growth and centralizing trend continued throughout President Roosevelt's Administration.

While the country had gone through many economic panics before, the Great Depression vividly demonstrated that many problems could not be solved by states acting alone.59/ In the 1930's, "the states lost their confidence, and the people lost faith in the states."60/ The attitude of the Roosevelt Administration was perhaps best described by one of its members, emeritus professor of Political Science at Harvard University, Samuel Beer: "I vividly recall our preoccupation with persuading people to look to Washington for the solution to problems and our sense of what a great change in public attitude this involves."61/

While governor of New York, however, Franklin Roosevelt had emphasized the ability of the states to help solve the problems wrought by the Depression. On the second working day of his Presidency, he called a meeting at the White House with a bipartisan group of 20 governors and 11 governors' representa-

---

58/ They went from $232 million in the last year of the Hoover Administration to more than $1 billion in the second year of the Roosevelt Administration.

59/ House Committee on Government Operations, Report of Commission on Intergovernmental Relations, op. cit., p. 14.

60/ Terry Sanford, Storm Over the States, (McGraw Hill Book Company, New York, 1967), p. 21.

61/ Cited in Deil S. Wright, "New Federalism: Recent Varieties of an Older Species," draft of an article for a symposium on federalism in the American Review of Public Administration, July, 1982, p. 4.

tives.62/ His plea for state executive cooperation in combating the crisis at hand shifted the governors from their traditional mode of being "firmly fixed against collective action."63/ By unanimous resolution, the governors pledged cooperation with the President. Bringing the governors together also helped Roosevelt "rally public support for his Administration," and "most important for the governors, Roosevelt was offering the state executives a role in the greatness of the times."64/ Indeed, governors were instrumental during the dramatic events of the early days of the New Deal. Concurrently, the 1930's brought about a rapid increase in the federal-city relationship. Because states and municipalities had their revenue raising capacity crippled by economic hard times, localities formed an axis with the federal government.65/

During the New Deal era, the Supreme Court began interpreting the Constitution more broadly, thereby giving credence to the federal government's involvement in managing the economy, and providing grants-in-aid to state and local governments. In 1934, the Federal Housing Administration was created to provide middle-income families greater access to home mortgages. The government, for the first time, became involved in economic development through the creation of the Tennessee Valley Authority and the Rural Electrification Administration. As a result of new programs in the areas of slum clearance, public housing, public works, and job creation, it soon became accepted that public welfare was a federal responsibility.66/ During the 1930's, federal domestic spending67/ increased more than sixfold -- from

---

62/ Glenn E. Brooks, When Governors Convene (Johns Hopkins University Press, Baltimore, 1962), p. 30.

63/ Ibid., p. 31.

64/ Ibid.

65/ Larry Sabato, Goodbye to Goodtime Charlie (Lexington Books, Lexington, Massachusetts, 1978), p. 185.

66/ James L. Sundquist, Making Federalism Work (The Brookings Institution, Washington, D.C., 1969), p. 7.

67/ Excludes major national security, international affairs and finance, veterans service, and benefits, and interest on the national debt.

1.2% of gross national product to 7.1%.68/ Federal aid to state and local governments rose from $100 million in 1929 to $1 billion in 1939.69/ Expansion continued after World War II. The Employment Act of 1946 gave permanence to the federal role in public welfare. And, with the 1949 urban renewal program came even broader support for enlarging the federal role in urban affairs.

While the Supreme Court's broadened interpretation of the Constitution was an impetus to the expanding role of the federal government, an even greater impetus was the unification of the nation's mayors.

An an outgrowth of the crisis of shrinking revenues in cities, the U.S. Conference of Mayors was formed in 1932. It was to be a clearinghouse and forum for mayors to exchange information on ways their cities were coping with the effects of the Depression. While mayors previously had made sporadic efforts to unite for common causes, the Conference would have a lasting impact on Washington and its attitude toward cities. Quickly, the mayors became an effective voice and were able to convince, not only the Executive branch, but also the Congress of the need for federal aid to the cities.

Twenty-five years later, the nation's counties would learn from the mayors that they too could have an impact on Washington. In 1957, the National Association of Counties was formed to represent the nation's counties and to get their "fair share" of the federal pie. Public interest groups representing state entities did the same, and this furthered the trend toward a centralized government. States and cities thus formed lobbying arms in Washington in order to solve their problems.

* * * *

Financing of the New Deal set a precedent for yet another lucrative revenue source for the federal government -- deficit spending. The practice was advanced by the new economic theories of

---

68/ U.S. Bureau of the Census, Historical Statistics of the United States, Colonial Times to 1970 (Washington, D.C. 1975), pp. 224, 1115.

69/ Ibid., p. 1125.

John Maynard Keynes, and President Roosevelt justified the national debt by saying "we only owe it to ourselves." The federal income tax, however, had not been extensively used. As late as 1939, only five percent of the population paid income taxes.70/ For one thing, per capita income dropped from $698 to $553 during the 1930's.71/ Also, the income taxes being imposed adhered to the understanding surrounding adoption and ratification of the 16th amendment that "only the rich will pay."72/ The first income tax law of 1913 applied to only the wealthiest 3% of the population, and the rate was a mere 1%. The tax was slightly progressive, but even at the very pinnacle of wealth, the total levy was only 7%.73/

Even those incredibly low rates -- by today's standards -- were cause for concern by those who worried about the effect of a federal income tax on state and local governments. The professor of public finance at Harvard University at the time, Charles J. Bullock, called the maximum rates "clearly excessive." He wrote that "as the experience of all countries shows ... the limit of safety for income taxation is probably ten percent." Because the federal government of 1913 had set a 7% marginal tax rate, "the United States has appropriated 70% of the total possible proceeds of direct taxation on large incomes," Professor Bullock projected. He concluded that "Congress has acted with a total disregard of the interests of the states, and apparently on the assumption that only the claims of the federal treasury require consideration."74/

With the crisis of World War II, the needs of the federal treasury became paramount, and the income tax would be universal-

---

70/ Richard Goode, The Individual Income Tax (The Brookings Institution, Washington, D.C., 1976), p. e.

71/ Internal Revenue Service, Statistics of Income.

72/ Buenker, The Ratification of the Federal Income Tax Amendment, op. cit., p. 183.

73/ Richard Goode, The Individual Income Tax, op. cit. pp. 3, 4. See also, Bob Gleason, "When the States Gave the Income Tax to the Federal Government," Intergovernmental Perspective, Fall, 1985, pp. 10-12.

74/ Charles J. Bullock, The Federal Income Tax, Proceedings of the Eighth Annual Conference Under the Auspices of the National Tax Association, Madison, Wisconsin, 1915.

ized. By 1945, the percentage of the population covered by the federal income tax was 74.2%.75/ This, too, was in keeping with one of the philosophies behind the 16th amendment -- that the income tax be imposed in times of national emergency. While the percentage of the population paying the tax dipped slightly after the war (to 58.9% in 1950), it gradually rose again. By the close of the 1970's, well over three-fourths of the population were required to pay the tax.76/

By the time World War II ended, the federal government was relying on the income tax as a primary revenue base, and added the new "fundraising" mechanism of deficit spending. Over the next three decades, this would squeeze out the revenue raising capacities of states and localities, as there is a finite revenue pool for governments in general. States and localities would grow even more dependent on the federal largess. World War II caused a burst of growth in the bureaucracy, and a vast centralization of power along the banks of the Potomac. Washington's grip on the public agenda was strengthened by weakened state governments in the aftermath of the Depression. One author wrote in 1949 that:

> "State government is the tawdriest, most incompetent, and most stultifying unit of the nation's political structure. In state governments are to be found in their most extreme and vicious forms of all the worst evils of misrule in the country. Further, embedded between the municipalities at the bottom and the federal system on top, state government is the wellspring of many of the principal poisons that plague both."77/

States were also characterized as corrupt, and ignorant of social needs.78/ State legislatures were malapportioned, causing unjust representation. The governors being elected were considered "second rate politicians." At the same time,79/ states were actively and adamantly seeking federal aid.

75/ Goode, The Individual Income Tax, op. cit., p. 4.

76/ Ibid.

77/ Robert S. Allen, (ed.), Our Sovereign State (Vanguard Press, New York), 1949, p. vii.

78/ Sabato, Goodtime Charlie, op. cit., p. 7.

79/ Harold J. Laski, The American Democracy: A Commentary and an Interpretation (Allen and Unwin, London 1949), p. 146.

President Eisenhower was deeply troubled by this trend and at the 1957 National Governors' Conference he admonished the state executives. He said:

"Every state failure to meet a pressing public need has created the opportunity, developed the excuse, and fed the temptation for the national government to poach on the states' preserves... Opposed though I am to needless federal expansion, since 1953 I have found it necessary to urge federal action in some areas traditionally reserved to the states. In each instance, state inaction, or inadequate national need, has forced emergency federal intervention."80/

His tone was in stark contrast to when he had first spoken to the Governors' Conference in 1953. He then said:

"I am here because of my indestructible conviction that unless we preserve, in this country, the place of the state government, its traditional place -- with the power, the authority, the responsibilities, and the revenue necessary to discharge those responsibilities, then we are not going to have an America as we have known it; we will have some other form of government."81/

Also in 1953, Eisenhower established the Commission on Intergovernmental Relations (commonly referred to as the Kestnbaum Commission after its chairman) to study the problem of imbalance in the federal system. This led to formation of the Advisory Commission on Intergovernmental Relations -- an organization which exists today, providing important research for federal, state and local officials. The Kestnbaum Commission issued its report in June of 1955, concluding that the country should:

"Leave to private initiative all the functions that citizens can perform privately; use the level of government closest to the community for all public functions it can handle; utilize cooperative intergovernmental arrangements where appropriate to attain econo-

---

80/ President Dwight D. Eisenhower, Address to The National Governors' Conference, Williamsburg, Virginia, June 24, 1957.

81/ President Dwight D. Eisenhower, Remarks at the Governor's Conference, Seattle, Washington, August 4, 1953.

mical performance and popular approval; reserve national action for residual participation where state and local governments are not fully adequate, and for the continuing responsibilities that only the national government can undertake."82/

Eisenhower also appointed a high level staff aide to attempt to realign federal-state relations. His call to the governors was to join the federal administration in devising an action plan with three responsibilities:

(1) To designate functions which the states are ready and willing to assume and finance that are now per-formed or financed wholly or in part by the federal government; (2) to recommend the federal-state reve-nue adjustments required to enable the states to as-sume such functions; (3) to identify functions and responsibilities likely to require state or federal attention in the future and to recommend the level of state effort, or federal effort, or both, that will be needed to assure effective action.83/

Notwithstanding Eisenhower's efforts and admonishments, he was not very successful at returning power to the states, and the events to unfold after he left office would far over-shadow all the centralization that had occurred to date. The growth of grants-in-aid would be explosive, matched by the growth in reve-nue usurpation, and the federal judiciary would batter the prin-ciple of federalism and separation of powers. As in earlier times, the issue of equitable balance in our federal system would be caught up in a swirl of socioeconomic forces. The New Frontier and Great Society would usher in an era of frantic so-cial engineering.

* * * *

82/ The Commission on Intergovernmental Relations, A Report to the President for Transmittal to the Congress, June, 1955.

83/ Carol S. Weissert, "Significant Developments in Federal-State Relations," Book of States, 1976-1977, Council of State Governments.

-223-

In 1953, President Eisenhower had appointed Earl Warren as Chief Justice of the United States. And for the next 16 years, the Warren Court would redo the landscape of American jurisprudence. Deeply affected were the operations of state and local governments.

In <u>Gideon v. Wainwright</u> (1963),<u>84</u>/ for example, the Court held that the due process clause of the Fourteenth Amendment extended to state as well as federal defendants the Sixth Amendment's guarantee that all persons charged with serious crimes will be provided the aid of an attorney. In <u>Malloy v. Hogan</u> (1964),<u>85</u>/ the Court held that the Fifth Amendment provision against self-incrimination is extended to state defendants through the due process clause of the Fourteenth Amendment. And in <u>Painter v. Texas</u> (1965),<u>86</u>/ the Court held that the Sixth Amendment guarantee of the right to confront and cross-examine witnesses is applied to state defendants by the Fourteenth Amendment's due process clause. As Professor Philip B. Kurland said, "If the road to hell is paved with good intentions, then the Warren Court was the greatest road builder of all time."<u>87</u>/

The attitude was mirrored by the executive and legislative branches of the federal government. It was perhaps best described by Theodore White in his 1982 publication, <u>America In Search of Itself</u>.

> "Each program was pressed through Congress in the name of virtue. No single program could be denounced, vetoed, or buried in committee without the objectors being shamed for their indifference to the call of conscience. Who, for example, could turn his back on the distress of the handicapped -- and if a regulation under the Rehabilitation Act of 1973 required that all mass transit systems (which drew money from the Federal Mass Transit Act) provide ramps, wheelchair lifts, and special aids for the handicapped, who would quibble about what it might cost? Who could object to scholarship loans to college students? Or object to a national recognition of the contribution of artists,

---

<u>84</u>/   372 U.S. 335.

<u>85</u>/   378 U.S. 1.

<u>86</u>/   380 U.S. 400.

<u>87</u>/   Philip B. Kurland, "Earl Warren, The Warren Court, and Warren Myths," 67 Mich. L. Rev. 353, 357, (1968).

writers, musicians, orchestras, dramatists, dancers, actors, to the nation's well-being? Or object to a program to cure narcotics addicts? Or object to the full, final equality to be granted to blacks and other minorities? Who had the courage to choose among all the calls of virtue and goodwill? And Congress, for almost twenty years, chose not to choose, but to enact them all."88/

So the Congress was asserting the national government's authority in an astonishing array of areas traditionally under the purview of state and local governments. By its very name, the Great Society was to be national. There were not to be 50 Great Societies existing in the states, but a Washington-led social revolution.

In a sense, the federal system was becoming, de facto, what Alexander Hamilton had advocated. The states and localities were being stripped of their autonomy, and their elected officials were becoming mere administrative agents for programs instituted by Washington.89/

Federal grants-in-aid -- with their strings attached -- induced state and local governments to solve social problems brought to national attention, like civil rights, poverty, urban unrest, and environmental concerns. No matter how intrinsically state or local the problem, evidence that it was common and widespread was

---

88/ Theodore White, America In Search of Itself, (Harper and Row, New York, 1982), pp. 103, 136.

89/ According to James L. Sundquist, a Senior Fellow at the Brookings Institution, during the Johnson Years:

"...the American federal system entered a new phase. Through a series of dramatic enactments, the Congress asserted the national interest and authority in a wide range of governmental functions that until then had been the province, exclusively or predominantly, of state and local governments... The dramatic expansion of the range of concern of the federal government in the 1960's can be seen as the elimination of an historic trend -- the final burial, perhaps, of traditional doctrines of American federalism that, for a long time, had been dying hard."

See Advisory Commission on Intergovernmental Relations, "A Crisis of Competence," Report No. A-77 (GPO, Washington, D.C., 1981), p. 27.

-225-

"seen as" sufficient justification for federal action. Increasingly, state and local officials looked to Washington for leadership and the resources to deal with nearly every problem from rat control to sewer extensions.

Despite the efforts of Presidents Nixon and Ford to limit the strings attached to federal aid -- through revenue sharing and block grants -- categorical programs proliferated throughout the 1970's. In 1960 there had been approximately 50 categorical programs. By 1970 there were 132, and by 1980 there were over 500. The dollar amount exploded from $7 billion to $95 billion between 1960 and 1980.

Beyond doubt, the dramatic shift in power had been made possible through two financing mechanisms that did not exist at the founding of the republic and thus were not embedded in the Constitution: deficit spending and the income tax. During the 1960's and 1970's, the budget had only one surplus (1969).90/ And, by 1980, the income tax accounted for 60% of all federal receipts91/ -- 78% when social security (a tax on income) is included.92/ As a 1982 report by the Congressional Research Service stated: "If grants-in-aid are the engine that drives the modern federal system, the federal income tax is the fuel that powers it."93/

The federal government's massive growth had its roots in the 1960's and early 1970's period of high economic prosperity. The proliferation of government spending, however, continued long after our ability to finance programs had undergone dramatic change.94/ Demographically, our population grew older.95/ The

---

90/ Office of Management and Budget, Budget of the United States Government, Fiscal Year 1984, pp. 9-55.

91/ Corporate income taxes are included in this figure, and account for approximately 13% of the total.

92/ Office of Management and Budget, Budget of the United States Government, Fiscal Year 1984, op. cit., pp. 9-40.

93/ Oshourn, "Federalism," op. cit., p. 33.

94/ Susannah Caulkins and John Shannon, "The New Formula for Fiscal Federalism: Austerity Equals Decentralization," Intergovernmental Perspective (Advisory Commission on Intergovernmental Relations, Washington, D.C., Winter 1981, Vol. 8 No. 1), pp. 23, 29.

(Cont'd)

post-World War II baby boom began to approach middle-age, and the wonders of modern medicine increased life expectancy. This shifted demand in what services people want -- particularly toward Social Security.96/ The claim of entitlement programs on gross national product rose by two-thirds during the 1970's -- from 6% to 10% of GNP.97/ Overall, non-defense claims expanded by 50% -- from 12% to 18% of GNP.98/ Real growth in government continued even though the economy had gone from real growth to inflation-related artificial growth. The federal government was no longer feeding off a bigger economic pie, it was diverting huge amounts of money from the private sector, mortgaging the nation's security by cutting defense, and wrecking the economy with massive deficits.99/ Just as the imbalance in wealth of the late 1800's and early 1900's caused a backlash of the Progressive Era, the imbalance of the 1960's and 1970's caused a backlash of conservatism.

Deficit spending came under universal criticism. "Bracket creep" forced middle income taxpayers to pay rates once reserved for the rich.100/ Tax limitation initiatives, such as Proposition 13 in California and Proposition 2-1/2 in Massachusetts, coupled with the election of distinctly more conservative Congresses in 1978 and 1980, sent a clarion message that the people were demanding that fewer dollars go to the public sector.101/ Citizens had lost confidence in the ability of government to solve social and economic problems, and they wanted government to come home to the state and local level.102/ All of this set the stage for a new era of fiscal federalism.

95/ Ibid., p. 24.

96/ Ibid., p. 25.

97/ Office of Management and Budget, The President's FY 984 Budget Freeze and Reform Plan, p. 10.

98/ Ibid.

99/ Calkins and Shannon, "The New Formula for Fiscal Federalism," op. cit., p. 25.

100/ Ibid.

101/ Ibid., p. 24.

102/ Ibid.

Ronald Reagan's mandate was to cut taxes, reduce the rate of growth of domestic spending, provide regulatory relief to all segments of society, and fulfill his campaign promise that "everything that can be run more efficiently by state and local governments, we shall turn over to state and local governments, along with the funding sources to pay for it."103/

As the nation embarked on its third century, it was obvious that the question left open in the Constitution -- the tensions that would exist between units of government -- had not been resolved. The great national debate over the way America was governed would take on new dimensions and hold new possibilities in the 1980's and beyond, for while the national government had been failing, a remarkable transformation was taking place in state governments. During the 1960's and the 1970's they had become more democratic, sophisticated, compassionate and efficient.

103/ Ronald Reagan, Acceptance Speech, Republican National Convention, July 17, 1980, Detroit, Michigan.

October 28, 1987

EXECUTIVE ORDER

- - - - - - -

FEDERALISM

By the authority vested in me as President of the Constitution and laws of the United States of America, and in order to restore the division of governmental responsibilities between the national government and the States that was intended by the Framers of the Constitution and to ensure that the principles of federalism established by the Framers guide the Executive departments and agencies in the formulation and implementation of policies, it is hereby ordered as follows:

Section 1. Definitions. For purposes of this Order:

(a) "Policies that have federalism implications" refers to regulations, legislative comments or proposed legislation, and other policy statements or actions that have substantial direct effects on the States, on the relationship between the national government and the States, or on the distribution of power and responsibilities among the various levels of government.

(b) "State" or "States" refer to the States of the United States of America, individually or collectively, and, where relevant, to State governments, including units of local government and other political subdivisions established by the States.

Sec. 2. Fundamental Federalism Principles. In formulating and implementing policies that have federalism implications, Executive departments and agencies shall be guided by the following fundamental federalism principles:

(a) Federalism is rooted in the knowledge that our political liberties are best assured by limiting the size and scope of the national government.

(b) The people of the States created the national government when they delegated to it those enumerated governmental powers relating to matters beyond the competence of the individual States. All other sovereign powers, save those expressly prohibited the States by the Constitution, are reserved to the States or to the people.

(c) The constitutional relationship among sovereign governments, State and national, is formalized in and protected by the Tenth Amendment to the Constitution.

(d) The people of the States are free, subject only to restrictions in the Constitution itself or in constitutionally authorized Acts of Congress, to define the moral, political, and legal character of their lives.

(e) In most areas of governmental concern, the States uniquely possess the constitutional authority, the resources, and the competence to discern the sentiments of the people and to govern accordingly. In Thomas Jefferson's words, the States are "the most competent administrations for our domestic concerns and the surest bulwarks against antirepublican tendencies."

(f) The nature of our constitutional system encourages a healthy diversity in the public policies adopted by the people of the several States according to their own conditions, needs, and desires. In the search for enlightened public policy, individual States and communities are free to experiment with a variety of approaches to public issues.

(g) Acts of the national government -- whether legislative, executive, or judicial in nature -- that exceed the enumerated powers of that government under the Constitution violate the principle of federalism established by the Framers.

(h) Policies of the national government should recognize the responsibility of -- and should encourage opportunities for -- individuals, families, neighborhoods, local governments, and private associations to achieve their personal, social, and economic objectives through cooperative effort.

(i) In the absence of clear constitutional or statutory authority, the presumption of sovereignty should rest with the individual States. Uncertainties regarding the legitimate authority of the national government should be resolved against regulation at the national level.

<u>Sec. 3</u>.   <u>Federalism Policymaking Criteria</u>.   In addition to the
fundamental federalism principles set forth in section 2,
Executive departments and agencies shall adhere, to the extent
permitted by law, to the following criteria when formulating and
implementing policies that have federalism implications:

(a) There should be strict adherence to constitutional
principles.   Executive departments and agencies should closely
examine the constitutional and statutory authority supporting any
Federal action that would limit the policymaking discretion of
the States, and should carefully assess the necessity for such
action.   To the extent practicable, the States should be
consulted before any such action is implemented. Executive Order
No. 12372 ("Intergovernmental Review of Federal Programs")
remains in effect for the programs and activities to which it is
applicable.

(b) Federal action limiting the policymaking discretion of the
States should be taken only where constitutional authority for
the action is clear and certain and the national activity is
necessitated by the presence of a problem of national scope. For
the purposes of this Order:

(1) It is important to recognize the distinction between
problems of national scope (which may justify Federal action) and
problems that are merely common to the States (which will not
justify Federal action because individual States, acting
individually or together, can effectively deal with them).

(2) Constitutional authority for Federal action is clear and
certain only when authority for the action may be found in a
specific provision of the Constitution, there is no provision in
the Constitution prohibiting Federal action, and the action does
not encroach upon authority reserved to the States.

(c) With respect to national policies administered by the
States, the national government should grant the States the
maximum administrative discretion possible.   Intrusive, Federal
oversight of the State administration is neither necessary nor
desirable.

(d) When undertaking to formulate and implement policies that
have federalism implications, Executive departments and agencies
shall:

(1) Encourage States to develop their own policies to achieve
program objectives and to work with appropriate officials in
other States.

(2) Refrain, to the maximum extent possible, from establishing uniform, national standards for programs and when possible, defer to the States to establish standards.

(3) When national standards are required, consult with appropriate officials and organizations representing the States in developing those standards.

Sec. 4. Special Requirements for Preemption. (a) To the extent permitted by law, Executive departments and agencies shall construe, in regulations and otherwise, a Federal statute to preempt State law only when the statute contains an express preemption provision or there is some other firm and palpable evidence compelling the conclusion that the Congress intended preemption of State law, or when the exercise of State authority directly conflicts with the exercise of Federal authority under the Federal statute.

(b) Where a Federal statute does not preempt State law (as addressed in subsection (a) of this section), Executive departments and agencies shall construe any authorization in the statute for the issuance of regulations as authorizing preemption of State law by rule-making only when the statute expressly authorizes issuance of preemptive regulations or there is some other firm and palpable evidence compelling the conclusion that the Congress intended to delegate to the department or agency the authority to issue regulations preempting State law.

(c) Any regulatory preemption of State law shall be restricted to the minimum level necessary to achieve the objectives of the statute pursuant to which the regulations are promulgated.

(d) As soon as an Executive department or agency foresees the possibility of a conflict between State law and Federally protected interest within its area of regulatory responsibility, the department or agency shall consult, to the extent practicable, with appropriate officials and organizations representing the States in an effort to avoid such a conflict.

(e) When an Executive department or agency proposes to act through adjudication or rule-making to preempt State law, the department or agency shall provide all affected States notice and an opportunity for appropriate participation in the proceedings.

Sec. 5. Special Requirements for Legislative Proposals. Executive departments and agencies shall not submit to the Congress legislation that would:

(a) Directly regulate the States in ways that would interfere with functions essential to the States' separate and independent existence or operate to directly displace the States' freedom to structure integral operations in areas of traditional governmental functions;

(b) Attach to Federal grants conditions that are not directly related to the purpose of the grant; or

(c) Preempt State law, unless preemption is consistent with the fundamental federalism principles set forth in section 2, and unless a clearly legitimate national purpose, consistent with the federalism policymaking criteria set forth in section 3, cannot otherwise be met.

Sec. 6. Agency Implementation. (a) The head of each Executive department and agency shall designate an official to be responsible for ensuring the implementation of this Order.

(b) In addition to whatever other actions the designated official may take to ensure implementation of this Order, the designated official shall determine which proposed policies have sufficient federalism implications to warrant the preparation of a Federalism Assessment. With respect to each such policy for which an affirmative determination is made, a Federalism Assessment, as described in subsection (c) of this section, shall be prepared. The department or agency head shall consider any such Assessment in all decisions involved in promulgating and implementing the policy.

(c) Each Federalism Assessment shall accompany any submission concerning the policy that is made to the Office of Management and Budget pursuant to Executive Order No. 12291 or OMB Circular No. A-19, and shall:

(1) Contain the designated official's certification that the policy has been assessed in light of the principles, criteria, and requirements stated in sections 2 through 5 of this Order;

(2) Identify any provision or element of the policy that is inconsistent with the principles, criteria, and requirements stated in sections 2 through 5 of this Order;

(3) Identify the extent to which the policy imposes additional costs or burdens on the States, including the likely source of funding for the States and the ability of the States to fulfill the purposes of the policy; and

(4) Identify the extent to which the policy would affect the States' ability to discharge traditional State governmental functions, or other aspects of State sovereignty.

Sec. 7. <u>Government-wide Federalism Coordination and Review.</u> (a) In implementing Executive Order Nos. 12291 and 12498 and OMB Circular No. A-19, the Office of Management and Budget, to the extent permitted by law and consistent with the provisions of those authorities, shall take action to ensure that the policies of the Executive departments and agencies are consistent with the principles, criteria, and requirements stated in section 2 through 5 of this Order.

(b) In submissions to the Office of Management and Budget pursuant to Executive Order No. 12291 and OMB Circular No. A-19, Executive departments and agencies shall identify proposed regulatory and statutory provisions that have significant federalism implications and shall address any substantial federalism concerns. Where the departments or agencies deem it appropriate, substantial federalism concerns should also be addressed in notices of proposed rule-making and messages transmitting legislative proposals to the Congress.

Sec. 8. <u>Judicial Review.</u> This Order is intended only to improve the internal management of the Executive branch, and is not intended to create any right or benefit, substantive or procedural, enforceable at law by a party against the United States, its agencies, its officers, or any person.

RONALD REAGAN

THE WHITE HOUSE
    October 26, 1987.

# # #

Implementation Status Report

FEDERALISM EXECUTIVE ORDER No. 12612

August 1988

This report summarizes the status of agency implementation of Executive Order 12612, entitled "Federalism," which the President issued on October 26, 1987.

The Federalism Executive Order sets forth substantive federalism principles, criteria, and requirements, and establishes various procedures to ensure that these principles, criteria, and requirements are adhered to in policymaking by executive branch agencies. As a general matter, the Order leaves to agency discretion the details of implementation, and requires as a minimum that the head of each agency designate an official to be responsible for ensuring compliance. In addition to other assigned duties, the federalism official must determine which agency policies have sufficient federalism implications to warrant preparation of a Federalism Assessment. The Order specifies minimum requirements for the contents of Assessments, leaving it to individual agencies to determine whether they will adopt any additional requirements.

While the Order's emphasis regarding implementation is on agency self-enforcement, the Order does provide that, as a part of its regulatory and legislative review functions under E.O. 12291 and OMB Circular A-19, the Office of Management and Budget will ensure that agency policies are consistent with the Order's substantive principles, criteria, and requirements.

All major agencies have taken substantial steps to implement the Order. A survey of the activities of some of the major agencies follows.

The Department of Agriculture is an example of an agency that has opted for a comprehensive and formal approach to implementation. The Secretary designated the General Counsel as federalism official and issued a Secretary's Memorandum giving general implementation guidance based on the requirements of the Order and directing that the Order be given to all employees involved in formulation or review of policies with federalism implications. The Department subsequently issued guidelines identifying the implementation responsibilities of various officials and providing guidance on preparation of Assessments, documentation and analysis requirements, and clearance procedures.

The Department of Commerce designated as federalism official its Deputy Assistant Secretary for Intergovernmental Affairs. It created a "Committee on Federalism," which has developed an implementation plan. Under the plan, senior staff persons appointed in all department components will be responsible for day-to-day coordination of implementation. An educational package will be distributed to program directors summarizing the Order and describing the process of making Assessments. All components will submit to the Federalism Committee a list of current and proposed programs and policies that may require an Assessment; independently, the Office of Program Planning and Evaluation will perform the same task. The Office of General Counsel will conduct a review of current laws preempting state and local governments, and will also review all existing Commerce regulations that may require an Assessment.

The Department of Education designated its General Counsel to be its federalism official. It is following Department-wide guidelines on complying with the Order. The Regulatory Action Memorandum, which is a required part of the Department's clearance progress for regulatory proposals, will now include a section entitled "Effect of Federalism," and legislative submissions to OMB will include such a section if the proposal has a significant federalism effect. The guidelines also define when a policy fits the Order's definition of a policy having federalism implications. The Department's Regulatory Review Task Force is conducting a review to identify new and existing programs and activities that will be affected by the Order; the Task Force will supervise implementation of the Order with respect to the identified programs and activities.

The Department of Energy followed its designation of the agency federalism official, with a comprehensive plan for implementation of the Order that was developed and reviewed by senior department officials. The implementation plan establishes the process for the review of all matters affected by the Order, and provides for the revision of relevant DOE orders to prescribe the Federalism review as an intrinsic element of agency policy making. Detailed guidelines to execute the plan have been prepared and are awaiting final approval.

The guidelines will require all proposed legislation, regulations, and other policy oriented activity to be reviewed for their Federalism implications by the appropriate policy level official in the office of primary interest who is authorized to take the action itself. Those matters identified as having potential impact on State sovereignty will be referred to the federalism official for a determination of the need for an Assessment. As and when prepared, the Assessment will accompany the legislation for the Circular A-19 submission to OMB, and be included in all rulemaking documentation.

The Environmental Protection Agency has designated its Assistant Administrator for Policy, Planning and Evaluation as its federalism official. The Agency is preparing implementation guidance, which will expand upon existing EPA structures and processes. The existing Agency-wide Steering Committee, which oversees rule-making activities, will consider the federalism effects of a proposed regulation at several key stages of the development process. For rules that require Assessments, EPA will summarize the Assessment in the preamble to the proposed rule that appears in the Federal Register, and a copy of the Assessment will be publicly available as part of the regulatory docket. EPA is considering ways to expand the use of its State/EPA Committee (a delegation of 15 State environmental managers who meet regularly with the Administrator) as a forum considering federalism issues.

The Health and Human Services designated as federalism official the HHS Assistant Secretary for Planning and Evaluation. At the same time the Secretary gave formal instructions on application of the Order and then asked officials to use the issuance of the Order as an occasion to look for new ways to enhance the role of the States as primary providers. Subsequently, the HHS federalism official issued detailed Department-wide instructions. The instructions provide guidance on circumstances under which an Assessment is necessary; provide for technical assistance to HHS staff involved in drafting Assessments and making initial determinations under the Order; require central review, in the office of the federalism official, of Assessments and other determinations; and establish threshold criteria to prevent preparation of unnecessary Assessments (i.e., criteria on what constitutes significant federalism implications in various HHS contexts), giving examples on applying the criteria.

The Department of Housing and Urban Development designated as federalism official its General Counsel. The Department has developed a Notice for publication in the Federal Register which would implement the Order for the policy formulation and implementation functions of HUD. The General Counsel will review each policy initiative that is subject to review under the Order and will determine which policies have sufficient Federalism implications to warrant preparation of a Federalism Assessment. The Federal Register Notice will provide detailed information on HUD's policies concerning (a) review and analysis of HUD policy initiatives with Federalism implications, (b) the contents of the analysis, (c) consultation with State officials, and (d) special provisions concerning preemption of State law by Federal statutes and regulations. The Notice further provides for the Secretary to personally consider Federalism Assessments at any appropriate decision point in the policy formulation and implementation process.

The Department has just recently performed Federalism reviews on the Department's FY 1989 legislative program. These reviews provide an example of how the Department has applied the Order.

The Department of Interior has issued a memorandum from the Secretary summarizing the Order, naming the Department's Legislative Counsel as federalism official, and attaching an implementation plan. The plan (1) requires appointment of a Federalism Review Officer in each Assistant Secretary's office to review all proposed policies for federalism effect and to consider whether to prepare an Assessment; (2) provides that the Assistant Secretary for Policy, Budget and Administration will review federalism determinations on regulatory matters and raise conflicts to the federalism official for resolution; (3) discusses the substance of the federalism principles in the Order, giving examples in the Interior context; (4) provides criteria for determining whether proposed actions have significant federalism effects; and (5) gives guidance on how to prepare Assessments.

The Department of Justice is an example of an agency that undertakes relatively few regulatory or other administrative actions with federalism implications. The Attorney General has sent to the heads of all Department components a memorandum enclosing the Order, asking them to make the Order's implementation a high priority, designating as federalism official the Assistant Attorney General of the Office of Legal Counsel, and drawing special attention to the Federalism Assessment requirement. The federalism official's office has been working with the legislative office on implementing the order in the legislative context.

The Department of Labor has designated its Assistant Secretary for Policy as its federalism official. As a first implementation step, that official asked each agency head within the Department to designate a policy level person to be in charge of implementation in that agency. The Department federalism official met with the agency federalism official to review the Order, and subsequently provided them with a brief statement of guidelines on implementation. Under the guidelines, whenever an agency official believes a policy may have significant federalism implications, the official is to send a draft of the policy to the Department federalism official for review, and if that official determines it has sufficient federalism implications, it will be brought to the Department's Policy Review Board for immediate consideration.

The State Department has designated its Coordinator for Intergovernmental Affairs as the federalism official and a State Department attorney to monitor federal activities affecting State and Local government. The Office of Intergovernmental Affairs will also be a part of the clearance process for any State Department communication with State and Local government.

The Department of Transportation has designated its General Counsel to be its federalism official. Senior officials of the Department discussed at a recent conference the federalism principles contained in the Order and their application to DOT issues. The Department has issued guidelines requiring DOT agencies to make preliminary federalism determinations on all actions covered by the Order. The guidelines define the methodology to be used in determining whether there are sufficient federalism implications to warrant preparation of an Assessment, how to prepare an Assessment, and the review of Assessments within the Department. They also include guidance on preemption and on consultation with the States. In addition, the Department has issued a comprehensive Department-wide manual on the Order.

ABOUT THE AUTHOR

During President Reagan's first term, Richard Williamson served on the White House senior staff as Assistant to the President for Intergovernmental Affairs. As President Reagan's senior advisor on federalism issues, Williamson helped design, promote and implement Reagan's efforts to decentralize government.

In 1982 the <u>New York Times</u> called Williamson "the chief theoretician and energizing force" of Reagan's new federalism. And the next year <u>Washington Post</u> columnist David Broder wrote that Williamson, "more than anyone else in the White House nurtured President Reagan's dream of handing off some of Washington's power and responsibility to the state and local governments of the land."

When Williamson left the White House staff, President Reagan said that he has been "my right hand in our struggle to restore the rightful balance between levels of government. They say that until now no government in history has ever voluntarily reduced itself in size, but with Rich's help that's exactly what this government has begun to do. We have brought back the themes of decentralization, diversity and accountability to the national dialogue."

Mr. Williamson, a partner of the international law firm of Mayer, Brown & Platt, has practiced law in his native Chicago and Washington, D.C. In addition to serving as Assistant to the President for Intergovernmental Affairs, he has served in many other government positions -- as a congressional aide on Capitol Hill, Special Assistant to the President and deputy to the White House Chief of Staff, member of the Federal Advisory Commission on Intergovernmental Affairs, Vice Chairman of the Administrative Conference of the United States, and on the Illinois Economic Board. Mr. Williamson also has served as U.S. Ambassador to the United Nations Offices in Vienna, Austria; Assistant Secretary of State for International Organization Affairs; and on the President's General Advisory Committee on Arms Control.

Mr. Williamson is the author of numerous articles in professional journals and periodicals, many of them on intergovernmental affairs issues.